Alexander Innes Shand

Mountain stream and covert

Sketches of country life and sport in England and Scotland

Alexander Innes Shand

Mountain stream and covert

Sketches of country life and sport in England and Scotland

ISBN/EAN: 9783743345379

Manufactured in Europe, USA, Canada, Australia, Japa

Cover: Foto ©ninafisch / pixelio.de

Manufactured and distributed by brebook publishing software (www.brebook.com)

Alexander Innes Shand

Mountain stream and covert

MOUNTAIN STREAM AND COVERT

*SKETCHES
OF COUNTRY LIFE AND SPORT
IN ENGLAND & SCOTLAND*

BY

ALEXANDER INNES SHAND

With Illustrations

LONDON
SEELEY AND CO. LIMITED
38, GREAT RUSSELL STREET
1897

PREFACE

I AM greatly indebted to the proprietors of *Blackwood's* and the *Cornhill Magazines*, of the old *Pall Mall Gazette*, and of the *Saturday Review* for permission to reprint these articles, which attempt sketches of sport and rural life in Great Britain in bygone years. Some have been rearranged in chapters, and slightly remodelled. The most recent is the article on "Coverts," which Messrs. Longman very kindly allow me to use, although it appeared only the other day in the *Badminton Magazine*. Of the other chapters, i–vii, x–xiii, xvii–xix, xxiii–xxvii, are from *Blackwood's Magazine*; viii, xx, xxii, from the *Pall Mall Gazette*; ix, from the *Saturday Review*; and xiv–xvi, from the *Cornhill Magazine*.

ALEX. INNES SHAND.

OAKDALE,
  EDENBRIDGE, KENT.

Dedicated

TO MY OLD FRIEND, DONALD MACPHERSON,
GAMEKEEPER AT STRALOCH AND BARRA,
ABERDEENSHIRE,
IN MEMORY OF CLOSE COMPANIONSHIP
AND MANY DELIGHTFUL DAYS.

CONTENTS

CHAP.		PAGE
I.	COUNTRY LIFE IN LITERATURE	1
II.	A HIGHLAND LAIRD	28
III.	AN ENGLISH SQUIRE	42
IV.	A KENTISH PARISH	60
V.	A KENTISH PARISH: HOP-GARDENS AND FARMS	71
VI.	A KENTISH PARISH: SPORT AND BIRD-LIFE	85
VII.	A KENTISH PARISH: THE RESIDENTS	92
VIII.	THE DOWNS	110
IX.	TRAMPS	119
X.	THE AMATEUR TRAMP IN ENGLAND	133
XI.	THE AMATEUR TRAMP IN SCOTLAND	147
XII.	FISHING IN RIVER, STREAM, AND LOCH	155
XIII.	SOME WRITERS ON THE GENTLE CRAFT	177
XIV.	AUGUST ON THE MOORS: A SHOOTING LODGE	197

CONTENTS

CHAP.		PAGE
XV.	AUGUST ON THE MOORS: THE MORNING START	205
XVI.	AUGUST ON THE MOORS: THE DAY'S WORK	213
XVII.	"THE MOOR AND THE LOCH": THE NESTOR OF SCOTTISH SPORTSMEN	225
XVIII.	AMONG THE WILD FOWL	238
XIX.	IN FOREST AND ON HILL	243
XX.	AFTER DEER	256
XXI.	THE COVERTS	265
XXII.	CURLING	283
XXIII.	THE ATTRACTIONS OF WINTER WEATHER	291
XXIV.	WINTER IN THE NORTH	305
XXV.	WINTER FERRETING	316
XXVI.	WINTER FOWLING	322
XXVII.	WINTER IN THE SHIRES	329

LIST OF ILLUSTRATIONS

WILD SWANS ON LOCH SPYNIE
    Archibald Thorburn *Frontispiece*

OTTER AND SALMON. *Sir E. Landseer* *To face page* 16

PTARMIGAN MOTIONLESS AMONG THE LICHEN-COVERED STONES
    Archibald Thorburn ,, ,, 32

HOUNDS LEAVING THE COVERT
    F. C. Turner ,, ,, 50

A KENTISH HOP-GARDEN. *George Morrow* ,, ,, 72

HUNTERS AT GRASS. *Sir E. Landseer* ,, ,, 104

THE TRAMP. *George Morrow* ,, ,, 126

GROUSE FIGHTING ON THE MOORS
    F. C. Turner ,, ,, 148

SALMON FISHING. *Lancelot Speed* ,, ,, 164

THE SETTER ON THE GROUSE MOOR.
    A. Cooper, R.A. ,, ,, 210

LIST OF ILLUSTRATIONS

GROUSE-SHOOTING.	*A. Cooper, R.A.*	*To face page*		220
DEER DISTURBED BY GROUSE.	*Sydney Steel*	,,	,,	244
THE STAG AND HIS FRIENDS.	*Sydney Steel*	,,	,,	262
BLACKCOCK AND SETTER.	*A. Cooper, R.A.*	,,	,,	274
CURLING.	*Lancelot Speed*	,,	,,	286
DEAD PTARMIGAN.	*A. Cooper, R.A.*	,,	,,	312

MOUNTAIN, STREAM AND COVERT

CHAPTER I

Country Life in Literature

BECAUSE of the climate we so naturally abuse, there is no place like England for the pleasures of the country—rain and sunshine, snow and frost, bring out a world of beauties in an enchanting variety of landscape. There are lakes and streams that are swarming with fish, in spite of the growth of manufacturing industries; game abounds in field, fell, and wood, notwithstanding occasional indifference to preserving it; and a succession of invigorating sports falls in with the several seasons. It is no *amour propre* of patriotism that makes us believe that in these matters we are far better off than our neighbours; and indeed they are ready to acknowledge it themselves, by cultivating the tastes that are instincts with Englishmen. You have only to cross the Channel to be conscious at once of a change. There is as charming scenery among the orchards of Normandy as any to be found in the hop-gardens of Kent. The granite precipices of

Penmarch, and the Pointe de Raz on the Breton coast are nearly as wild as anything in Devon or Cornwall. Where the line of railway from Liège to Cologne is carried along the slopes of the valley of the Vesdre, you look down on meadows and rushing streams that remind you of the pastoral picturesqueness of Herefordshire. But everywhere you are struck by the sharp lines of demarcation that are drawn between the country and the towns. Here and there you may come upon an isolated *château* that looks as if it had been transplanted from some neighbouring *boulevard*, and then adapted to its rural site by being fitted with turrets and bartizans. If there is a park, it is shut in from plebeian intrusion by forbidding walls of stone; and the highest praise you can possibly bestow on such a place is, that there are turf and flower-beds reminding you of England. No thought of coveting it ever comes across your mind, except in so far as it may be the sign of an easy fortune. On the contrary, you are inclined to pity the owner, and to wonder what in the world he does when he goes there. Doubtless he has the means of amusing himself indoors, so far as the cellar, *salle-à-manger*, and a billiard-room can help him. The ladies, in toilets of affected simplicity, may saunter on the terrace of an evening, and sip their coffee in a frescoed temple covered with creepers, looking down on the water-lilies in a formal fish-pond. But theirs, after all, is only the life of the town, with all that is dullest in the country superadded. The brand-new stucco of the façade—that formidable wall, with its gilded grills and its bolted posterns—are disagreeably suggestive of antipathies of class, and the absence of those kindly feelings that are insensibly fostered in the course of generations by a neighbourly intercourse between the landlord and his people. The foreign proprietor can seldom hunt, and there is little for him to shoot. The fields look all that is desirable for partridges, but they are cut up in infinitesimal patches among a society of jealous little owners, who would open full cry on their more wealthy neighbour if he followed a pack over their patrimonies. His woods may be attractive to the artist, but they have none of the undergrowth that shelters ground-game ; and if he went in for pheasant-breeding, he would have to bring up his birds by hand in wired-in aviaries like those of the Jardin d'Acclimatation.

Go where you will abroad, there are the same signs of conspicuous segregation between the men of the country and those of the town ; and the exceptions only prove the rule. In Brittany and some other of the more wild and woodland provinces of France, there are still seigneurs who live in their ancestral *châteaux*, devoting themselves to the chase of the wolf, and having off-days among the hares, the wild fowl, and the partridges. But they are a class by themselves, and the wolf-hunting is supposed to be mattter of necessity, so that the dignity of master of the hounds is frequently an official appointment. Volunteers flock to the rendezvous clad in garments of sheep-skin and armed with antiquated weapons, heavily loaded with slugs and

B.B. No authority can repress the excitement or keep the vociferous field in check, when the game is fairly afoot; and fatal accidents are of frequent occurrence when a hail of shot is drifting through the covers. It is much the same in Germany; and there things have been getting worse than they were, since the peasants swept the country of game in the civil troubles of 1848. Some great land-owners in Bohemia, Northern Bavaria, and elsewhere, have wonderful quantities of hares and pheasants. In the neighbourhood of their vast woodland preserves you see each outlying patch of grain protected from the ravages of deer and wild boars by *chevaux de frise* of stacked thorn-bushes. But even there sport is the monopoly of an aristocratic few, who seclude themselves in their domains for a short hunting season; as the Kings of Bavaria or Italy, the Emperor of Austria, and the Arch Dukes, enjoy the chase of the chamois or izzard in the magnificent solitudes of their mountain hunting-grounds. Elsewhere you have occasional grand days among the game with comparatively pitiful results; but there is little of those everyday country sports which are so keenly appreciated by thousands of Englishmen. Indeed the evidences of life of any kind are few and far between. Nothing can be more beautiful than the Black Forest, for example: you may walk on day after day from Baden-Baden towards Stuttgart, through noble woods of feathering beech-trees, or grand glades of clean-stemmed pines; that, with the light falling in streams through their boughs on the bilberry carpet beneath them, remind you of the labyrinths of long-drawn aisles in the most superb of Gothic cathedrals. Every here and there you come out on some sequestered valley with fields that are waving with the hay-crops and the ripening grain, sloping down to the sides of some murmuring brook that babbles along between its banks in a series of rushes and cascades. But you may walk onwards day after day, and seldom raise a hare or flush a covey. Game there must be, no doubt, for you find it frequently figuring on the dinner-table. But it has a perverse knack of keeping out of your way, and cannot in any case be very abundant. The roes and the foxes that lurk in the recesses of the woods either see or scent you as you approach through the open ; for naturally, in the absence of undergrowth, they get preternaturally shy and suspicious.

As for human habitations, the country is fairly populous, and human habitations there are ; but there is scarcely a trace of the existence of a squirearchy or of a comfortable class of gentleman farmers. Here and there in the depths of the forest you come on the picturesque huts of the charcoal-burners or woodmen ; now and again you stumble out upon a clearing with some sylvan lodge, the dwelling of the forester, whose duty is to keep an eye on them, and whom you have possibly come across in the course of the morning with a *dachshund* or two at his heels. Generally, however, the people are huddled together, and each of the greater valleys has its village. Nothing can be more quaint than the many-gabled houses with their rustic woodwork interlaced through the rough lime walls, hanging along the slope in the single street that leads down to the little *place*, with the village inn and the post-house. There is a pleasant odour of fresh hay and newly-milked cows; everybody seems in easy circumstances, and the local authorities look after the poor; but it is plain that they must labour hard to live, and that life shows its serious side to all of them. Not a man of them who does not place the *summum bonum* of recreation in a Sunday or saint's day that is celebrated by free indulgence in beer and tobacco, or a longer chat on local politics. Naturally that marked feature is brought out conspicuously in those writers of the nations who are the most keen to appreciate all that is most enchanting in the scenery of their respective countries. Our remarks on the Schwarzwald, though the results of a long familiarity with it, might have been borrowed almost *verbatim* from the pages of Hackläader, who narrates in his "Pictures of Travel" the very excursion we have been imagining. Perhaps no French novelist of our own time or of any other excelled more absolutely in delicate landscape drawing than George Sand, and at the same time she had made herself the unrivalled mistress of the subtle refinements of rustic character. Her whole heart went out in her writings; she made her enchanting studies either from memory or observation of scenes endeared to her by happy associations; and her dreams of the most perfect lot on earth were closely linked with a life in the country. In "Flamarande," one of her latest works, her love for nature is as fresh, and her pen as forcible, as in " Le Meûnier d'Angibault " or " La Petite Fadette." Yet even George Sand in her inimitable descriptions gives us the idea of an enthusiastic and emotional amateur looking at the beauties of nature through an æsthetic medium, as she might admire them on the canvas of a Corot or Jules Breton. You see the old *château* lost among the woods and rocks, tenanted now by the family of the farmer who has succeeded to its ancient lords. You see the lonely mill among the meadows and the water-courses, among osier-beds and clumps of the drooping alders and sedges, swarming with the water-hens. You are wrought insensibly into easy sympathy with the hopes and hardships, the griefs and the joys, of the hard-working people who have their homes there. You are made to fancy that retreat among such soothing influences would be more tranquillising to the jaded spirit, and quite as satisfactory in the long run to the *blasé* hermit, as the gloom and asceticism of the mediæval convent ; and that a short sojourn in summer would be no disagreeable variety even to men and women of the world, though the fare might be simple and the post irregular. But the very longings with which you are inspired must arise from some passing impulse of misanthropy. You are to court solitude from an ephemeral passion for it, and you are to woo peaceful nature in a dead calm of seclusion. You are to change your every habit, and divorce yourself from your every-day routine. You are to abandon the congenial but demoralising society of your equals for the improving company of virtuous and unsophisticated peasants, as you might give up your Bordeaux or Burgundy for a course of goat's milk. Such books are idylls and pastorals in prose, and there seems a dash of the artificial and theatrical in them. But there is, and there is not. They are only artificial and theatrical in so far as they are true to foreign facts, and founded on an intimate though idealised knowledge of the feelings and habits and social relations of our good friends on the Continent.

Nothing can more forcibly illustrate our meaning than a comparison of the fascinating books we have been referring to with the inexhaustible rural literature of England. What a variety of volumes come crowding together on our memory, written by men who have lived in the English country, and loved it, although many of them had to quit it for more serious pursuits for the best part of the year! What an infinity of friends they have made themselves among folks they have never met in the flesh; and what an endearing popularity they have attained, because they have struck the sympathetic chords in the bosoms of so many thousands of their country-people! If they have been read and read again by successive generations, it is because they have expressed with unstudied and instinctive eloquence those feelings that are universally struggling for utterance; because by the force and minute fidelity of their descriptions they have recalled to us some of the brightest associations of our lives. Not only when they have written with that definite purpose, but incidentally as essayists, biographers, and romancers; and even when their passion for the country has run away with their pens, their rural digressions are most readily forgiven them. The country is become a stock theme with literary professionals although their individual experiences may have lain among bricks and mortar; although their ornithological observations may have been mainly confined to the street sparrows; and although they would be sorely puzzled by the call of the partridge, and mystified by the cry of the landrail. They have practised writing of these things because they know they take; and if they write with talent, Cockneys as they may be, their country episodes may be far from unsuccessful. Take Dickens, for example. Is there anything much better in the inimitable "Pickwick Papers" than the day with the partridges on Sir Geoffrey's land, when Mr. Pickwick followed the sport in the wheelbarrow, though the author's evident inexperience crops out everywhere? or the spring morning among the rooks, at the bright Kentish homestead, where Mr. Winkle so nearly "does for old Tupman"? But the standard books are of course by men who have taken naturally to themes with which they are familiar, or by men who have been driven to change the gun for the pen by the depth and intensity of their own enjoyment; who in the geniality of their natures have felt irresistibly impelled to communicate the pleasures that came so keenly home to them.

We might go to work on an interminable catalogue

of authors of what may be termed the rural school. But we may be satisfied with passing allusion to a few that ought to be familiar to everybody. There is old Izaak Walton, whose name, so long as our world exists, seems likely to pass current as a household word among generations of anglers who have never read a word of him. Old Izaak was a Cockney himself, so far as living in a city can make a Cockney. But in Izaak's days even London had its limits : we fancy there was really a green at Clerkenwell and a bubbling fountain ; and a brisk morning walk from the bustle of Cheapside brought you out among trees and brooks and meadows. What can be more exhilarating than your sympathetic sense of the sharpness of the change from the smoke and noise of the streets he has left behind, to the freshness and silence of the fields towards Hoddesdon ? The pictures of rustic felicity are the more perfect that the smoke of the capital is hanging on the horizon, and that a faint hum of traffic is borne to their ears from the neighbouring high road, as the anglers listen to the carolling of the milkmaids, while casting their lines in the slow-flowing stream, or sitting in the sanded parlour of the little hostelry discussing their fish and the details of catching and cooking them. We find the fresh and quaint simplicity that is the charm of Walton's style reproduced in the " Natural History of Selborne," if we make due allowance for the lapse of time and advances in the literary art and general enlightenment. Devoted as we are to Gilbert White, the extraordinary attraction he has for his readers must always remain something of a mystery to us; and it is only to be explained in any plausible way by those inborn tastes to which he addresses himself instinctively. No one would have been more astonished than the retiring Sussex parson, had it been predicted to him that in jotting down his everyday notes, or in penning his letters to Pennant and Barrington, he was raising himself an imperishable monument, and bringing his parish into undying notoriety. There are scores and hundreds of villages in England to the full as attractive as Selborne, which enjoy no greater reputation than can be given them by a county gazetteer. But as for Selborne, how many of us there are who seem to know the place, as if they had passed their days under the Hanger! White happened to possess a natural literary gift, which has done all the more for his fame and his parish that he exercised it in absolute unconsciousness, and never dreamed of cultivating it. He had a passionate attachment for nature, which made him indefatigable in his observation of her; and a variety of unconsidered touches in his desultory correspondence and his diaries have worked a thousand details indelibly into our memories. How many of us there are who owe such lights on natural history as we possess almost entirely to the interest that was excited by that unpretending and antiquated volume! Since then we have had such fanciful theories exploded as the general hibernation of swallows in the depths of the Sussex ponds or the rifts of the chalk cliffs; but it was White who taught us to distinguish the black swifts screaming and circling round the church tower from their more numerous congeners who build under the house eaves, and the martins who flit about the face of the sand-banks. We may smile at the innocence of his un-travelled raptures on "that magnificent range of mountains, the Sussex Downs"; but as we ride over the ranges that have inspired the pens of such accomplished admirers of nature as Mr. Blackmore, and our older acquaintance Mr. Harrison Ainsworth, it is the recollections we owe to the "Natural History" that give a zest to the ride by awakening our observation. We remember what White had to tell about the curlews and the wheat-ears, and those restless red-legged choughs that are fluttering about the fissures in the precipices. He could even warm us into a feeling of personal regard for a misanthropic reptile like "the old Sussex tortoise"; and he has left particular pollards as landmarks in the memory, which you begin anxiously to inquire after on a visit to Selborne.

That White made his book what it is, is the more remarkable when we remember that it is merely natural history. How many men there are who pass months of each autumn in the country, unconsciously enjoying it in absence of knowledge, and never deigning to confess to an interest in anything that falls beneath the category of game! White was a clergyman of the old school and could handle the gun on occasion, but he was very little of a sportsman; and so gentlemen of inferior genius to his ought to write with a good many points in their favour, when they are not only naturalists but sportsmen to boot. Among the most popular of his successors in kindred fields, Scrope, Colquhoun, and St. John, will naturally suggest themselves. No one of the three falls very far short of him in ardent admiration of nature, while the range of their several experiences was infinitely broader and more exciting. Nothing can be more exhilarating than the buoyant sea air on the Sussex Downs, laden with the land-scents from the thyme and the furze-blossom : nothing more picturesque in the way of lowland landscape than the deep woodland lanes worn out in the Selborne chalk, or the lonely ponds in Woolmer and Alice Holt forests. But what is life among them after all, with their tamer partridge and wild-fowl shooting, to that of the sportsman who has the run of the Scotch deer-forests or of the broad waters of the Tweed or the Tay? Scrope's stories of his adventures in the forest of Atholl, where he was made welcome year after year by the princely hospitality of "the Duke," read with a flavour of Cooper's Indian romances, although far grander scenery is thrown in for a background. Pedantic he may be occasionally ; and the formal dialogues with his pupil which blend instruction with entertainment sound somewhat like those of Sir Humphry Davy in "Salmonia," or chapters from "Sandford and Merton." But there is not a taint of the oil of the study lamp when he is really fired with the spirit of the sport. When he describes the rough stalk and the deadly shot ; the slipping of the deer-hounds on some wounded animal, or the hart turned to bay under the waterfall

—we can feel the throb of his pulses and hear the beating of his heart. There were heads in the land, too, in those days—heads of ten, with brow, brae, and trae antlers in perfection, such as are seldom to be seen nowadays save hanging upon the walls of the shooting-lodges. Deer have increased with over-preserving, but rifles of precision and improved practice have been doing their work, and the harts that promise to be the pride of the forest are seldom suffered to attain maturity. "Life has little better to offer than this," Dr. Johnson observed on one occasion, when thoroughly enjoying himself in the Highlands, devoted as he was to Fleet Street. The deer-stalker might say as much with far more reason when following his solitary sport in the valleys of the Tilt and the Bruar, and about the skirts of the witch-haunted hill of Ben-y-gloe, while he had the refinements and luxuries of society within his reach at the Castle of Blair or the lodge in Glen Tilt.

Talking of the deterioration in the heads of deer, and *àpropos* to general changes for the worse in the wild life of the moors and mountains, in consequence of the ever-increasing demand for shooting-quarters, we may refer to a delightful little *brochure* by Mr. Colquhoun on the *Feræ naturæ* of the British Isles. For keepers have been increasing too, and persecuting everything they are pleased to call vermin with a zeal that is born of ignorance and prejudice. There are beasts and birds for which we have nothing to say. Kill down hooded crows and magpies as fast as you will; there will always be enough of these scourges left, and their mischievous hunger for eggs places them beyond the pale of toleration. Weasels and polecats, and *id genus omne*, are only too well able to take care of themselves, and should be trapped without scruple or mercy. Hill-foxes are altogether out of place, seeing that they fly so far in the face of their nature as to burrow like rabbits in impracticable cairns, and that there is no possibility of putting them to their legitimate purpose. But every one who has a soul above sheer slaughter must regret the disappearance of those magnificent birds of prey that lend so characteristic a charm to mountain scenery as they float like specks in the air against a cloudless sky, or stoop down over the heather in lessening circles. The eagle and peregrine falcon may take toll of the game, but, so far as we are concerned, they should be welcome to what they can capture. After all, the hares are their great resource, and the blue hares are positive nuisances; nor can there be any objection to their disputing with the shepherds the "braxy" to which they occasionally condescend. Unhappily the protesting against their being put to the ban, can literally be nothing but the voice of one crying in the wilderness, so long as ornithologists offer fancy prices for specimens and an eagle's egg will fetch a sovereign. Were we driven to make a choice, we could more easily spare the ravens; and yet there is something romantically appropriate in the hoarse croak and the uncanny antics of a lonely pair of these demon-like birds in the recesses of some sombre glen that is seldom illuminated by the sunbeams. We should never grudge the otter his fish, though his habits of feeding are decidedly wasteful, so long as we had the pleasure of seeing him slip silently off the bank of the stream and dive oilily into the water, leaving a trail of bubbles behind him. Nor can anything be more weird of an autumn night, when the moon is shining fitfully through a grey drift of clouds, than the long, mournful cry of the wild cat from the loose boulders among the fir-trees on the banks of some lonely loch. We delight to see the grey forms of the badgers rooting like spectral pigs in the dusk, when the screech-owls are just beginning their music. So we respond heartily to the lament of Mr. Colquhoun when he tells us how hawks and eagles, otters and wild cats, marten-cats and badgers, have been disappearing from the Luss country on the banks of Loch Lomond and elsewhere, since he used to shoot as a boy over his father's domains.

Take them all in all, however, the books on Highland shooting and Scotch natural history that please us the most are decidedly those of Mr. St. John. An Englishman by birth, he was long domiciled in Scotland, because it was there that he could indulge his bent to the uttermost. Fond of society, and formed to live in it, he gave it up for the greater attractions of the wilds. For long he would persist in asserting that he had no vocation for the pen. Yet no man has written better on his favourite subjects, with the

Otter and Salmon. *By* Sir E. Landseer.

single exception of Gilbert White. A keen sportsman and devoted admirer of nature, he was the most practical and observant of naturalists. Nothing can be more vivid or sympathetic than his first work, "The Wild Sports of the Highlands"; but in point of method and accuracy he surpassed it afterwards in his "Natural History and Sport in Moray." and his "Tour in Southerlandshire." In his choice of residences he found admirable head-quarters for a man of his particular tastes. At one time he rented Invererne, on the Morayshire coast, a house lying between the cultivated country and an unfrequented waste of woods and sandhills; and then he removed to a mansion with a great old-fashioned garden in the outskirts of the town of Elgin. Now he was off on expeditions into the neighbouring mountains, as when he made that famous stalk of his on the "muckle hart of Benmore," or when he narrowly escaped being buried under an avalanche when looking for ptarmigan in their winter plumage. Now he was filling a mixed bag nearer home with a miscellaneous variety of lowland game, picked up in the course of a hard day's walking. Now he was stalking swans or geese on the Loch of Spynie or the shores of the bay, creatures even harder to come at than the wary red deer; now he was watching for wild duck in the dusk, as they streamed over his lurking-place in their flight from the sea to their feeding-grounds. He carried a gun in the season, and was a deadly shot; but the number of head he killed was quite a secondary consideration with him. By preference he would turn his steps towards that waste of sandhills where the foxes, left to forage undisturbed, grew to be "as large as wolves"; where the rabbits they fattened on had gnawed the furze-bushes they gambolled among into all manner of fantastic shapes; where, in fact, wild creatures of every kind had it all their own way, and where the cautious observer could study their habits as they followed the promptings of their instincts, unconscious of the presence of man. Or he would break off from so-called sports altogether, to stroll along the sea-shore when the tide was out, where the seals were basking on the rocks, or disporting themselves among the waves, and crowds of clamorous sea-fowl and water-fowl were picking up their living among the pools, the sand-eels, and the sea-weed. He was always on the look-out to welcome the earliest arrivals from foreign latitudes, to see the swans come trumpeting into the bay to settle down in a stately fleet upon its waters, or to mark the streaming flight of the grey or lag geese as they headed for some well-known haunt away among the inland lochs. It was most unlikely that any unfamiliar stranger would escape his wakeful attention; he marked each peculiarity in the form or plumage, and never rested till he established its identity. We cannot answer for other people, but to us he has given an infinity of new ideas on the birds that frequent these northern counties. Nearer his home, too, about his doors, and in his "policies," he was Gilbert White over again. The birds that were happy enough to settle under his wing enjoyed the immunities of absolute sanctuary. He went about poking after their nests as ardently as any of those boys of his who were brought up in his tastes. He can tell you almost to a day when it is their habit to set about nest-making. He can detect the presence of the shyest of them by their note; and should any stranger turn up unexpectedly his voice betrays his incognito, although he should keep himself modestly concealed. In short, we could expatiate for ever on St. John, but we have recalled enough of him to show what an enjoyable life may be led by a man of his fortunate turn of mind.

Nor have we time to linger with Stoddart and Stewart among the Scottish lochs and salmon-rivers, or the silvery trouting-streams of the Highlands and Border. But we cannot come southward again without an allusion to the veteran Christopher North in his Recreations. All accomplished as he was—politician and philosopher, essayist, romance-writer, and poet—Professor Wilson was a born sportsman, if ever there was one. In spite of their joyous and humorous exaggeration, nothing in the "Noctes Ambrosianæ" is so piquant as the passages where the merry party warms up to the recollection of some grand day with the gun or the rod. As when the Shepherd gives the reins to his glowing imagination in recounting his exploits on the way from Mount Benger to Tibbie Shiels', where he found the water everywhere in such magnificent cast and the fish in so grand a humour for taking. Or the scene at Tibbie's, *à la* Sneyders or Landseer, when the gillies come in and shoot out their loads of feathered game in unstudied studies of colour, at the corners of the little parlour. But it is in his Sporting Jacket in those Recreations of his that Christopher is simply perfect, beginning with the boyish reminiscences of the moorland parish where he was under the roof of the manse ; where such game as he cared for then swarmed like the midges on some mountain tarn, and you could not throw a stone into hedge or cornyard without sending a cloud of sparrows into the air. How humorous is the description of the exploits of himself and his comrades with the rusty pistol that was their common property—we think we remember something of the same kind in the introduction to the "Old Forest Ranger," also written by a Scotchman—or with the ancient single-barrel of portentous length and recoil that used to be supported along the shoulders of two of the party, while a third volunteered for the duty of discharging it ! So he leads us on through such feats of irregular shooting as his stealing in upon the heron struggling with the eel, since "we too can crawl silent as the sinuous serpent," to the finished exploits of the full-grown youth who drops his birds almost unfailingly to the fatal double-barrel, as he strides over the heather behind his highly-trained dogs, and who can throw a fly that falls light as thistle-down. There is nothing North touches that he does not adorn, even when the touch is a mere passing allusion. How one chuckles over the match he rode on Colonsay, when he cleared the impossible leap, or got jammed up among the north-country nowt; or over the coursing of the old hare that is the pet and playmate of the cottar's family, although she is more than suspected of being a witch—a suspicion that gains additional confirmation each time she shakes her fud at "the lang dogs," as she sets herself to breast the braes in earnest!

Scotland is *par excellence* the land of sport and scenery, in spite of a rough climate and treacherous temperature. Yet we can understand that there must be many who may prefer for a permanence the softer and richer beauties of the landscapes of merry England. It is the southern part of our islands we would naturally contrast with the half-inhabited aspect of continental Europe, as we have attempted to describe it. Go where you will in countries that are most essentially English in their character, there is the same sense of home-like enjoyment in a wide variety of easy existences among classes that shade insensibly into each other; nor does the enjoyment appear to be diminished very perceptibly even when united to great wealth and to grandeur, It may possibly be sour grapes, but we believe it on searching self-examination to be our sincere persuasion that we are grateful for not having been destined to dwell in mansions so magnificent as Chatsworth or Blenheim. Yet to say nothing of the enchanting country that generally surrounds them, the lords of such princely seats are not altogether to be pitied. Country gentlemen like their neighbours, in spite of the length of their rent-rolls, the plurality of their mansions, and a certain formal state that is the inevitable adjunct of their great positions, they manage to divert themselves with much the same pursuits as the more moderately-acred squire. To appreciate the attractions of their historic homes, and the sylvan beauties of their parks with the masses of secular timber, one ought to read Howitt. We own to having been early prejudiced in his favour, for his " Boy's Country Book " was one of our boyish delights ; but seeing how his " Book of the Seasons " and his " Visits to Remarkable Places " have asserted their influence on us in our maturity, we cannot believe that we admire him unduly. It is not only his bewitching panoramas of scenery, wonderfully true to nature as they are, when he invites you to an excursion across the brown moors of the Cheviots, or plunges with your waist-deep into the luxuriant bracken under the boughs of the oaks in some deer-park in the Midlands ; or when he leads you away to some deserted and half-forgotten old hall like Compton Wyniates—to some spectre-haunted Norman hold that looks grimly forbidding in the gloaming, like the ancient castle of the Lumleys ; or when he takes you on a brisk walk through the Black Country to the humble birthplace of an artist like Bewick, on the beautiful banks of the Tyne, past grim rows of colliers' cottages. But he thoroughly enters into the life of the English country-people of all ranks, reflecting their feelings with unfailing fidelity ; he sympathises with the pursuits of the squire and the farmer; bred a Quaker as he was, he has a friendly word for the worthy parson whose lines have fallen in these pleasant places; and, above all, he has a kindly feeling for the peasant and the working-man. It is writers like Howitt and Thomas Miller who love to bring out the home-like features of our rural life in their most attractive aspects; who make it a sacred sentiment to cherish the little that remains to us of old English manners and customs. Howitt is the more loth to see England stripped of its traditional poetry and romance, that he is so heartily alive to the benefits of our material progress, and the vast development of our manufacturing industries. Because the sea-breeze is tainted with the fumes of the chemical works, he abstracts himself all the more devoutly at the shrine of the Venerable Bede at Jarrow; and his fancy is the more lively among the ruins of Tynemouth, that he is looking down on the smoke of grimy Shields and on the shipping that crowds the river. And it is wonderful how much of rude romance he contrives to find among people you might set down as essentially prosaic; making no ostentatious exhibition of the interest he so evidently feels, he wins the confidence of the most reserved: whether he may have dropped into casual conversation with some dusty wayfarer, or have turned aside to ask his way of a cottager, or is gossiping pleasantly with some prim old lady, the *châtelaine* of some ancestral show-place. And as Providence helps those who help themselves, he is always in luck in his especial objects. He is perpetually stumbling in the course of his wanderings on feasts or fairs, or anniversaries or border games, and he is sure to make friends among garrulous merry-makers, storing his memory with their old-world tales.

If we desired to do the honours of England to a foreign friend, whether he came over the Channel or across the Atlantic, after giving him a glance at the immensity of London or the bustling prosperity of the port of Liverpool, we should invite him to accompany us on such a driving tour as Mr. Black describes in his "Adventures of a Phaeton." He might growl at the climate on the days when it was wet or windy; but he would have to confess in candour, in any average summer, that our watery atmosphere was not without its advantages. We have often revelled in the marvellous transparency of the air in districts like the upper valleys of the Alps, or even the higher plateaux of central Germany. Sitting before the door of your mountain inn, in the Engadine or the Oberland, you fancy you might distinguish the chamois at their gambols on the opposite snow-slopes; while in the German uplands you can almost count the buttons on the coat of the *bauer* who is driving the waggon with the team of oxen against the distant sky-line. But there is a wearisome monotony of effect in the brilliancy of that extreme limpidity. It cannot compare with the rich variety of lights among the softened shadows and changing colours of an English landscape, as you look down over waving crops, verdant meadow, and rolling woodland, through a faint transparency of haze and under a shimmering of fleecy clouds, from such a height as Richmond Hill or the terraces of the Crystal Palace. The stray showers and the heavy night dews keep everything fairly fresh and green, even in the dryer seasons. The very high-roads wind and dip as they are engineered in accordance with the undulations of the ground, in place of unrolling themselves straight on end like so many kilometres of sad-coloured ribbon, between their regular borderings of dust-peppered poplars. As to the labyrinths of woodland lanes in the home counties, you had better take your bearings before you commit yourself to them, if you have not chartered an experienced pilot. Now they have hidden themselves out of sight and well-nigh out of sound between deep banks that are watered by bubbling land-springs, and under the cool shade of the boughs that interweave themselves thickly overhead. The wheels grate lightly over gravel that reminds you of a gentleman's approach, although here and there you go jolting over the gnarled roots. Before you have wearied of the dim religious light, and begin to long for a glimpse of the glorious sunshine, you are emerging on some stretch of purple heath, or are breasting the slopes of some breezy down. The crest of each eminence and each turn of your road opens up a new infinity of prospect, as the eye travels along the lines of leafy undulations to some range of hills that hangs dimly in the distance. Nor are the broad pastures of the Midlands, or the wilder and more open landscapes of the Yorkshire Ridings, less lively in their way. You may miss the tangled luxuriance of hedgerow, the rich flowers or the fruit in the apple and cherry orchards, the hop-plants twining themselves from pole to pole, like the trellised vines of the plains of Italy ; but you have an exhilarating sense of life and freedom among those wide stretches of glorious galloping-ground divided by their stiff ox-fences and bull-finches, with the halls and manor-houses sheltering among their covers, and the willow-bordered streams meandering peacefully along the bottoms.

If there was little in the formal French *château* to excite any emotion of envy, we must own it is altogether a different thing when you are out on your wanderings in rural England. It must be a contented spirit indeed that is not being perpetually tempted by the hall or the rectory house, by the luxurious cottage or the comfortable homestead. Wedded as you may be to the ways of the town —inspired by some devouring ambition, or hotly excited in the fever of money-getting—you fancy, for the moment at least, that you might be perfectly happy if you were settled in one of those seductive abodes. It may be partly that the simpler and sounder part of our nature is asserting its instincts ; and it seems so easy to take kindly to a country life when a soothing languor has settled down on the smiling landscape, and you see everything around you in its rosiest colours. Of course it is long odds that you are altogether deceiving yourself, as a little cool reflection reminds you. You are like the veteran winebibber who tries to take to water-drinking : you have spoiled yourself for the calm of bucolic enjoyment all the year round. You would be perpetually sighing for the familiar excitement, and *ennui* might haunt you the more that you were relieved from the worst of your worries. But to those who have been bred and born to it there is assuredly nothing like a life in the country, at all events when that country is in the British Isles. You have but to look at your country friends and be convinced. Their ruddy faces and elastic or comfortable figures are the signs of light hearts and well-preserved health ; and if there are exceptions they only prove the rule. It can hardly be otherwise. Fresh air and good digestion, with the habit of exercise in the open air, make them strong to support or cast aside the sorrows that eat away the springs of a more artificial existence. The occcupations by which they get their living would be the recreations of other men ; and while they harmlessly excite themselves over sports and trifles they are apt to attain a serenity of temperament that almost borders on stolidity. So it comes about that farmers can slumber peacefully, and know no abatement of their vigorous appetites, while the rain is beating down on the hay or the wheat, while the drought is playing the mischief with the root-crops, or the foot-and-mouth disease has broken loose among the flocks of their neighbours. So landed proprietors sit lightly under mortgages and settlements, and easily console themselves with a growl or a grumble under unwelcome shortcomings on the rent-day, or even in a bad season for the birds.

CHAPTER II

A Highland Laird

WE have run over some of our favourite books on the country, and now we are tempted to try some random sketches of one or two of our familiar country friends. Take the Highland laird to begin with. His ancestors down to his grandfather were always hard up for cash, though they were lords of a wide extent of barren acres. His lands lie along one of the most lovely of the winding sea-arms on the western coast; and fifty years ago, or even less, the wreaths of blue peat-smoke might have been seen curling up from the hamlets or clachans in half a score of glens. The people who eked out the scanty produce of their crops by the profits of "the fishing" sat at small rents for the best of reasons. A considerable portion of the rent was paid "in kind"—in chickens, in peat-cutting, and other services; and in an unfavourable year, when the crops had failed, or the fishing, the pecuniary transactions were chiefly the other way. The laird had not only to forgive his people what they owed, but to feed them into the bargain. So there was a good deal to soften the separation to him when emigration came into fashion among his neighbours, and he decided to try the experiment. He was reluctant to part with the Donalds and the Duncans and their families, whose fathers had sat under his, and followed them to the field in clan feuds and civil broils from time immemorial. But it was clearly for the good of both parties; and he was bound to consider the prospects of his children as well as the feelings of his clansmen. Sheep-farmers from the south were shifting northwards, and there was a great and growing demand for grazing. Highland shootings were coming into favour with southern millionaires, and lands where leave to shoot used to be had for the asking were fetching rising rents in the market. So droves of the aboriginal Celts were consigned to the good offices of a shipping agent on the Broomielaw, and sent forth from the Clyde to try their fortunes in the Canadas. To this day you may trace the foundations of their houses in valleys, by the sides of the mountain brooks, and along the loch and the salmon-stream that winds through the haughs of the strath.

Doubtless this emigration to another continent was for the best. At all events, the present laird has no reason to regret it from a pecuniary point of view. He draws £1,500 a year from the sheep-grazings in Strathernan and Strathbran; and the grouse-shooting over the same ground is worth about as much more to him. He has £1,800 on a long lease for his deer-forest of Auchnaclosky ; the landlord of the inn at the mouth of the Ernan pays him a handsome price for the salmon and sea-trout fishing there ; while he disposed of some outlying hills at what was then deemed a fabulous price, although already he regrets his precipitation in parting with them. In fact, for his many square leagues of rock, heath, and bog, interspersed with patches of mountain grazing, he draws the income of a fine property in the most fertile of the English counties. But with all that he has not stinted himself and his friends in the amusements to which he is keenly devoted. He has kept in his own hands an ample range of the woods and the heather that stretch away from immediately around the house ; and he can boast of as pretty a shooting in every sense as any gentleman of his means in the Highlands. Probably rather by chance than from design the house was set down in a charming situation ; and, thanks to the modern additions he has made, it is as roomy and comfortable as he could wish, though by no means architecturally attractive. It stands in the middle of feathering birches on the romantic banks of Lochlyle ; and out of the broken ground that extends behind it rises a range of bold, heathery uplands that lose themselves high overhead in a mountainous jumble of rocks and precipices. In a creek below you may see the masts of the little cutter that transports him easily to his more distant beats ; while half a dozen of broad-bottomed boats in the boat-house are eloquent of excellent fishing. Although

his seat is pretty much at the back of the world;
although his precarious posts are delivered to him
by boat and steamer, and the landscape is wild enough
in all conscience—yet the climate on the lower levels
is anything but ungenial, as is shown by the shrubs
that thrive in luxuriance in his wife's romantic little
flower-garden. As for the game, in point of variety,
he has nearly everything that man need desire. You
have magnificent roe-drives in the woods and the
rough ground that lie along the shores of the loch.
You may walk up the graceful animals like hares
among the bracken under the birches; and many
a merry day the laird has there in autumn, when he
has them running in rings round his post among the
tree-trunks to the music of his lively little beagles.
Along the scattered corn-fields in the strath at the
loch-head, there are plenty of coveys of the small
hill-partridges, where you may amuse yourself pleasantly
enough when the weather is wet and the grouse are
wild; while as you wade through the marshy ground
that is overflowed from time to time by the river, you
have the snipe getting up in wisps all about you. As
for the grouse, of these there are any reasonable
quantity. The beats are long—it is nothing to walk
six or eight miles before you think of uncoupling the
dogs—and the walking is rough; but then you can get
fair shooting till late in the year, for the coveys are
in no hurry to pack. And such shooting as it is, for a
man who has the soul of a poet or the eye of an artist!
As you gradually mount higher and higher the views

become grander and more extensive. Lochlyle, with its sheltered bays and wooded islands, unfolds itself in all its length beneath you, running out and in among the purple hills, and losing itself from your sight in land-locked little harbours. Inland you follow the course of the strath, with here and there a solitary house or a shepherd's shieling; while as you ascend higher still into the zones of the ptarmigan you open up rocky vistas through the surrounding heights, through which you get glimpses of the carse-lands in the distant Lowlands. The mountain air has a perceptible scent of the brine and the sea-weed, as well it may have, for it is salt water you are looking down upon in Lochlyle; and the surge of the Atlantic is breaking at the back of those splintered peaks that hem in the horizon away to the westward.

More exciting, perhaps, than the best of the grouse-shooting, is a day up there among the ptarmigan in the late autumn, when they are beginning to change to their winter plumage. Not that the shooting them is difficult, for the birds are always in extremes. At first they get up wild enough, and go circling round the mountain-tops high in the air like swift flights of carrier-pigeons; but when you have flushed them several times they will cower down motionless among the lichen-covered stones, from which their mottled feathers are scarcely to be distinguished. But there is a strange pleasure in the crisp keenness of the air, the magnificence of the bird's-eye views over the panoramas that unfold themselves around you, and

Ptarmigan motionless among the Lichen-covered Stones. *By* Archibald Thorburn.

the glimpses of solitude-loving beasts and birds that you are likely to get if you are in luck. In spite of the persecutions of the agents of ornithologists, more than one pair of golden eagles have their eyries in the hills that overhang Lochlyle; and they may often be seen sweeping round overhead, as if they felt themselves monarchs of all they surveyed, although they prudently keep themselves well out of rifle-shot. There are sea-eagles, too, among the rocks that hang over the ocean, and a pair of peregrine falcons have built since the memory of man in an inaccessible cliff in the laird's deer-forest. Ten to one you may catch sight of a sleek though sinewy old mountain-fox, taking himself leisurely off in the broad daylight to his quarters in one of the many cairns around you. You have startled him probably from his slumbers in the heather where he laid himself up after a heavy meal and a long night of successful foraging. There is a handsome price set upon his head, and it is hard to say whether the shepherds or the keepers hate him with a more perfect hatred; nor is there any better fun, by the by, to be had on an off-day than drawing one of these stone-heaps for a vixen and her litter, with a few frantic couples of varmint-terriers. Before you get to the crest of the lower hills, the mountain-hares have been lolloping up before you by dozens, like rabbits disturbed at feeding-time on the skirts of a low-country warren. Troublesome as they are to the best-broken dogs, you feel you could very easily spare them; yet they make capital subjects for a Highland *battue*, when you have the lower grounds driven in a narrowing circle of beaters towards the guns that are stationed on the heights above. You may roll them over then by hundreds, or even by thousands; and it must be owned they come as a godsend to the Highland kitchen, where the soup is made on the liberal receipt of the Ettrick Shepherd—half a dozen hares to each tureen.

Walking over the grouse-ground you come upon sheep in each grassy hollow; and although they may be sufficiently picturesque objects, with their shaggy fleeces and their curling horns, yet they are decided nuisances in many ways. The shepherds may be on bad terms with the gillies, and may revenge themselves on the grouse-eggs and the young broods, which they naturally come across in the course of their peregrinations. The collies in any case are always disturbing the ground; and on the very day you have devoted to a favourite beat you find that the herds of sheep are being driven in, and gathered in flocks to be numbered. In the solitudes of the forest of Auchnaclosky there is no nuisance of the kind. There you are absolutely alone with nature, and the red deer, and the "vermin" that are carefully kept up in order to keep down the grouse. Auchnaclosky consists of a conglomeration of half-inaccessible hills, split up by the deep precipitous valleys that lead to nowhere in particular. Unless you were as much at home in these as the laird himself, or the keepers who have charge of that portion of his grounds, you would be perpetually landing yourself in *culs-de-sac*, and being lured on into ugly scrambles where retreat is difficult and advance impossible. The forest is "grand ground," as any connoisseur will tell you. Although by no means large, it is amply stocked, for there are famous preserves on three sides of it; and in the depths of its valleys there is splendid feeding that seduces the deer from extraordinary distances. But the stalking is as difficult as well may be. In the first place, you may sweep your range of vision with the telescope, overlooking, after all, a number of animals hidden out of sight, who will be sure to spoil the stalk on the victim you have selected. Then unless you have the head and foot of a chamois-hunter you are not at all unlikely to come to grief: while the actual exercise—toiling up rocky heights, only to come down again; hanging on to ledges of rocks by the eyelids; dragging yourself along stony water-courses at a frightful expenditure of skin and homespun—is safe to try the temper and to test the stamina of the strongest. Finally, it is difficult for the most experienced of stalkers to make due allowance for the caprices of the wind. It twists and turns in the most tantalising fashion in the folds of the hills and the recesses of the corries; and just as you are crawling up wind, as you fondly imagine, and congratulating yourself on a highly successful cast, you are disagreeably conscious of a side puff on your cheek that must infallibly carry the alarm to the quarry. But all the difficulties that would be insurmountable drawbacks to many people are only additional attractions to the laird. Many is the night he has lain out under the "Shelter Stone" with a bundle of heather for a pillow, his plaid for bed-clothes, and a sandwich and his whisky-flask for sole refreshments; although now, chiefly in deference to the sybaritism of his friends, he has set up a tiny lodge in the wilderness, where they can be tolerably comfortable on occasion.

Though the laird in these latter days occasionally takes his family to town for a month or so in the season, his habits are very different from those of the gentlemen who make a dash at the moors or the forests for a few weeks in the autumn. He lives on his territory all the year round; sport in its different shapes is pretty much his sole avocation; and he is most hospitable in filling his house with guests who take his annual invitations almost as a matter of course. It is odd indeed if they cannot find plenty to do; and even if they should be kept close prisoners by the weather, there are a library and an excellent billiard-table and agreeable young women within doors. There is capital mixed shooting on the lower ground, or what may be called the lower ground by comparison. The birch-woods that come feathering down to Lochlyle are famous places for black-game and woodcocks; and when a flight of woodcocks arrives with the first frost, the laird sends expresses forthwith to his neighbours, who are looking out in keen expectation. These gentlemen gather in fast with their attendant gillies, and the party sets out in line after breakfast from the very door of the house. Now it is a hare that gets up, now a couple of roe who have been crouching in their lair with ears laid back and heads buried in the heather, hoping in vain that the *vacarme* would go by. Now they stumble among some partridges that rise only to scatter and drop again ; and then in the corner of some thicker patch of cover they possibly have the agreeable distraction of a brilliant little bouquet of pheasants. A little farther, and they are in the best of the woodcock ground. Small streamlets, half choked with the frost, come trickling down among rime-covered rushes ; the cry of " mark-cock " makes itself heard more and more frequently in every variety of Gaelic gutturals ; and then follows the shot or the succession of shots, as the crescent-winged bird goes zigzagging softly away among the scattered tree-stems in some clearing in the copsewood. Or there is a whir and a loud rustle through the trees, and the heavy blackcock is brought up in his rapid flight, to come down with a crash among the branches that interlace themselves over the brook below.

In winter, when there is little else to be had, there is duck and wild-fowl shooting ; and that in spring and early summer is followed by the salmon-fishing. The laird prides himself on his skill with the rod rather more than on his prowess with the rifle ; and he is as well off for water as he ought to be, considering the variety of it that there is on his domains. Trout swarm everywhere; and though the little yellow-bellied fellows in the brooks and rivulets seldom run more than four to the pound, they are wonderfully strong for their size. As a rule, however, except for an occasional dish for breakfast, very little attention is paid to these, although now and then the boys will condescend to ply the otter among the shoals of still smaller fry in one of the mountain tarns. But there is unrivalled sea-trout fishing at the head of the loch, where the tide runs into the river; and the lower pools of the Ernan are famed far and wide for salmon. Where the hills have closed in on the level strath, the Ernan winds along among the rocks and the birch-woods, now tumbling over half-submerged shelves in an infinity of white tiny cataracts—now rushing along in a narrowed bed in a succession of black, bubbling swirls—now eddying fretfully under the bank, beneath the overhanging roots and the heather. It is no easy matter to make a cast in some of these pools, where you have to balance yourself in fishing-boots on a slippery shelf, with the branches of the trees behind bending down over your shoulder; and you dare not cut them away, for fear of the salmon resenting it. But the laird handles his heavy rod in these circumstances as if he had been born and bred up to the calling of an acrobat: he casts a long line out underhand, with the skill that has been born of much experience; and the sober-coloured fly is pitched, with miraculous dexterity, right into the very ripple it is meant for. But when the fish does come at it with a resolute rush, and the long line runs out with a rattle, the situation of the angler may be critical, not to say positively perilous. Fighting every yard of the water on a system of tactics that changes with the necessities of the case, it is a question when to humour the salmon, when to force him, and when to head him up the stream by dint of firm persuasion. Instinct suggests the most dangerous dodges to him, and he seems to be thoroughly aware how awkwardly his enemy is hampered. "Show him the butt" may be an excellent maxim; but how are you to do it when you are doubled up among the trees, with the top of the rod rustling against the branches? He makes a dash straight for the sea, as if he had no idea of stopping till he got there; and if you are too brusque in your hints that he had better not hurry, it is a sovereign to a shilling that something gives way with you. He is doing everything he knows to test the soundness of your tackle, if he is foiled in that determined rush. He is winding the line about among the stones, grazing it against their sharp edges, or else he is down with his nose in the gravel, grinding at the hook for dear life. Possibly he takes to sulking—a sore trial to the temper—when he absolutely declines to pay any attention to the stones that are hailed down in his direction. And it is worse still when he will insist upon your following him, although the track along the banks is well-nigh impracticable, even when the scrambler has both hands at his disposal. But the trials and anxieties increase the value of the triumph, when at last he begins to own himself beaten, and when you can see the scales of silver glancing to the light as you guide him gently within reach of the gaff. Not a pennyweight less than sixteen pounds, in prime condition, clean run from the sea, and covered still with the sea-lice he has brought with him. A fish like that deserves a dram ; and the laird takes a hearty pull at his flask before passing it on to his gillie. Nor has he seen the last of him, as he is happy to think, when the salmon is sent promptly off to the kitchen ; and the well-spread table of a well-conducted Highland mansion is far from being one of its least agreeable features. The cook is something of a *cordon bleu*, and never at a loss for materials. What haunches and necks of hill-flavoured venison ! and to our mind, the red deer, with the sauce of a Highland appetite, is no whit inferior to the park-fed fallow deer. At all events, there is no saying a word in detraction of the saddles and cutlets of the mountain mutton. We have adverted already to the tureens of hare-soup, that should be delicately flavoured with port or Madeira ; and then there are the grouse of the season, that have just been sufficiently hung, without sacrificing the piquancy of the bitter of the backs—grouse *en salmi*, and in pies, and split and " brandered " ; the woodcocks fat as butter, with their melting trails ; the black-game, that make an agreeable variety ; the snipe and the ducks ; the salmon, served in the sublime simplicity of the water that boiled him, and in cutlets, and in curry, and in kipper ; the pink-coloured sea-trout and the white little burn-trout by no means bad in their way as a *pis aller* for breakfast ; herrings from the loch, delicate as those of Loch Fyne ; and fresh haddocks from the neighbouring ocean that might hold their own with those of Dublin Bay. Considering that the laird has an excellent cellar, and that the family has always prided itself on its claret in especial, since his grandsire and forebears were in the habit of smuggling it, it must be owned that a man might find worse quarters, although Lochlyle may be scarcely a paradise, so far as its climate is concerned.

CHAPTER III

An English Squire

PERHAPS the Highlands have most fascination for a man with a dash of the adventurer in him, who is hard and sound in mind and body ; who loves to brace his sinews in exposure and with severe exercise ; who does not object to an occasional touch of hardship ; who can make himself happy among well-chosen books as the companions of his leisure hours, when he is not living in a house that is filled with congenial company. But there is much to be said, on the other hand, for the life of the English squire. It is true that, so far from being monarch of all he surveys, and a good deal more, he is rather "crowded up," as the Yankees would say. The lands of his neighbours cut here and there into his own ; and when he flushes birds upon farms not very far from his house, they are apt to drop beyond his boundaries. But then he has plenty of pleasant society in a neighbourhood that is full of quiet, domestic beauties, if it has not the grandeur of the shores of Lochlyle. The hall may stand a trifle low. Those who built the oldest part of it, in the days of the Tudors, had a habit of coming down like rats to the water. But the suspicion of damp that hangs about the little river and the lake fosters timber and shrubberies into the richer luxuriance, and gives a brilliant freshness to the grass and the foliage. The house is a long and rather rambling building, where you have never far to mount to your room, though you may have a long way to walk along the corridors and up the quaint oak staircases; and the mullioned windows, with their lozenged lattices, are embowered in their masses of roses and creepers. The doors open on a broad terrace looking over the velvet lawns and variegated flower-beds to the undulations of the beautifully timbered park, that seems to shade away imperceptibly into the woodlands beyond. Scattered clumps of venerable trees throw out their gnarled boughs over great beds of bracken and bramble, where the fallow deer stand buried to their heads and horns; while there are groups of cattle that are scarcely less ornamental. Everything bears evidence of careful overlooking and liberal expenditure. The oaken fences of the park are kept up to perfection; and there is hardly a weed or a rut on the broad gravel drives, which provide easy and well-paid employment for half the old people in the village. The village itself is a show one. A low-aisled Norman church, with ivy-grown tower and moss-covered lich-gate, and superannuated yews all rent and torn by time, scattered about among the simple tombstones; a rectory half hidden out of sight among great shrubberies of laurel; quaint-gabled cottages in blooming gardens—cottages that are either as old as they seem or else admirable modern imitations; an old-fashioned inn, with a great bow-window and a broad gravelled space before the door, where the sign is swinging from an overshadowing elm tree; and better than all, a general look of contentment and cheerful comfort, which tells of confidence in kindly friends and happy relations with generous landlords.

The estate is a model of good English farming of the olden time, with just so many modern improvements introduced as may be compatible with preserving its picturesque appearance. Farm houses with spacious kitchens, and with sumptuous parlours that are only used upon state occasions; rambling steadings round great straw-yards, where the cattle are ruminating up to their bellies in litter, and where pigs, constrained to cleanliness in spite of themselves, are grunting and gorging themselves in supreme felicity; a shady horse-pond well stocked with ducks and geese, flocks of fat poultry picking up a leisurely living among the wheat-stacks, and flights of pigeons cooing on the tiles. There has been little grubbing of hedgerows or straightening of roads. The lanes meander about among thorn-bushes, matted with the wild clematis and overgrown with the wild hop and honeysuckle. There is turf enough between the hedges and the cart-way to pasture the horses of whole caravans of tramps and gipsies; and, in fact, you may often see them hobbled there, while the kettles are slung before the tents in some nook out of the wind or the sunshine. The fields are cut up in all manner of waving lines and fantastic patterns, by copses and hangers and outlying spinneys, linked together by lines of trees growing out of the straggling hedges. It is scarcely what you would call a partridge country. There is more grass than wheat; and the root-crops on the higher lands, especially in a dry season, would seem mere spectres of profitable cultivation to a gentleman who farms in the Lothians. With so much that is primitive, even in the way of woods and furze and hedgerows, it is impossible to lay your hand on the birds at the precise moment you are looking for them; and when you do find them it is long odds that you fail to mark them in their longer flights. Yet they are there in plenty, as you may be very sure; for there are a wealth of breeding-places, and endless corners where they can bask, and delightfully dry elevations where they can take refuge from the rains in the spring. The fields are carefully bushed as you may see, and there is an ample strength of keepers; though the villagers, who have lived like their fathers on the estate, are but little addicted to poaching.

But the feature in such a south-country shooting is the pheasants; and the land looks as if it had been laid out with a special eye to their delectation. Till they come to a sudden and violent death, the wild broods have pleasant times of it, with the dense undergrowth of bramble, where nothing but a fox or some prowler of the weasel species can make its way ; with the gorse covers where the foxes are carefully preserved, in the hope that they may stick pretty much to the rabbits ; with the great patches of bracken in the park and along the lanes ; with the long, dry, grassy-covered ways, that run under the roots of the hedges. And then the numbers that are brought up under fowls. The head-keeper is hand-in-glove with the farmers, and their good-wives are always willing and eager to supply him with sitting-hens. Spring after spring he shifts his breeding-ground, but it is always on some sunny, sheltered aspect in the immediate neighbourhood of his cottage and the kennels. There the long lines of coops are set out in the rank grass that is carefully mown immediately in front of them ; and he or one of his subordinates is always on sentry duty to guard against the descent of hawks or jackdaws. How he has gone questing about in search of the early eggs before the voracious rooks and magpies have had time to anticipate him ! What a pretty sight it is, when the young ones are hatched and come running out of the grass to his call ! And later, before the first of October, when their plumage is in its bloom, and they begin to take a conscious pride in it, how ornamental they are in the stubbles and on the cover-side ! How he can reconcile it to his feelings to see these pets of his shot down is a question between himself and his conscience—on the same principle, we suppose, as the motherly poultry-woman cherishes her ducklings to come in with the peas. But it is certain that there is a

AN ENGLISH SQUIRE

great charm in pheasant-shooting, however one may abuse the *battues*, for which we have no great love ourselves. There are few things pleasanter on a fresh autumn day, when the foliage has been thinned by rain, and the frosts have opened daylight through the broken-down undergrowth, and when the leaves that are still hanging on the trees are glowing in their gorgeous autumnal tints. Nor can anything be more lively than working quietly behind a couple or so of spaniels, when they are forcing the wandering birds out of the hedges and running them through the outlying covers.

Rabbits may be a curse to the farmer when they are suffered to breed to excess, but we know no better fun than rabbit-shooting, over spaniels or terriers. So the squire thinks, who lets his land at easy rents to the tenants, making no secret of his tastes, and is liberal in distributing what he kills among the farmers and the poor people in his cottages. And when a frost in the winter keeps the hounds at home, he is often to be seen, with keepers and ferrets, a terrier or two, and a retriever, bending his steps towards some well-known burrow. Many of the gravelly banks that enclose his plantations are mined and countermined in all directions. The difficulty is to persuade the rabbits to bolt, when they have so many opportunities of dodging their pursuers. But a couple of ferrets or more are put in, at the risk of having the rabbit taken in front and flank, and compelled to succumb to the blood-suckers below ground. You hear a subterraneous rumbling and rattling and scrambling that now seems to draw near the mouth of some hole, and the next moment rapidly recedes from it. At last the persecuted victim takes heart of grace, and shoots out of some unsuspected bolting-hole, altogether hidden among the grass and the fallen leaves. The terriers who have been watching for him with cocked ears, cannon up against each other in their eager rush, and you have to shoot clear of them, and shoot quickly, before the nimble game disappears under some convenient branches. There is an extreme satisfaction in a rabbit rolled over by a clean shot, more especially when his impetus has carried him out of sight, and you are at a loss to know whether you have killed or missed him. In the open park the sport is comparatively simple. The rabbits burrow in the mounds of turf under the roots of the venerable thorns ; while on occasion they even scramble up the hollow trunks, and come tumbling out of unsuspected orifices on high, to the extreme astonishment and disgust of the jackdaws.

Whatever our individual opinion may be, it is certain the squire would never hesitate between his English home and a principality in the Highlands. His heart may be in the Highlands, among the deer in the season, and possibly his person too ; but if he were sent to the Highlands to settle he would have to leave his horses behind him to begin with. Except a pair for his lady's carriage, and the serviceable beast he drives in his dogcart, the laird keeps nothing but the "shelties" that run loose in his "parks," and bear him out to his remoter beats, or bring home his deer or the heavy game-hampers. The squire's stables, so far as they go, are among the most complete in the county, and the horses that fill their stalls are as the very apples of his eyes. He does not live in the "shires," as may be surmised from our descriptions of the scenery. He does not profess to have an interminable string, the half of them on the sick-list or eating their heads off, so that he may hunt himself with second horses five days in the week, allow for casualties and the caprices of a stud-groom, and mount a friend or two on occasion. But the best part of his neighbourhood may be described as "a fair hunting country," though it is a trifle cramped about his own domains; and he takes care to mount himself that he may be carried comfortably with a stone or a couple of stones to spare, though prices are high enough in any case, and go up in arithmetical progression for every pound above a certain point. He does a little in the breeding way himself. One of his largest tenants is regularly in that line of business; and more than one dealer makes a point of breaking his journey at the neighbouring inn on his way homewards from Horncastle or elsewhere. There are worse places to smoke a cigar in of a winter morning, when the hounds are frozen up hard and fast in their kennels, than the warmed and well-ventilated seven-stall stable, when the old head-groom goes stripping the clothing, passing his hand along the muscular thighs and hocks, the well-ribbed-up barrels, and the powerful loins and quarters. The squire has seldom to pay excessive prices for his horses, considering their looks, because, rather than not, he would have something that wants riding; but with his light hand and firm yet flexible seat, they soon fall into his ways, and seldom dream of refusing. If there is a fault in his style of going, it is that he goes a trifle too straight, and takes it out of the animals he rides instead of trying to save them. Enthusiastic pheasant-preserver as he is, Gorhambury Gorse and the Hazeldean woods are among the surest draws in the country, and the squire's well-deserved reputation for hospitality makes his mansion one of the most popular meets. Then the grand entrance-hall, the great dining-room, and the breakfast-room, are all laid out with tables *en suite*, and every one with the slightest pretensions to admission is made welcome to cut and come again among the viands that load the side-tables and buffets. Then the home-brewed, that reminds one of Trinity audit, is broached for those who are kicking their heels outside, and the gardener must endure as best he may the inroads that are made on his turf and his shrubberies. There is nothing that borders on the riotous or boisterous, for with all his hospitality and frank good-humour, the squire has a strong sense of decorum; yet nothing can be more jovial than the mixed multitude that files off at the tail of the pack when it follows the huntsmen to the nearest fox-cover.

The taste for horseflesh has been in the family for generations. Our friend's grandfather was a famous gentleman-whip in the days of the Regency; and the walls of the billiard and smoking rooms are hung at this present moment with a variety of portraits of himself and his horses. In drab driving-coat, curl-brimmed hat, and belcher scarf, he is springing his team of bays over Five Mile Bottom; he is doing the Park behind Trojan and Traveller, the grey and the chesnut, in his mail phaeton; he is sending along Marigold, his wonderful trotting mare, in a cloud of dust before a mob of spectators, from a perch between a pair of gigantic yellow wheels. That light of old coaching-days, as well as his son who came after him, used to help to horse the Highflyer, and drive it too. *Eheu, fugaces!* these times are gone. The great posting-house of the "Wheatsheaf," half a mile from the lodge gates, where a dozen of coaches used to change horses daily, and which had stabling for a hundred pair and more, has been tenanted for long by an ordinary farmer, and the racks and mangers have gone to wreck and ruin. The surrounding agriculturists have to consign to more distant markets the oats they used to shoot into its well-stored bins, and the hay that was weekly delivered by the waggon-load. But the present man does something to keep up the family tradition. When he takes his carriage-horses to town, connoisseurs will still turn to look at them. His park hack is a model of symmetry, and cost him considerably more than the best of his weight-carriers; while necessarily he is an eminent member of the coaching club, and the critics are hard put to it when they set to picking faults in his turn-out. Consequently there is always something worth looking at in his paddocks; and nothing can be prettier in the way of pets than the colts and the fillies of illustrious race that come whinnying at their master's heels, seeking to rub their silken muzzles on his shoulder, and hunting after apples or sugar in the broad pockets of his shooting-coat.

Except, perhaps, the occupants of the kennels. At the hall they still shoot over dogs, for the country is little adapted to walking in line. And the squire's setters are so many pictures. What action they show when you see them out! what dash and fire, and yet what perfect training! They are rather dearer to the keeper than his own children, and yet he is a most affectionate parent. Broken by gentleness and not brutality, in their wildest swing they always keep their eye on their master, answering to the slightest wave of his hand. "Handsome is as handsome does"; but their steadiness and splendid action are as admirable as their animated eyes and silken coats, their sinewy loins and feathering sterns. Then there are the Sussex spaniels, that make such merry melody after the pheasants and rabbits; and the lively little terriers, with their prick ears and game limp; and, last but not least, the curly retrievers, with a staid demeanour beyond their years, and a world of sagacity in their thoughtful faces. And everybody and everything about the place—farmers and cottagers ; servants, from the bailiff, the forester, and the chief butler, down to the smallest helper in the stable-yard ; horses and dogs, pigeons and ornamental water-fowl—are all devoted to the master ; so if his lot is not an enviable one, we should like to know a lot that is.

But after all, and without so many worldly advantages, there are others of our country acquaintances who are at least as happy as either the squire or the laird. The rector, for instance, who holds the lucrative little family living, and ministers to the spiritual and temporal wants of a small and scattered population, who have known him and whom he has known from his childhood. He discourses to them out of the pulpit with an intimate personal knowledge of their necessities. In time of health, as in seasons of sickness, he has always a warm greeting everywhere. If there is a bit of a tift in a family, or a difference between master and servants, it is the parson who, of course, is called in to settle matters ; and if all the parishes were ministered to like his, the lawyers might starve for lack of litigation. Off go the hats in the length of the village street when the broad-brimmed, black wideawake and the pepper-and-salt suit are seen coming down the causeway. The women are bobbing and ducking in their doors, inwardly hoping that the rector may turn aside to them ; and the children are for ever getting in his way, looking out for a kindly word or a caress. The young men regard him with mingled love and veneration, for there is not a bat among them that can hold its own against his round-hand bowling ; and when his eye is in, and he takes to judgmatical cutting and driving, he teaches the panting field the secret of perpetual motion. He is not only the leading member of the club, but its very generous patron, though his kinsman, the squire, is hereditary president. He is the life and soul of the cricketing suppers and the other entertainments he gets up for those who do not care for the willow. He would be the last to rob a poor man of his beer, and is on the best of terms with the village landlord, though he sets his face against anything like excess, and takes care that the merriment of these social meetings shall never degenerate into anything unseemly. He used to shoot at one time, but he has given it up ; and now he contents himself with the fishing, to which he is devoutly attached. Not a man in his own or the adjoining parishes can come near him in the delicate skill with which he lures the wary fish out of these still and pellucid waters. But with all his healthy activity and delight in the open air, not the least pleasant of his hours are those he passes in his library. The little room with the great bay-window looking out on the brilliant flower-beds is a marvel of quiet literary luxury, with the well-chosen volumes assorted in the cases and the periodicals and journals that litter the tables. For the rector was a scholar, and took creditable honours, in spite of an early attachment to the cricket-field ; and he was a Fellow of a distinguished college to boot before he was fortunate enough to fall in with his wife. Simply eloquent and pointed as his sermons are, it is only as matter of good sense that he does not make them more learned and more elaborately ornate. For when he takes pen in hand to address himself to a cultivated circle in the pages of one of the leading quarterlies or monthlies, it travels over the pages in a rush of inspiration, and wins him admiration from the most fastidious critics. It only rests with himself to remove to more sensational spheres of usefulness; nor is there any reason, with his piety and his gifts, his manners and his excellent family connections, why he should not legitimately aspire to the highest places in the Church. But he has the sense to know when he is happy and serviceable, and is very reluctant to change. In all human probability he will live and die in the parish he was born in, and be gathered peacefully to his fathers in the family burying-ground under the aged yew tree at the end of the chancel.

Nor may the life of a well-to-do farmer be less desirable in its way, allowing for differences in education and station. Cares and anxieties he has, of course, but, as we observed already, he comes to carry them lightly; for if he sits at a reasonable rent, has a snug sum put away in some safe investment, and has credit or a floating balance at the county bank, experience tells him that things will come right in the end, on the average of a succession of fluctuating seasons. Early to bed and early to rise, eating largely, and knowing nothing of nerves or digestion, passing the livelong day in the open air among the up-turned furrows and breezy fallows, his health is robust and his spirits equable. Unless matters go very badly indeed, he acquires a happy knack of regarding everything as all for the best. If the rain does harm to the hay, it is just what he wants for the roots or the shooting corn-crops; and if prolonged drought is parching his herbage and forcing him to make premature inroads on his hayricks, at least it is ripening the wheat in perfection. If the length and the breadth of the islands were before us to choose, we scarcely know where we should prefer to farm. Though the weight of the winter snowdrifts might lie somewhat heavy on our mind, we fancy we might be happy as a Dandie Dinmont in the dales of the Scotch border or among the moorlands on the Cheviots. We can imagine the pleasure of the early walk among our flocks over the grassy hills or the heathery uplands, with the silence only broken by the bleating of sheep, the whistle of the plover, or the cry of the curlew. We can conceive the intense excitement of lambing-time, when hopes are blossoming into fruition, and the young ones are dropping into the folds by pairs; the lively scenes of the washing and shearing; the drafting off the surplus stock for despatch to the Falkirk Tryst or some other of the markets. But then for a skilled and scientific agriculturist, whose soul is in his pursuits, we know there can be nothing like a great farm in the fertile Lothians or the Carse of Gowrie, lying round its superb steading. Everything that can be done is done by steam-power; everything is ingeniously made the most of; the latest discoveries in

AN ENGLISH SQUIRE

agricultural chemistry have been pressed into the capitalist's service; and in the course of a walk over his ground you may study the best and most practical of modern mechanical inventions. Yet the introduction of steam would not seem to have materially reduced the number of hands in the farmer's employment, nor those teams of sleek and powerful horses whose work appears to agree with them so well, But steam and skill and science have conspired to bring the land to the highest pitch of cultivation; the waving fields of golden grain are a sight to gladden the eye and heart, as is the straw in the bulging stack-yard, when the best of them have been cut and carried; and as for the turnips and mangels, as compared to what you see in the southern counties, they are as Indian jungle to an English pheasant-cover. Notwithstanding which, in point of picturesqueness and climate, and cheery surroundings, a man of æsthetic temperament might not unnaturally prefer the south; but as we have already passed some time there with the parson and the squire, we must not go back on a visit to the farmers.

Nor, after all we have been saying of farming and shooting, do we care to loiter among shepherds and keepers. Yet the men who have betaken themselves to such healthy occupations are much to be envied, since their tastes and the manner of their bringing up has kept them below disturbing ambitions. Contrast their happy circumstances with those of the most highly paid labourers and mechanics—the colliers who may be in the habit of working all day and sleeping all night;

who seldom except of a Sunday have a look at the noonday sun; with their chances of being crushed, or imprisoned alive, or scorched and stifled in an explosion of choke-damp, and the certainty of having to breathe in foul air at a suffocating temperature, while hewing and picking with unnatural contortions. Or with the fate of the Sheffield cutler, or the Manchester cotton-spinner, or the Spitalfields silk-weaver; or even with that of the men whose occupations are not absolutely unhealthy, but who have to huddle up their families in a small room or two in some crowded court, and who are almost driven to drink as an antidote to the noxious atmosphere. If the keeper does not live near the black countries or some great manufacturing town, where the poachers go abroad in gangs and do not shrink from bloodshed on occasion, the worst hardship he has to put up with is a healthy midnight walk to see that all is right in the covers, with the possibility, perhaps, of a chase and a round at single-stick should he chance to come across some trespasser. He is paid for taking the pleasures that cost his employer dear, and on the whole he has a greater variety of amusement. For he rarely goes on his rounds without his gun, ready to knock over a hawk, or a magpie, or a hooded crow, or to take a snap-shot at a stoat or a weasel. He has never been taught that trapping may be cruel, and we are sorry to think it would be next to impossible to persuade him of it; and, cruelty apart, it must be confessed that there is a good deal of interest in circumventing the different wild animals, whose in-

AN ENGLISH SQUIRE 59

stincts make them portentously distrustful. As for the mountain shepherd, his avocation is as innocent as poetic; and the morbidly sentimental Cockneys who set their faces against all manner of field-sports, can have nothing in the world to say against him.

CHAPTER IV

A Kentish Parish

WHAT an infinite variety of pictures may be suggested by a single word! A parish may lie anywhere between Cape Wrath and Beachy Head, the Land's End and the lights of Cromer. It may be wild moorland, and forty miles long, with a cottage kirk a world too wide for a scattered congregation of shepherds and keepers. It may be bleak cornland, painfully reclaimed from a shivering waste of dreary peat-bogs, where the farm-steadings, though substantial, are all built for use, and the nearest approach to ornamental landscape-gardening is the belt of firs or the clump of "bourtree" bushes. It may embrace a smiling strath in the Lowlands, or a range of rich green hills on the Border, watered by a thousand streams and rills, and peopled in each lap of the landscape by its bleating flocks. It may be overcrowded with grimy colliers, who have honeycombed it with their mines and defaced its natural beauties with the smokes of their countless fires. It may be in the soft green Midlands, where the broad stretches of

A KENTISH PARISH

pasture, shut in by their ox-fences and blind bullfinches, are associated with fields of magnificently-mounted men following the streaming pack at flying speed ; where each cover and gorse thicket may have its litter of foxes, and every mansion of any pretension its grand ranges of hunting stables. It may lie among the wheat-stubbles and mangel-wurzels of the eastern counties, where countless coveys are basking on the sunny banks, and each corner of wood and spinney in the season sends up its constellation of rocketing pheasants ; or it may be down among the meres and decoys of the fens, where fogs envelop everything in a vapoury mantle, and the amphibious inhabitants are happily half fever-proof. Or among the tors and moors of Devon, where herds of shaggy ponies run wild with the sheep and the red deer ; or among the rocks and blasted heaths of Cornwall, where one half the parishioners hazard their lives underground, while the other half are tempting Providence on the surges of the tempest-driven ocean. It may be half hidden out of sight in woodlands and hedgerow timber, with lanes winding like covered ways under masses of impenetrable foliage ; or it may be a wide expanse of featureless plain, the horror of mountaineers and the paradise of coursers.

Or if you turn from the country to the town, the fancy takes a fresh departure. Man and his handiwork have come to the front, and nature is only existing on sufferance. Here you have forests of masts, and there you have stacks of factory-chimneys. There are great blocks of warehouses and offices where there is bustle through the day, and silent solitude in the night-time; fashionable quarters frequented by the wealthiest aristocracy in the world, that are as gay in the season as they are depressing out of it; modern suburbs, with their flimsy villas; rookeries where the morals and misery of the wretched inmates sadden the souls of hard-working curates; river-side districts where dock-labourers, watermen, and water-thieves are lounging loosely by dozens about the doors of the public-houses; cathedral towns, where luxurious orthodoxy reposes in cloistered shades among the lawns and gardens of the close; county towns, where the purity of the peaceful streets is only soiled by the invasion of agriculturists on the market-day; watering-places, where the flower of the incumbent's flock is here to-day and gone to-morrow. In short, the sketches of types might be multiplied indefinitely were we to set memory and imagination to work instead of dashing off these random suggestions; and there is scarcely a parish where the story would not be worth the sketching, however unassuming the pretensions of the artist.

But we flatter ourselves that this particular parish in Kent is decidedly more characteristic than the average, not merely because it is not swamped in any speciality, but because it numbers amongst its residents people of many sorts. It can boast neither of mines nor manufactures, and it is miles away from the sea, though within scent of the briny breezes. It is thoroughly rural, though within reach of the town, and not only of a town, but of the city of London.

A KENTISH PARISH 63

So that its population is getting to be somewhat mixed, and yet in its outlying nooks and corners there are worthies who go jogging from the cradle to the grave, just as their fathers and their grandfathers did before them. Oakenhurst is scarcely more than a score of miles, as the crow flies, from London Stone or St. Paul's Churchyard ; occasionally we come within the radius of the city smoke, though far more often we are fanned by those Channel breezes ; and forty years ago, to all intents and purposes, it must have been well-nigh as much out of the world as if it had lain in the Cumberland dales or down in the fen country. A venerable gentleman of fine though decayed *physique*, who is now laid up in lavender in the almshouses, will babble to you by the hour, if you will only listen, of the days when he used to work the Pig and Whistle. Of course there were no railways in those good old times—even now they come no nearer than four miles on the one side and half a dozen on the other—and his Pig and Whistle maintained communications with the coaches at the great posting-station of Lowbeech. But at Lowbeech your Highflyers, Comets, and Eclipses never condescended to pick up casual passengers, being invariably filled outside and in. And accommodation, even in the heavy coaches, was always precarious, so that it was altogether a toss-up how or when the towns-folk of Oakenhurst were forwarded to the metropolis. Thus, as the journey was an affair of doubt and time, most of them wisely stuck to their homes, transacting their business by post or carrier. As for the gentry, of course they drove up in their own carriages, baiting half-way at the "Bull" at Brackenbury. The "Red Lion" at Oakenhurst, and the "Godwin Arms" did but an insignificant business in post-chaises; but post-chaises were always to be had in profusion at the famous establishment of the "Hop Pole" at Lowbeech, where the sixty coaches changed horses in the twenty-four hours, and relays of postilions were perpetually on duty. The "Red Lion" and the "Godwin Arms" had tolerably lively times on the market-days, when the farmers were talking hops or wheat while their good wives were laying in haberdashery or groceries. Otherwise the place must have stagnated in a comfortable sort of fashion. Most men managed to pay their way, and few cared to press a neighbour; indeed, where everybody was gossiping on everybody's affairs, credit could rarely be granted recklessly. And to say nothing of the neighbouring squires, who made a point of dealing with the local shopkeepers, the prosperous residents in certain solid brick mansions set a good deal of money quietly in circulation. Now the approach of the railways has changed all that, without carrying the place off its legs in a rush of traffic, and Oakenhurst, though it still affects airs of prosperity, has rather been slipping down between two stools.

Should it succeed in raising the requisite capital for the branch line from Lowbeech which it has latterly begun to sigh for, it is probable that there may be brighter days in store for it. For the parish only needs to be more accessible, and to become more generally known, to be a favourite resort of jaded Londoners. Nothing can possibly be more lovely than the rich variety of its scenery ; and among its many attractions of hill and dale, park and farm-land, waste and wood, the only thing that perhaps is lacking is water. Not that it has not a river of its own, which rises in the springs above the town ; but the Flete runs away into the bottom of the Lowbeech valley, where its infant water-power turns the wheels of some paper-mills ; and elsewhere there is little but rush-grown pools stagnating in hollows among the hanging woods.

Oakenhurst is but twenty miles from town, and yet its landscapes are as wild, and its surface as broken, as in ever a parish in the English lowlands. The land is held on short leases ; nobody has any idea of high-farming ; and it is but here and there that there are fields flat enough or big enough to make it worth one's while to employ the steam-plough. Generally speaking, the enclosures follow the rolling outlines of a jumble of bluffs and wooded eminences, running in and out of the charts and copses, and cut up into the most irregular and fantastic patterns. Never was such a country for hedgerows. There are snaky, sinuous jungles of thorn and ash, holly and hazel, interlaced with bramble of the most luxuriant growth, and festooned with honey-suckle, dog-roses, and briony. The birds build in them by myriads, while rabbits and ground vermin multiply among their roots. In many places, with their natural *chevaux de frise*, they set the inroads of the most resolute bird-nesters at defiance ; and when you are out with the gun you must make many a tedious detour, since there is no struggling through them save at the regular " gaps." And through these labyrinths of savage shrubbery the narrow lanes wind their tortuous courses, seldom seeming to trespass on the continuity of a hedge, and never turning aside from the steep of a hill. Now you are ascending a sharp, gravelly incline that makes deadly wear and tear of horse-flesh ; now you are descending the opposite slope, where the most reckless expenditure of drags and *sabots* scarcely suffices to lock the waggon-wheels. Every here and there from some crest, if you are in luck, you have a peep of some enchanting prospect from under the boughs of the oaks or the beeches. Now on the hill the drooping branches of the trees are brushing the waggon-tilt on either side ; and then again in the flat farm-land in the bottom, hedges and ditches run back into the fields, leaving broad margins of rich green sward, where caravans of gipsies picket their cattle in plenty.

Then as to the timber. Oakenhurst is bounded on the north by a bare ridge of chalk hills that ought to be downs, but which, for the most part are cultivated. It is to be hoped that the crops repay the farmers, but it is certain that the oat-fields in their rankest luxuriance give but scanty covert to the coveys of partridges ; while the turnips are a trifle smaller than Portugal onions, and the mangel are as moderate-sized garden carrots. In the shelter of these chalk hills is a wooded

A KENTISH PARISH

flat surrounding the little town; to the south of the town there rises abruptly a precipitous line of wooded heights; while away from these stretches the whole width of the Weald, studded with the spires of innumerable churches. Everywhere on the lower ground, as on the lower slopes of each eminence, the oaks are flourishing in all their grandeur; the hedges are full of them, as they throw their limbs across the lanes, and cast the great breadth of their shadows far into the neighbouring pastures; while in the parks that lie locked in the folds of the hills are stately clumps of magnificent beeches. As for the numerous ridges, when they are not crowned by the charts—a purely Kentish feature, of which we shall speak by and by— they are broken by black groups of Scotch firs, which remind the traveller of Italian stone-pines. There are dense thickets of spruce, straggling with their self-sown seedlings into the skirts of the heather; and each nook of the fields and each dip of the ground is lined with a copse or a matted spinney. Much of the wood is regularly cut every seven years or so to serve for hop-poles, wattles, and hurdles. The great knotted roots, shooting out in a dozen or more of tapering saplings, look as if they had held their own in the soil from time immemorial. And each second spring after the periodical cutting a flush of primroses covers the ground, while legions of fairies might play hide-and-seek in the beds of anemones, daffodils, and bluebells.

But although the sylvan scenery is as enchanting as could be desired, with glades as tempting to dryads and fauns as those asphodel beds to English-bred fairies, and groves of oak trees festooned in mistletoe, where Druids might have celebrated their mystic rites, it is the charts that are the speciality of the parish, and indeed of that side of the county. The Kentish chart is a thing *per se*; it is something between the Highland moor and the common, with a dash of such scenery betwixt Highland and Lowland as you come upon in the middle course of the Spey. Oakenhurst chart forms a bare plateau on the brow of the southern range of wooded hills; but bare only in the single sense that, looking up to it and across it, you see the daylight lying lower there than everywhere else upon the sky-line, between a broken and jagged palisade of firs. In reality, although it stands high and exposed, though it is swept by the winds from every quarter, it grows the more hardy forms of vegetation in the very richest luxuriance. The seedling firs are shooting up thickly around its borders, growing sparser and still more sparse as they push forward their unprotected outposts. And in the midst there are sheets of the purple heather, broken here and there by patches of bracken, and by thickets of bramble that are loaded with blackberries when the summer has been followed by a warm autumn.

 The chart is common land and public property, so far as pasturing, fuel-cutting, and the other servitudes are concerned; though the lord of the manor has the right of sport, with some minor privileges that are very generally ignored. We presume that, properly speaking, nobody can have been entitled to settle there in permanent habitation. But as matter of fact, around its somewhat indefinite boundaries there are a variety of singularly picturesque cottages, which must date from a tolerably remote antiquity, notwithstanding their rude and slight materials. The inmates have comparatively easy times of it. They have their little gardens and their beehives, and the bees that are swarming among the foxgloves and heather bloom make honey as fragrant as any from Hymettus. They have the pigs they either feed on the refuse of their vegetables or turn out to grub and forage for themselves should there be breaks in the fences of the adjoining beech-woods; and they may keep half a dozen of sheep or a cow, which take the free run of the common. They have their tiny orchards of apple and plum trees that seem to have run half wild, though they bear heavy crops all the same; and these spots that culture has reclaimed and embellished make a pretty contrast to the savage surroundings.

Then in the middle of the chart there stands the weather-beaten windmill with its skeleton arms or great brown sails—a conspicuous object from half a score of the surrounding parishes; and the miller's view must be almost worth his rent if he chance to be an amateur of the beauties of nature. Far away to the south stretches the rolling expanse of the weald, till the eye, as it travels in sky and space over the slopes swelling against the horizon opposite, catches the faint outline of the southernmost downs. And wherever the eye can reach it embraces a natural garden, crowded with the peaceful signs of a happy and prosperous population. Through the green of the woods in the middle distance rise the white cowls of the hop-kilns; the wreaths and threads of light-grey smoke are curling up from the hamlets and scattered farmhouses. Here and there, beneath a somewhat thicker cloud, you mark the roofs and chimneys of a considerable village. On the highest ground, far away to the left, are the glistening villas of a fashionable watering-place ; and everywhere you distinguish more or less distinctly the spires or towers of the parish churches.

CHAPTER V

A Kentish Parish: Hop-gardens and Farming

BUT what charms you the most in the foreground are the hop-gardens—for, next to our charts, our hops are our speciality; in fact, it is only the dispassionate admirer of the picturesque who would be disposed, as we say in Scotland, "to even the one to the other." Unfortunately the days are gone by when the hop-grower could make a fortune. When a heavy import duty gave the home counties and Worcestershire a monopoly of this speculative crop, a single happy hit put the grower in clover for some seasons. It was by no means his best time when a generally good year had been raising prices all round. On the contrary, he drew his prizes in the lottery when his garden was the exception to almost universal failure, and then he would make his own terms with the brewer. But now the English hops have gone the way of the English wheat, and free admission from South Germany and America depresses the prices to a moderate level. Moreover, we have heard it whispered that the keenness of competition has made the brewers less scrupulous, and when hops are dear they are said to balance their budgets by simply putting a weaker infusion into their vats. Be that as it may, and whatever be the position of the growers, the hops are still the blessing of the gatherers. Go through a Kentish parish in the hopping time, and the roads and the dwellings are alike deserted. Each cottage door is carefully secured, and neither for love nor money will you find a soul to deliver a message or do an odd bit of work. Every man, woman, and child, from failing age to helpless infancy, is about and busy in the gardens. The bedridden have to do the best they can ; and even the dying, should they choose to be lingering perversely, may be left to smooth their pillows for themselves. Only the other day we heard a story very much to the point. A friend's bailiff was riding quietly across the chart, when he pulled up to a feeble appeal from a solitary cottage. A poor woman had dragged herself to the window, and was supporting herself with an effort against the sill. She had known that morning that she was on the eve of her confinement, but neither relations nor friends could be prevailed upon to stay by her ; and now, having been taken in labour—for we cannot say she was surprised—she addressed herself to the bailiff as a family man, and implored him in charity to send some one to her assistance. Each family goes forth with the infants packed in perambulators, and gathers round its separate bin. The result of the day's picking is weighed and paid for by the measure. For once the smaller children in an overflowing household are made profitable, since each may clear a couple of

A Kentish Hop Garden. *By* George Morrow.

HOP-GARDENS AND FARMING 73

shillings a day. But it is not the profit alone that makes the hopping so pleasant. The annual outing is looked forward to as a holiday, and townsfolk and tradesmen of comparatively good position are wending their way to the gardens with the rest. Nothing can be gayer than the scene when the sun is shining brightly. Each bit of colour in the motley groups throws its light on the landscape with telling effect. A mile away you may hear the merry voices, for the tongues go even faster than the fingers ; and the very babes, who are laid out in shawls under the hedge, are clapping their hands and crowing in chorus.

But though all the world turns out to the hopping, and although our parish is more populous than most, the supply of labour comes short of the demand for it. Hence it is that in many a sheltered nook, where there is wood and water, shade and sun, you stumble in upon some gipsy-like encampment. Generally speaking, though our visitors come from eastern London, they are very decent people on the whole. Year after year they return to the same employers to take up their quarters on the familiar ground. Some amount of exposure they must submit to, but there is little overcrowding, and few temptations to immorality, as is too often the case elsewhere. You may meet their messengers late of a Saturday evening carrying home the provisions from some village shop ; but it is probably a long walk to the nearest public-house, so the people prefer to rest after the toils of the day. Many of them take a pride, besides, in encroaching on their wages as little as possible. They make their fire in the open, and boil the kettle on the sticks they had gathered in the lanes or dragged from the hedgerows—and a cheery family they seem as they gather round the common platter. Their clothes may be ragged enough, and the hair of the mother and her daughters is wofully unkempt; but it is pleasant to see the thin faces of the children filling up and bronzing with their country outing. Indeed we believe that, on the whole, these wandering hop-pickers are a greatly maligned race. Last season, for example, owing to miscalculations as to the opening time, the South-Eastern Railway Company ran its Sunday hopping-train a week too soon. For a whole week a body of impecunious vagabonds and adventurers were lounging about the streets of Maidstone, which is of course one of the great capitals of the hop-districts. Yet there were few complaints of their behaviour, and fewer charges before the magistrates.

We said that æsthetic amateurs of nature might place the charts before the hop-gardens, but on second thoughts we are by no means sure of that. For there is no more graceful climber than the hop; though the exuberant suckers may be nipped from the roots, otherwise it is suffered to grow in untrained luxuriance; and then in admiring it you have the *arrière pensée* that it is not only ornamental but eminently useful. The very scent of the hop is suggestive of mighty home-brewed, and the invigorating pale ales of our skilled professionals. The hop is a genuinely English plant, and it is hard to say how much of our national glory and

HOP-GARDENS AND FARMING 75

prosperity may be attributed to its successful cultivation. It puzzles us to surmise how the sturdy heroes of the Armada days and the Spanish and Low Country wars fought so well as they did, considering that we are told by the Rev. Mr. Harrington, who wrote his lively memoirs in Queen Elizabeth's time, that England then produced 25,000 tuns of wine annually—and such wine as it must have been! And the choicest of these hop-gardens are in the most enchanting situations, on the steeps of hills, yet in the middle of woods that break the winds which are so fatal to the bines. Often flinty, the soil would seem unfit to grow even thistles; and the more laboriously it is tilled and manured the more do the flints come to the surface. After all, however, that is the less astonishing, since it is the same with some of the rarest vineyards that yield the world-famed vintages of the Gironde. And from these picturesque eminences, looking down through the natural vistas, you get a series of panoramic glimpses of the glories of the Weald framed in a long succession of flowery archways.

But we have lingered long enough in the hop-gardens, so by way of changing the scene we may take a look at the cottages and farmhouses. If the farming is picturesque, with the irregular fields and copsy hedge-rows, with the crops of thistle and yellow ragweed, and the ditches overgrown with grass and bindweed, so are the farmhouses. They have nothing in common with the bare, neat, substantial steading of stone and lime that you see in the Carse of Gowrie or the north-eastern Scotch counties. Almost invariably they are embowered in orchards, and unpleasantly buried among venerable trees, if the tenants are at all susceptible to damp. Wherever you can struggle out into the open anywhere on the surrounding heights, you get a glimpse of tall, angular stacks of chimneys of Elizabethan character. Ten to one, it is not till you are turning the corner of the nearest lane that you catch the curving lines of the eccentric gables. The steep-pitched roof is yielding under the weight of years, and possibly of great masses of the ivy that clutches at the tiles with its knotted fingers, and forces its tendrils through the interstices to twine them round the rafters of the attics. Where roof and walls are free from the parasite, they are covered with a growth of mosses and lichens in the most mellow tints of yellow and orange. The upper half of the walls is in weather-tiling, the lower is blackened brick that begins to shows signs of crumbling. The glass in the lozenged casements dates from days when the art of the manufacture was in its infancy. You ascend to the entrance-door by a flight of much-worn steps, to find yourself landed in a spacious passage that very frequently is groined and arched. To the right is the capacious kitchen, with its whitewashed walls and vast cupboards, and great smoked beams overhead. There is plenty of room for an easy chair on either side of the daïs in the chimney-place; you might roast a sheep, if not an ox, at the logs that might be piled upon the old-fashioned dogs; and looking up past the flitches suspended in the funnel-shaped opening, you may get a glimpse of

HOP-GARDENS AND FARMING 77

the blue vault of heaven overhead, where the stars are faintly sparkling at noonday. A door behind opens into the dairy, with its fragrant odours of butter and cream ; opposite is the living-room, so called, *lucus a non lucendo*, because it is only occupied on state occasions, when christenings, weddings, or funerals are going forward. Another straight, easy flight of steps slopes gently down to the cellar accommodation, where hogsheads of home-brewed may be stowed away by the score ; and it is not impossible that the staircase which leads to the upper storeys may be an absolute masterpiece of quaintly-carved oak. Indeed, not a few of these farms have been manor-houses in their time ; and even on those that never had loftier pretensions than at present, you read dates that carry them back to the civil wars, or possibly to the times of the Tudors.

Without, there is an air of ease and plenty, although sometimes, on more narrow inspection, it proves fallacious. But usually there are well-conditioned cattle placidly ruminating up to the hocks in the loose layers of bright yellow wheat-straw. Sleek calves are penned behind hurdles in the corners of the surrounding sheds ; fat black Hampshire hogs are grunting and grubbing among the fodder, or are reposing their corpulent forms in a sublime luxury of laziness. Great flocks of plump poultry and waddling troops of white Aylesbury ducks come crowding forward to your footfall in hopes of a shower of grain ; while the flights of pigeons are circling in the air, or settling down upon the shelves before their holes in the barn gable. Behind are ranged barn upon barn, with the rows of cattle-stalls and the stables; and the whole is backed up by the inevitable oast-house.

It would be hard to find a fairer or more refreshing scene, whatever be the season you view it in. Whether in spring, when the foliage is fresh and green, and the trees in the orchard are flecked with the white and pink blossoms. Or in summer, when the fruit has been setting and swelling, and the canopies of leaves cast cooling shadows. Or in autumn, when the barns and stackyards have been filled, and the waggons are rumbling homeward with their load of hops. Or even in winter, when the glare of the fires within casts its cheerful reflection on the panes in the casements, and the still fat though frozen-out fowls are huddling together under the lee of the house, beneath eaves that are fringed with their draperies of icicles.

The Kentish farmer is of many a class. The substantial small proprietor still survives, half thane half yeoman, sitting snugly on the soil transmitted to him by his ancestors, and proud, as Lord Lytton says in "Harold," of his five hydes of land: the yeoman who, according to the old local rhyme, could buy out with his yearly rent the citizen of Cales, the gentleman of Wales, and the knight of the north countree: the yeoman who figured as the immortal Mr. Warden of the Manor Farm in the pages of the "Pickwick Papers." Although in these days, when everybody is scrambling upwards, the Kentish yeoman has been changing into the squire, and consequently the race is

HOP-GARDENS AND FARMING 79

rarer than it used to be. Then there is the tenant-farmer of comfortable means, who sinks his spare capital in the hazardous hops, in preference to extending his holding or going in for a higher style of farming; who sends his daughters to boarding-schools and buys them second-hand pianos, and decks them out of a Sunday, with their mother, like the blooming lilies of the field. And there is the struggling holder who starves his land if he is not driven to retrench on personal necessaries. But whatever his means, or the balance at his bankers, or the state of his current account with his landlord, his features seldom show any signs of his anxieties, pecuniary or otherwise. The Kentish farmers lay flesh on their solid bones like their own oilcake-fed oxen, meet their neighbours half-way in hearty good fellowship, and are kindly and liberal masters to their dependents.

A certain " decentralisation " is a conspicuous feature in the farms. Although their acreage may be of no great extent, you come everywhere upon outlying cattle-sheds and barns. Follow some deep-worn waggon-track through the fields, and it leads you perhaps to a lonely hollow, with a shallow pool half overgrown with sedges, and thickly coated over with duckweed. The water-hens are swimming out and in of the cover, and in spring the alder copse is vocal with the notes of the thrushes and blackbirds, who have come to make their nests where they can bathe and drink at their pleasure. And throwing its shadow over the sombre pool is the great rough building of moss-grown tiles and blackened timber, that still answers its purpose somehow, although it has long been half tumbling to pieces For generations it has been the favourite haunt of the vociferous colony of night-owls that you hear hooting from the depths of the woods after nightfall. The martins have made their nests under the eaves by the dozen, and there are whole flying squadrons of bats hooked up by the claws among the cobwebs under its rafters. The number of these scattered barns tends to multiply the field-paths, by which any one with the *carte du pays* in his head may go straight as the crow flies in almost any direction. Such of these as lead from the hamlets to the church, and in the direction of the little town, are broad and well beaten, beyond possibility of mistaking. But there are many that seem to have been neglected or almost deserted in the course of time, although there must still be some traffic to keep up the right of way, or else the occupiers of the cultivated land they traverse have never thought it worth while to close them. You see a gap in the roots of an untrimmed hedge—a gap which, on closer inspection, proves to be fenced with a stile. And if you care to force your way, with the certainty of having your cheeks scarred by the bramble sprays, you find yourself all abroad on the other side. You are in a field of waving clover, or in a fallow unmarked by any traces of a foot-track. But if you take your bearings by the nearest farm buildings you are pretty sure to find a corresponding break in the bushy enclosure opposite. Seldom used and overgrown as they may be, these gaps and stiles are invaluable to the sportsman; otherwise, he would perpetually find himself "pounded" by barriers it is impossible to breach and tedious to turn.

Whatever be one's opinion of "the good old times," it is certain that our forefathers made wonderful workmanship. It may be nothing out of the way to see farms of great antiquity scarcely showing signs of decay in their solid strength. But here we have cottages scattered all about the parish, to say nothing of many others in the town, which must have been built several hundred years ago more or less, and are still as serviceable and weather-tight as ever. We are happy to say that the walls bulge and the roofs bend; for their waving beauty-lines, like their time-painted colours, indescribably heighten the artistic effects. And there is something in a picturesque cottage—you may even call it a hovel if you will—that strikes you more poetically than a hall or a castle. Man has been working humbly with nature in place of vaingloriously challenging her. Like the nest of the chaffinch, woven into the mossy bough, the cottage outlines and tints blend themselves with the surrounding beauties—the copse behind overtops the roof-tree, the heathery thatch has been plucked from the heath hard by, and it seems natural that the shoots of the untrimmed roses should struggle in where they can at the broken lattices. Contrast the lot of the inmates with that of the better-paid artisan and the labourer in cities; but can there be any question which is the more enviable? The cottager may not always be sensible of the sources of the pleasures that console him for his toils, yet he realises his blessings quickly enough if misadventure deprives him of them. Send him into a bare whitewashed ward in the parish union, stow him away in the steerage of a New York or Australian liner, even let him consent to take up his quarters with the well-to-do son who exchanged the country for the town when a boy, and the shadows of home-sickness settle heavily down upon him. It is then he remembers the brightness of the open prospect before his door, and the fresh breath of the breezes that braced him unconsciously against hardship and exposure. It is then his wife will sigh for the cottage door where she used to sit over her sewing or her spinning-wheel, listening to the hum of her industrious bees, in a bower of roses, wallflowers, and gilliflowers. They miss the song of the birds and the friendly twitter of the sparrows, and the neighbours they had known all their lives, with the kindly gossip and greetings. Nor, although never much given to moralising, can they recall, without some pricking of conscience, the indifference, not to say the ingratitude, with which they used to receive the attentions of the rector, and the help in time of sickness or distress they could count upon from the great houses around them. For we are bound to say that the Kentish cottager has little of the sturdy self-dependence of the Scotch peasant. You need never cast about for an excuse to prevail on him to accept a half-crown or a shilling. Should he have any morbid feelings of pride, he slips them into his pocket with the smallest donation, and goes off with your tip in the evening to the public-house, where he probably forgets to drink your health.

But if the circumstances of their surroundings conspire to make men poets, our parish ought to boast its Clares and its Bloomfields, although we have never heard that it prides itself on such worthies. We have at least a score of cottages in our eye, each of them absolutely enchanting—at all events when admired from a little distance; such cottages as you see in the Undercliff of the Isle of Wight, so far as the luxuriance of their simple gardens goes; such cottages in form and colouring as Birket Foster loves to paint. Here is one held by the lord of the manor on a six hundred years' least granted by her Majesty Queen Elizabeth. It stands opposite the finger-post at the corner of the cross roads in its carefully defined boundaries between the chart and the woodlands. It looks its age all over; yet its occupants, who are vain of its antiquity, notwithstanding their habits of grumbling, will assure you it is as good as new. There is a group of others within rifle-shot, half-way down an almost precipitous hill, facing the gravel-pit that is honeycombed by the sand-martins. The venerable black oaken beams are forming quaint patterns of tracery on the whitewashed walls, while the lines and angles of the foundations and ground-floors offer the most eccentric studies in perspective. We have already taken a look at the cottages on the charts, and you come on others almost more lovely, buried away out of sight in the woods. For we had forgotten to say that, on the southern boundaries of Oakenhurst, there is a wood that almost takes the proportions of a forest, considering that it lies in one of the home counties, and is skirted by the railway to Dover. Here are thickets, and there are glades, with hollies overgrown with honeysuckle and gnarled thorns that have been warped by time, with roots as much above ground as below ; while hidden in some swampy nook, like a wild-duck's nest among the sedges, stands the dwelling of some squatter, who is rich with his flocks of geese or the hogs he turns loose under the oak trees.

CHAPTER VI

A Kentish Parish: Sport and Bird-life

AS may be imagined, there is fair shooting in Oakenhurst. Pheasant-preserving pays very well in the great flat covers, cut up by rectangular rides; the cocks raise a perfect chorus of crowing of an autumn evening; and the birds may be seen pecking about by scores in the surrounding stubbles, to the temptation of the indifferent characters who hang about the Oakenhurst pot-houses. There is but little poaching all the same: a very moderate staff of watchers is found to suffice; and it is remarkable, indeed, how comparatively cheaply and bloodlessly the proprietors continue to do their preserving within easy reach of the London poulterers. Occasionally an astute labourer may go lounging about his work with some snares or wires in the pockets of his corduroys, or he may stretch his limbs of an evening after his labours with a gun in pieces under his smock-frock. But we never hear of the gangs of truculent ruffians with blackened faces, who beat up the preserves in the mining or coal districts, murdering or maiming for life keepers and members of the police force. As for the partridges, we have them in plenty ; but though the grass fields are bushed, there is little netting done, since neither by night nor by day can you ever be sure where to find a lot. The mangel and turnip crops are generally meagre : here and there may be a thick strip of clover or a flourishing patch of mustard ; but then the birds take by preference to standing corn, or, after that is cut, to the various permanent covers. Unluckily the season of the hopping coincides with the September shooting ; and during the hopping the sportsman is more at a loss than ever ; for the pickers are swarming and shouting in the gardens, and perpetually passing to and fro, setting the partridges in motion. The coveys learn to take long flights, skimming low over the undulating ground, rising and twisting aside at an angle as they come upon some fresh lot of labourers, and finally dropping out of sight beyond the ken of the markers. So, except on the flats in the valley beneath the northern chalk hills, we seldom or never make satisfactory bags, and we have long ceased to shoot over pointers or setters.

All the same, the sport is none the less enjoyable on that account for those who are content with a moderate day and do not object to serious exercise. We shoot in parties of three or so, with some keepers and watchers interspersed in the line, and a steady spaniel or two trained to retrieve. A sharp-sighted boy is posted here and there by way of *vedette* on some point of vantage. And though it is awkward shooting

SPORT AND BIRD-LIFE

among the trellised poles in the hop-gardens, and although the birds will rise wild from the close-shorn stubbles and from among the straggling roots, yet if we do mark them down in gorse or "short-cut," we are very likely to make up for lost time. And there is good fun on an off day among the pheasants in the hedgerows, with lots of rabbits thrown in. A gun on either side, and another ahead; a couple of spaniels routing in the ditches; a rustling upwards among the branches, a swishing to and fro of the topmost sprays, and up goes a rocketer to be cleverly grassed, if he does not play hide-and-seek with you behind the spreading boughs of some hedge oak. There is heavy firing, too, on a big "shoot" among the rabbits in the beginning of the winter, when the frosts have thinned the undergrowth and cut down the last of the leaves. Now you are picketed along the rides cut in the furze covers; now you are set in stations round a copse of oak and hazel saplings; now walking in line through the tree-stems in an open wood among the tufts of withered bracken; or, best of all, beating the face of a down dotted over with patches of furze and broom, where bunny, stopped short in his scuffle from his lair, is knocked head over heels to roll down like a ball, till the body is brought up of a sudden some hundred feet lower down. We could wish there were more snipe left; and ancient keepers delight in dilating on the flights of ducks and plumps of teals that used to haunt some of the ponds in the good old days ere the country was "spoiled" by ditching and draining.

But we own to being sceptical as to these tales, for water is the great want of the parish; and, as may be gathered from what has been said elsewhere, nobody has much reason to complain of improvements.

Indeed a good third of Oakenhurst is never likely to repay reclaiming, unless the day shall come when speculative land-jobbers shall cut it up into lots for suburban country-seats when the expanding metropolis has been brought a dozen of miles nearer. We can ourselves remember the time when hawks and gipsies had their haunts elsewhere on sites that are covered by semi-detached villas. But in the meantime, thanks to our charts and copses and hedgerows, hawks and owls of the more ordinary kinds are still common enough with us. As you take your walks abroad, you see the former sailing smoothly in circles overhead, or poised on their pinions in tremulous flutter, before swooping with outstretched talons on some victim; or if you chance to be strolling homewards in the dusk, the great brown owls go floating silently past overhead, their fine eye and ear far more intent on the movements of their prey on the ground than on the form or heavy footfall of the human intruder. The keepers will tell you, of course, that we have a great superfluity of vermin; and no doubt the keepers are right. Yet they would have less of our sympathy in the war that they wage did we not know that they never can exterminate their enemies. The foxes, of course, are sacred, and we admire the hawk tribe. We like to hear the harsh scream of the jay, and have a transient

SPORT AND BIRD-LIFE 89

glimpse of the brilliant plumage that reminds us of birds of tropical climates. We don't even object to the roguish magpie, balancing himself conspicuously on his perch with that jerk of his saucy tail. But there is no soft spot in our heart for the hooded crow, the bloodthirsty exterminator of the weak and the helpless ; nor yet for the polecats, stoats, and weasels, those sanguinary members of the sylvan secret societies. So that, like Catherine of Medicis before the gibbets of Montfaucon, we can gloat over the show on the " keepers' trees," although such maligned victims as the birds of Minerva had much better have been spared. Conspicuous among the relics of malefactors who have well deserved their fate, are the tails of the domestic cats run wild, that range the woods from the cottages where they harbour, and ruthlessly exercise free warrenry and venerie.

Small birds and singing birds swarm, as we have said ; and in the autumn, when the days are closing in and the leaves are coming down, and the first of the keen frosts is killing the bedding-plants in the gardens, mixed multitudes of birds of passage begin to gather into the hedges. There is fine feeding for any number of them among the hips, haws, and holly-berries that brighten the leafless twigs or the evergreens in a glow of scarlet and orange. Their rush before you for a score of yards at a time, if you come upon them while shooting down the side of a hedgerow, makes a rustle among the branches like the noise of many breezes. But far the most characteristic of the migrants that have a special fancy for our parish is the night-jar, who makes his haunt upon the heaths, and hunts in the higher fir-woods. Jesse remarks, in a note to his edition of White's Selborne, that these curious birds are far more rarely to be met with nowadays than in Gilbert White's time, in consequence of the great extension of enclosures. That is the reason why they have taken refuge and abound in parishes like Oakenhurst. Smoking the cigar on an upland lawn of a summer evening, you hear that wild, long-drawn jar, sounding from many directions around you. Nothing is more deceptive as to distance, except, perhaps, the cry of the landrail. But should you chance to be driving out to dinner in the twilight, or returning in the clear moonshine, as you let your horse pull you leisurely up the hill, where the road is climbing between the double banks in the spruce woods, you will see the night-jar flitting across, ahead, and zigzagging in his downy flight across the charts. Or you may catch sight of him on his perch on the topmost pine-shoot, his head well down and his tail in the air, while he is hard at work grinding out the rattle which vibrates far and wide in undulations of sound, according to the stillness and the condition of the atmosphere. Like the hedgehog and other harmless creatures, he is the subject of absurd superstitions, and of many injurious calumnies. So much may be said in extenuation of his calumniators, that his nocturnal habits give occasion to evil tongues ; and then, like most suspected characters, he rejoices in a variety of aliases—night-jar, night-hawk, fern-owl. They never call him the goat-sucker in Oakenhurst, probably because nobody keeps a goat ; but we believe that the keepers here, as everywhere else, shoot him down chiefly on account of his unlucky name of the night-hawk.

CHAPTER VII

A Kentish Parish: the Residents

WE have not much to brag of in the way of historical or archæological associations, although the Kentish Archæological Society once paid us a visit. They say that Henry the Eighth used to visit at the "Cross and Crozier," which subsequently changed its sign to the "King's Head," when he had "cut the Pope adrift," in the words of the "Ingoldsby Legends." And there is a grey stone half sunken in the ridge of Oakenhurst chart, where it is rumoured that he was wont to breathe his horses in riding southward to his flirtations with Anne Boleyn. It is certain, at least, that the woods of Hever, and the tall, tapering spire of its parish church, are full in view from that commanding eminence; although the moated keep and battlements of the Boleyn castle lie well out of view in an intervening hollow. There is an old mansion of the Cobhams too in Oakenhurst town, originally a vicarage, which stands in its encircling ponds in a blaze of flower-beds and a wilderness of flowering shrubbery. Nothing can be more cheery than the bright rooms with the great bay-windows looking out into the green meadows behind, yet so slightly removed from the bustle of the High Street. But there are rumours of secrets in the cellerage which have never been disclosed, or only disclosed to some trusted individuals. The terrace walk is said to be mined by subterranean passages, which communicated with the site now covered by the brewery buildings, but formerly a cloister of Carmelite nuns. And *àpropos* to the sign of the "Cross and Crozier," there were reasons for the ancient hostelry of Oakenhurst advertising itself by so markedly ecclesiastical a title. For half-way up the chalk hills behind, there runs the famous pilgrims' road. Chaucer's merry and motley band, and many another troop combining pleasure with religion, must have drawn bridle to bait at Oakenhurst. Many a sin-laden sufferer like Sweyn, the first-born of Earl Godwin, when he had donned the pilgrim's weeds under the ban of the Witan must have plodded along that lonely road. Even now the road is carried wide of human life, past solitary farmhouses, or under bleak downs, between thick hedges covered with hazel-nuts, leaving scarcely room for two vehicles to pass. Dotted about against the white chalk are black, bushy yew trees, in knots or singly. Some of these might be old enough to have furnished bows to the archers in the wars of France and the Roses. They say, too, that each yew marks a pilgrim's resting-place, as the cypress in the land of the Turk shades the headstone of a true believer; though it is hard to suppose that pilgrims could have tailed off and dropped so fast, in an age when few cared to carry austerity to excess, and when the staff, the scrip, and the scallop-shell were passports to charity everywhere.

The Established Church is in the ascendant with us, although rather in virtue of its *prestige* than anything else. The population has never been tossed on those waves of revival that have ruffled the souls of Highland parishes in Scotland; and all that Dissent can do is to hold on, without actually expiring of inanition. The irregular pastor, who is supported by the voluntary contributions of his flock, must have lean times of it, to judge by the beggarly show on the benches in his tabernacle. The shoemaker who delivers soul-stirring philippics of a Sunday, and who seldom lets slip an opportunity of denouncing the Muggletonian divine, is far better off. For he lives by the labour of his hands on the week-days, and preaches in an upper loft that is lent him and lighted for him by a seriously-inclined corn-factor; so that any money collected at the doors is clear profit for congregational purposes. Now and then, and especially in market times or about the hop-picking, one or two wandering missionaries, whose earnestness rather outruns their discretion, will set up an *al fresco* Ebenezer on the green before the church. But waiving the question of good taste—since the shrill treble of their hymns clashes with the tones of the organ—they generally have a listless congregation, or rather a slender gathering of spectators, with hands buried in their trouser pockets.

THE RESIDENTS 95

The parishioners who attend the church have no reason to complain of their parson. He is exemplary in both his private and his official relations ; and if his lines have fallen to him in pleasant places, and if his nest in the vicarage is tolerably well feathered, so much the better for the members of his flock. There is little destitution in Oakenhurst. There is an imposing pile of cottage almshouses, and the panels of the front of the gallery in the church are emblazoned with inscriptions recording the charitable disposition of crumbs of their property by men who had quite done with it, and whose dust is mouldering in the churchyard. How Walter Fakenham, gentleman, bequeathed the sum of £300, 3 per cent consols, in perpetuity ; the yearly proceeds to be devoted to supplementing the sustenance of six impoverished widows of fair fame—the selection of the said widows to be at the discretion of the vicar and the churchwardens for the time being, &c., &c. Still, the poor in England will be always with one, whatever the charitable funds they have to draw upon ; and this the good vicar and his lady are never suffered to forget. Every evening in the winter, and more or less all the year round, there is a larger or smaller *levée* of applicants assembled at his kitchen door. In the hard frosts, when the labourers are frozen out, the scene in the stable yard reminds one of the courts of the old convents in Rome or Naples, before the Italian rookeries had been swept away by the stern edicts of a latitudinarian Parliament. The vicar goes about in all weather almost as indefatigably as the parish doctors, and we can hardly say more in his favour than that. There is soup to be sent out to some sickly child, blighted by consumption before she has bloomed. There is a bottle of port for the elderly labourer, who has at last "caught his death of cold" while working in the ditches in all weathers. And there is quinine for the old folks who are suffering from the neuralgia which hangs about with the fogs in the bottom of the valleys.

If the vicar is proud of anything, it is of his prize Dorkings and of his church. Of the former we need say nothing. Has not their fame been sounded in the ears of the frequenters of the grand poultry shows everywhere between Islington and Sydenham? But the venerable church is really an interesting monument, with the tracery of its windows and the quaint sculpture of its gargoyles; with the soberly-blazoned windows and sculptured tablets that happily escaped the ravages of the iconoclasts; with its square grey tower dominating the chimneyed and gabled house-tops, between the downs and the woodlands—the tower capped at one corner by the lantern characteristic of earlier Kentish church architecture. Those storied tablets between the pillars of the aisles record the virtues and biographies of departed Godwins, while the flags of the chancel are inlaid with brasses of Godwins in chain-mail, their hounds reposing at their feet; of Godwins in slashed doublets and trunk-hose; of female Godwins in ruffs and pointed stomachers. In a low, long niche in one of the side aisles lies the cross-legged effigy of Ranulph de Oakenhurst, whose maternal ancestor was one of the numerous brothers-in-law of the mighty Conqueror; whose banner streamed against the Saracens in the crusade of Richard Cœur de Lion, and who is said, by the most authentic county histories, to have had excellent reason for expatriating himself in his high-handed proceedings with his vassals and his serfs. Although it is honourable, lying in the sacred fane, yet, speaking for ourselves, we would rather repose in the peaceful "God's acre" that slopes gently to the southward, towards the limpid brook that bubbles at the bottom. If phantoms charmed away expectation by admiration of the lovely scenes they had failed to appreciate when in the flesh, nowhere could they find a more entrancing waiting-place. Yews that were set in the soil many a century ago, have flourished in the dust of innumerable generations. Some of the mighty trunks are tumbling to pieces in decay, being rent with the weight of their ponderous boughs. They are studded, like the timbers of a dungeon-door, with the clamps and fragments of rustful iron bands that have burst and since been replaced by others. The melancholy blackness of these venerable trees is relieved by the brighter foliage of the thorns, which are clothed in the freshness of spring with a bloom of variegated blossoms; and it is the pretty fashion of the place to deck the grave with the flowers which grow so freely in the cottage gardens, so that on an Easter Sunday and some other high days, the moss-grown tombstones of the forgotten forefathers of the village are lightened with the rosy reflection from the adornment of the fresher graves.

From the church to the public-houses, to the inns, and to "the hotel," is a not unnatural transition, seeing that the most frequented of these look out on the triangular green whose base is bounded by church and churchyard; and notwithstanding the well-deserved popularity of the vicar, we must add in conscience that these hostelries are the most in favour. The Oakenhurst tradespeople complain of the hardness of the times—of keen competition with shopkeepers in London—and they grumble over the blight of the co-operative societies, which is preying like a cankerworm on their modest profits. But in spite of a general mutual indebtedness and rumours of bills of sale over goods that are bought on credit, they continue to keep a fair amount of conviviality going. There is a little informal club of cronies which meets almost nightly in the "Godwin Arms." The parlour set apart for the use of the members looks out on the stable yard behind, and summer and winter the shutters are scrupulously put up at a certain hour, to screen the interior from the eyes of the curious. The good ladies of the members may regard the gathering with dislike, but they are aware that it is distinctly *de rigueur* to belong to it; and if husbands keep unholy hours, and sometimes make unnecessary noise in mounting the staircase to the nuptial chamber, the wives are "squared" and soothed with the finery they are fond of flaunting in. The uninitiated know nothing authoritatively of the proceedings. The landlord and James the elderly waiter are bound over by self-interest to extreme discretion. But should you happen to be hanging about in the inner lobby while your horses are putting to, you recognise familiar voices exciting themselves in warm disputation, while a rush of spirituous fragrance comes to your nostrils when the door is opened for the execution of orders. The best of us may be overtaken under the seductions of good-fellowship, but the presence of Mr. Baggs, churchwarden for the congregation, and of Mr. Garbett, the parish clerk, ought to be a guarantee for the habitual respectability of the proceedings. The general tone of politics among the Oakenhurst *bourgeoisie* is Conservative, but Knocker the coachbuilder is a red-hot Radical, who never cared to conceal his sympathies with the Commune; and should he get to loggerheads with such fiery spirits as Shortrib the butcher, and Spavin the veterinary surgeon, that would sufficiently explain the animation in his arguments. We have reason to fear, too, that debts of honour will sometimes get awkwardly mixed up with commercial transactions. For not a few of the gentlemen are dead hands at loo and "vanjohn" —indeed round games at cards and little suppers are a favourite form of entertainment in their private residences; while Spavin and the Godwin bailiff are professed betting men, having their books on each meeting from Croydon to Lewes.

There is a different society altogether of market-days. Then the access to the bar is blocked up with bulky farmers, with jolly, hearty faces, and cheeks like Kentish pippins, in broad-skirted coats with voluminous pockets, and breeches, gaiters, and square-toed boots. Though there is a sprinkling of the younger generation of agriculturists and speculative corn-factors, who run up to town periodically to have dealings with brokers in the borough, who disport themselves in smart cutaway velveteens and gorgeous neckties with horseshoe pins. The talk of these younger bloods is of horse-flesh and music-halls as much as of corn and hops and bullocks. At the farmers' ordinary it is a case of cut and come again, amidst the merry roar of stentorian voices, the clink of tankards and the jingle of glasses ; when Boniface, the dapper little landlord, has come staggering in under some ponderous sirloin, and the table would groan under its burden if it were not warranted up to any weight. Then Maltby of the brewery will be voted into the chair, or Grindley the great miller and hop-grower, or old Mr. Pigswash from the Moat farm ; while Skinner, the lean, weasel-faced lawyer, will drop in from his office over the way, and get value for the price of his dinner by doing some strokes of business on the sly. It takes all Mr. Skinner's tact to be equal to the embarrassments of the situation ; but he has the knack of always looking after the main chance, with an appearance of devil-may-care *bonhomie* that imposes on people, although it scarcely deceives them. The farmers, who have very good reason to respect his sinister powers, eye him askance, and are extraordinarily civil ; but every now and then

THE RESIDENTS

—*in vino veritas*—they will blurt out a frank bit of their minds, and make him flush into vindictive anger, notwithstanding his practised self-control.

There is less to say about the Red Lion, since it chiefly lays itself out for a class of stranger customers. There the room for commercial gentlemen has the importance which is given to the market room over the way. There are sure to be three or four bagmen's double dog-carts drawn up under the shed in the courtyard, and there is a pile of leather-strapped cases in the passage. The owners of these are eating, drinking, and getting cheerful, previous to going on their way rejoicing, after paying their round of business visits. And in summer the "Red Lion" makes the most in way of advertisement of the unrivalled attractions of the neighbourhood, tempting down quiet holiday-makers from town by offer of fishing and reasonable board. In the latter it is said to perform nearly as much as it promises. As to the former, it is quite marvellous how little the Cockney will be contented with, when everything except the fishing is to his mind. For, with the patience which should be the badge of the much-enduring race, you will see the citizen fisherman going by day after day to whip the few hundred yards of water which the host of the "Lion" rents of Squire Godwin; and each evening you may mark his complacent return, though his basket is lighter by his luncheon than when he started.

The "Royal Oak," the "Jolly Hoppers," and the "Fighting Cocks," form so many successive steps in the descending scale. The first is the resort of the smallest tradesfolk; the second, of the steadier labourers and carriers and waggoners in transit; the third, of all the village ne'er-do-wells, of tramps, and of the travellers who are under the surveillance of the police. As for the "Fighting Cocks," it is an unmitigated nuisance. In broad daylight, the benches before the door are often crowded with roisterers who remind you of the Borrachos of Velasquez or one of Jordaen's Flemish pictures. There is the gross laugh and the coarse language, the foul oath and sometimes the savage blow. Bold women with weather-battered faces and tangled hair exchange rough ribaldry with their lords and masters, who pass them the pewter-pots in their more generous moments, as the Bedouin throws the leavings of his feast to his wives. The dingy little drinking-dens within doors are the horror of the gamekeepers—for though, as we have said, there is but little poaching in the parish, it is here that anything of the kind is planned. And if the keepers were called as evidence to the landlord's character, unquestionably his licence would be promptly cancelled. One is familiar with the aspect of these rural boozing kens. A low-browed door, as repulsive to reputable customers as the similarly forbidding feature in the landlord; a dirty window, with curtains of faded crimson, to screen the questionable doings within doors; with a wooden stand at the corner, that bears by way of fruit clusters of battered and indented beer-pots. The place does a tremendous trade in the hopping-time, when messengers from all the

THE RESIDENTS

surrounding encampments crowd to it for the nightly supplies of their companies, and when occasionally an adult envoy tries to take away as much as he can conveniently carry in his person. We should be sorry to stake the character of English ale on the taps they draw at a place like the "Fighting Cocks." There may be chemicals that come cheaper than inferior hops even when you are brewing in the middle of the hop districts; and at all events "The Cocks," being a "brewers' house," is a convenient channel for disposing of the brewers' failures. When a man is smoking rancid tobacco, and muddling himself in his cups, his palate is even less fastidious than usual; but his stomach and his stamina must suffer all the same, however strong they may have been made by nature.

Appeals have frequently been made to the Squire on the subject of local public-house reform, but always unsuccessfully. Were he witness himself to any act that was overtly discreditable, he would speak his mind freely enough, and soon put abuse down by the strong hand. But whenever he rides down the High Street, disorder is hushed before the sound of his horse-hoofs; and he is known to hold tale-bearing in abomination, while he notoriously carries his Conservative instincts to an extreme. Possibly because he is an aristocrat to the backbone, he shows extreme consideration for the sensibilities of his dependents; he detests meddling in their affairs save in the way of kindness, and would never rob a poor man of his beer because he suspects that the beer is bad. If the poor man does not like the tap, he can carry his custom elsewhere. At all events, the Squire does his duty by him so far in showing what ale ought to be, when he is invited to the hospitality of Oakenhurst Place, at a harvest-home or any entertainment of the kind. The Squire is an excellent landlord, though he might be even a better one were he to attend more closely to the business of his properties. Perhaps he is hardly the less popular that he holds himself apart, since it is from reserve and want of readiness far more than from pride. He is getting on for the three-score years and ten, and for the forty years since he succeeded to an uncle and sold out of the Guards, he has been settled in solitude in the great house. As it happens, for three generations, and for nearly ninety years, the Squires of Oakenhurst have been bachelors. So that there is rather a depressing absence of sweetness and light in the great rooms of the old Elizabethan house. Here and there a modern easy chair, or a luxurious lounging sofa, have been introduced among the massive furniture that looks as if it would last to doomsday. But the heavy Turkey carpets have taken the tinge of the black oak panelling, and they are never replaced till they are frayed into tatters, owing simply to procrastination, not to parsimony.

In anything that falls in with his personal tastes or his stately ideas of the necessities of his position, Squire Godwin is magnificent. Although he seldom hunts of late years, since he has been feeling twinges of rheumatism, save when the hounds are drawing his

Hunters at Grass. By Sir E. Landseer.

Oakenhurst covers, he has always half a dozen of made hunters in his stables to mount himself or a friend. The steppers he drives in his chariot or mail-phaeton are matched to a hair. The pair of cobs which carry him about the estate, and which can easily be persuaded to take a fence on occasion, are models of breeding and solid symmetry, and do credit to their Norfolk pedigrees. There is always something worth looking at to be seen in the paddocks, where playful colts and fillies are grazing among pensioners more or less worn out. There is an unnecessary number of grooms and helpers under the corpulent old coachman, who acts as master of the horse; and they have their quarters under his immediate supervision, in rooms on one side of the cheerful courtyard that is finished off by the great clock-tower with the gilded cupola. The gardens are kept up rather as a matter of state; but the Squire passes more than once in the day along the sunny terrace-walks that leads to the keeper's cottage and the kennels. The occupants of these last are rather select than numerous; but the Oakenhurst breed of spaniels has long been famous, and the Squire would sooner give away the presentation to a living than part lightly with one of his ebony favourites. There is no prettier spot in the park than the slope below the hanging beech-wood, where the many-gabled cottage stands under the walnut tree. On the one side are the ranges of pheasant-coops that are shifted about upon the lawns that lie beyond the garden and the beehives; on the other the kennels on the little brook that is dammed back in a pool in the middle of the exercise-yard. And there most methodically, almost every tolerable morning about eleven, the Squire mounts the cob that has been sent forward for him, and starts upon a ride round his woods and home-farm. His constitutional shyness may be confounded with pride; but he is rather the kindly companion than the master with the keeper or forester or bailiff who goes striding along by his stirrup. There are some valued tenants, too, whose " forbears " have clung for generations to the soil, who are looking out anxiously for the greeting that almost invariably leads on to a chat. Though there are seven-years' breaks in all the leases, they know they are just as securely rooted as the Godwin family itself; and should they come under a passing cloud of misfortune, they count upon the Squire to see them clear of it.

The grand festivity at the place is the annual hunting breakfast; so much the better if there are two or more of these. Then the hounds and horses are crowded on the grand gravel sweep, and the long-drawn tables in the hall, the great dining-room, and the morning-room are a tight fit for the squadrons of guests. These meets on the Oakenhurst lawn bring men to the hunt who never turn out on any other occasion; and gentlemen who are given to craning at other times are apt after these to take lines of their own, in place of hustling each other at gates and gaps. In another style there is the harvest-home: when the bailiff has instructions to stretch a point, in the way of issuing his invitations ; when the beams and rafters of the huge barn disappear in the foliage of the evergreens, and festoons of dahlias and sunflowers ; when the barrel of home-brewed is broached ; when the oxen and fatlings are killed, and poultry and pigeons are slaughtered by the score ; when the Squire, though unaccustomed to public speaking, takes the chair, supported by his familiar friends—makes half a dozen of short but sententious orations amid vociferous applause, and then solemnly proceeds to open the ball, which is kept up with undiminished vigour through the small hours. And then there are the *battues* in autumn and winter ; when every man who has the faintest pretension makes interest to be enrolled in the regiment of beaters, when the toils of the day are broken by the repast under the greenwood tree, and when the triumphs of the bag are crowned in the evening by a sporting supper in the servants' hall.

We need not go the round of the surrounding houses that are still inhabited by families long settled in the county, and of the sundry substantial mansions in the town, occupied by scions of county houses, by retired officers, *et id genus omne*. All of these have stepped naturally into their places, and with all of them the Squire is on friendly or cordial terms. But his *bêtes noires* are the new men who have been encroaching on the neighbourhood in virtue of purchase, and the antipathies he cherishes in their regard are shared by the humble classes around. More than one of them have paid a heavy price for most beautiful situations with most incommodious residences. They have either pulled down the latter or transmogrified them out of knowledge, and very naturally. But the Squire cannot away with these brand-new turrets and battlements, so conspicuous in their ostentatious splendour from the familiar points in the landscape. Respectful admirer as he is of the fair sex, and the more so, perhaps, that he has never mated with any individual, he shrinks from the showy toilets which confront him in his family pew. Though he has no special pride in the produce of his garden, he dislikes seeing his gardener run hard by rare varieties of tropical plants at the Oakenhurst flower-show; and he takes the appearance of some pair of handsome carriage-horses, set off by unknown crests on the harness, as a personal insult to his stables. By nature he is really most kindly and good-humoured, and it is not in him to do an unkindly thing, unless under strong momentary provocation. So it is a sight for the student of humanity to see him when he is brought into involuntary contact with Mr. Veneer, the great furniture dealer from Bloomsbury, or with the respectable Mr. Solomons who is so thoroughly satisfied with himself, and who conducts pawnbroking operations on a stupendous scale. Both Veneer and Solomons are excellent people, and in a lifetime of close application to business have well earned an honourable retirement. But it may be a question whether they have not made a mistake in anticipating the railways, and coming so far afield. Purse-pride is their weakness, and certainly they get through a great deal of money. Their grounds are kept like villa lawns at Fulham; they have a wealth of pineries and graperies and forcing-pits; and the appointments of their sumptuous mansions are the most showy that money can procure. But they are lavish in the wrong place, and often parsimonious on trifles. They have a horror of seeming to be done, instead of sometimes submitting to it as a matter of course; and as their conduct is regarded most critically by humble applicants for their bounty, the occasional refusal of a shilling often effaces a long score of charity. Then their wives and daughters are in a perpetual dilemma, and have either to hold themselves apart in their solitary splendour, or else fall back on the society of the families of the more upsetting farmers, which might prejudice their social status to all time. Altogether, these new arrivals are a disturbing element in the parochial harmony—the more so that their settlement is a sign of the times, and that they excite uneasy apprehensions of revolution in the immediate future. For the probability is that in another generation, or even less, the ancient glories of Oakenhurst will have departed, although the influx of bullion and its free circulation may certainly bring material compensation.

CHAPTER VIII

The Downs

WHEN old Gilbert White goes into raptures over that "magnificent range of mountains, the Sussex downs," we may smile and think of making mountains of molehills; but none of us who know the country half as well as he did will be much inclined to quarrel with his enthusiasm. For the downs grow upon one, and theirs is far more the beauty of expression than of form. Rarely, indeed, is it a case of strong love at first sight; rather it is a friendship warming into affection as you become aware of countless lurking graces and alive to a bewitching play of feature in sun, shade, and storm. Unless to the little craft that run in and hug their shores, tacking and twisting by each waving beauty bend of the coast, the downs are a closed book to passers-by on the great waterways of the Channel. The sections of white cliffs show like so many blank title-pages, giving no clue to all that lies behind. Wind round their inland skirts by rail or road, and you look up to a rolling succession of mammoth barrows, strongly suggestive of the handiwork of gangs of mighty navigators in primeval days when giants were yet in the land. But once set yourself to breast their steep slopes, and your heart begins to beat with appreciation, fast as it throbs to the unwonted efforts. It is a sunny, sultry day, when on the Dutch landscape at their feet, you leave all nature gasping in the stirless air in a dreamy langour. You have painfully dragged your burden of melting flesh to their base, and your spirits sink as you despairingly measure the distance that divides you from their summit. *Excelsior!* and resolution brings its own reward, and a speedy one. The air grows lighter, cooler, buoyant, exhilarating, as you approach the ridge. After gulping it down in liberal draughts, you appreciate Mark Tapley's feelings on his first experience of a sherry cobbler, and become, in all particulars worth mentioning, a different man. You step out, casting off the dead weight you were carrying, and can almost imagine that, like Christian in the "Pilgrim's Progress," you ought to see a visible burden of material infirmities roll down the hill behind you. Nowhere else, we venture to say, does so trifling an exertion bring you so near to immortality. The air comes breathing round you with a strange rush of old associations of kindred pleasures—pleasures that you bought at a far greater expenditure of toil. Again you are slipping along the loftiest heather slopes of some savage Highland moor, and the shots fired from muzzle and breech-loader in a succession of vanished Augusts are waking the slumbering echoes in your memory. Or, higher still, you are striding over the short-clipped turf, picking your way through piles of granite blocks and erratic boulders, your gun swaying as a balancing pole, what eyes you have to spare from your feet cast far ahead to catch the first grey glint of the ptarmigan's pencilled wing. Or, loftier yet, you have climbed the snow slopes of snow-clad mountains, and are plunging over some *col* or *joch* in the Alps, through some *breche* in the Pyrenees, with glacier or desert born air winging your steps, the promise of a fresh country, at least a new watershed before you. On the downs your thoughts grow busy enough, ranging about as free and uncertain as the breezes, and were they monotonous, as they threatened to be at first start, your walk would still be an enviable one.

But monotony! why, they smile to you in the play of light and the colours of fountains falling among fireworks. Rich floods of sunshine would seem to have dyed their short brown sward with a lasting tinge of yellow. The dark shadows of the clouds fall trembling and flickering over the sea of light that comes rolling and surging over their slopes. Golden you would call the light were it not for the dazzle from the wheat stubbles hard by, where cultivation in its autumn dress is more gorgeous than simple nature. Not a breath of moisture is rising from the chalk and sand to dim the limpid purity of the air or break the sharp lines of the falling shadows. Like the swan floating in still St. Mary's Loch, each southdown

THE DOWNS

seems to graze by its double ; the furze bushes, rabbit-gnawed in unconscious imitation of the fantastically clipped yews of some trim old pleasaunce, reflect themselves with picturesque fidelity on the tawny brown of the natural lawn they dot. Mowed close enough it is by the cutting breeze, but the teeth of the sheep must bite closer still, for they seem to pick up a comfortable living somehow. Is it reality or fancy that exhibits their clodhopping guardian posing himself on the sky line of the cliff in an attitude that would tempt a sculptor? Assuredly there is poetry that harmonises with his surroundings in the floating fall of his coarse grey blouse as it coquettes with the playful winds. It was no admiration of the beautiful that made him seek that vantage post of his, but if you join him there you will say the rarest taste could not have chosen better. There is a bit of sea scenery that Gudin, in our idea perhaps the most effective of recent sea painters, would travel leagues to paint as we see it now. A bold, bluff headland strikes the eye, its pure white surface throwing back with a painful intensity of light the full flush of the noonday sun. It is flung out from the deep blue background of a waveless sea, that melts imperceptibly in the vague distance into a sky as blue ; not the transparent southern blue of the Bay of Naples or Sea of Marmora, but with a dash of English grey stirred through its colouring, thereby gaining in effect what it loses in brilliancy. Here and there a bright bit of sail catches the sun and breaks the surface—the reach lies rather off the great pathways of Channel traffic—bringing the scene into a sympathy with life. If you seek for animation in the foreground—though before a cliff so bold and a sea so limitless you scarcely care to occupy yourself with trifles—you have it in those Cornish choughs that float about the rock face far below, rising and sinking in ceaseless and successless efforts to find clinging place on its surface. For a pendant to this picture, and one not less attractive in its way, come back when the raw sea fog that steeps everything below in a briny vapour, is making a luxury of the exercise that sends your blood coursing through your veins. Every muscle comes in for more than its fair share of work, thanks to the slippery, sloppy turf, and every particle of film is cleared from your eye. The sheep are grazing in joyless stolidity as matter of business; their shepherd wrapped in his soaking capote is cowering down behind a dripping furze bush; his shaggy, queer-bred dog draws down the curling corners of his jowl, and tucks his stump of a tail away between his trembling legs. Heavy grey wreaths of cloud are clinging to the cliff; the deep leaden grey of the sea shades away in a light grey haze, and the grey tide comes rolling in with sullen splash on the strip of beach beneath. But the neutral tints are brightened inimitably by the gleaming crests of the breakers at sea, and the white curl of the rollers that are rattling in on the red shingle you see faintly shimmering below. Turner would have revelled in the effects, and probably before, in his latest eccentricities of style, he left so very much to the imagination, would have flung his brush at his canvas in sheer despair of reproducing them.

Perhaps it is because our artists "fear their fates too much," or modestly recognise their deserts to be so small, that they do not oftener stake their chances of fame against scenes like these; when a grand morsel of the sublime subordinates itself to a vague expanse of distance growing out of the very foreground —a distance to which nothing but genius can give the semblance of reality. But the downs abound in more homely studies, enchanting landscapes set in natural frames, fascinating nooks and "bits." Village churches, farms, and cottages nestle themselves shrinkingly out of sight, hidden so well away that few painters seem to find them. Standing upon some grassy bluff, some bastion of these uplands, glancing from yon Pisgah over the monotonous ranges stretching away before you, you get but slight glimpses at the promise they conceal. All you see are so many ridges bare or furze-crested, here a lighthouse, perhaps there a windmill. Dip into the first valley, and, agreeably disappointed, you brighten up to the fascinating surprises awaiting you: copses and thick-leaved woods hang lovingly over the brooklet that murmurs at the bottom. You passed cornfields before, and ought to have augured there must be farmhouses; but where all seemed so deserted that thought scarcely struck you at the time. Now the farmhouses are before you, and the patriarchs who own them with the flocks and herds that cover the neighbouring slopes, must live in a magnificence of rural luxury. Those homes of theirs are more like ancient manor houses, and, for all you can see, may have stood there since the civil wars, although in their bright bow-windows, opening on the beds of hardy flowers, they sacrifice to modern tastes and ideas. Round them, embracing perhaps an acre or more of grass and gravel, runs the strong wall of cemented stone, imitating, on a smaller scale, the bastioned enclosure of Pevensey Keep. All looks as if they had been planned to bid defiance to man and time ; as if they had fought a long and successful battle with the elements. The solid house, gabled and mullioned ; the vast massive barns that line the quadrangle and offer shelter to every sheaf of grain ; the very cart-sheds and pigsties look hard and weather beaten. The chimneys, low and square, and strengthened with iron stanchions, give as little hold as may be to the strong blasts they have to wrestle with ; the gnarled stems and limbs of the trees are toned into a grey in happy harmony with the colour of the buildings, and their leaves all have that same yellow tint so invariably characteristic of the downs. Every advantage the ground can give in the way of shelter has been taken. It is seldom we can suppose the winds working their way down into the hollow, but, once down there, it is hard to see how they ever get out again. That, we fancy, is the reason why the foliage of isolated trees is twisted round into the cabbage form, while their stems are stripped so bare and scoured so clean.

Everything has an air of being made snug in case of the worst, all top hamper is dispensed with as far as may be ; the very flocks of geese seem to be on the outlook for dirty weather, and never to be happy far away from home. Yet, withal, for picturesque comfort, give us these farms before any we have admired elsewhere in the British Isles. We would rather not speculate on the condition of their inmates in the short days of a sloppy winter, but no human lot is perfect. Then there are their long, low churches, with their squat, square-set towers, older, more massive, and more weather-worn than the homesteads—everything is long-lived here, man among the rest, as you may gather from the inscriptions on the bleached tombstones — the heavily buttressed little bridges, the wrinkled ivy stems beaten right into the cement and stone work, while where the ivy leaves would droop naturally below the arch the wind has done the work of the pruning knife ; the cottages cowering under the bank by some deep-grooved chalk lane, finding in their humility such comparative shelter, that strange species of hardy creepers hang in tough masses from their gables. Except for a colony of rabbits you send scuttling off to their quarters in a furzy sand-bank, or some wiry hare who goes lolloping up the slopes in his perfect training, shaking his fud at you in light-hearted defiance, anything like game is infrequent. Bustards vanished generations ago, and the curlews we may suppose have followed them. The rarity of graceful birds of prey, so far as our observation has gone, would sadden the spirit of Mr. Newton. Partridges do not seem to care to follow the wheatfields that came straggling up into the wastes, for cover in the way of root-crops is scarce and poor. But when meteorological science telegraphs a coming gale, then you may see those infallible storm prophets, the sea-fowl, go floating inland over your head, croaking impotent defiance to the storm they fly before. In the way of small birds, the downs, like their watering-places, have a teeming population resident and migratory. Chief of them are those captivating wheatears, the favourites of Gilbert White, which, when they are served to you with bread-crumbs, and the appetite given by their native air, will rank to all time, with ortolans and beccaficos, among sunny memories carried away by the cultivated stranger.

CHAPTER IX

Tramps

AMONG country sights in English spring and early summer one of the commonest is the tramp. At midday, you find him reposing on banks where oxlip and the nodding violet blow, in nooks overshadowed with canopies of lush wood-roses and eglantine. At evening the thread of smoke from his kettle fire wreathes itself in with the faint damps from the stream that flows past his bivouac. From early morning to dewy eve, and sometimes much later, our shady lanes and the rank luxuriance of our hedgerows are vocal with curses as with cuckoos. The tramp, although he penetrates the very sanctuaries of Nature, regards the beauties he rifles from a practical rather than an æsthetic point of view. Like the companion of his wanderings, she is his mistress but his drudge as well. She is more complacent to him than the austere authorities of the neighbouring Union, and laughingly tenders her lap to be lolled in with no associated nightmares of stone-breaking and oakum-picking. She pleasantly offers him the key of the fields, of the woods, of some solitary barn, or outlying cattle-shed. Her guests may not admire the rich green of the oak copse, but they know that it makes an undeniable screen against the light wind that has fixed itself in the east. The masses of foliage that cast their shadows on the grass from the gnarled oak boughs overhead will throw off any passing showers that may fall should the wind chop round to the west. The slanting rays that set the brown trunks all ablaze with gold are a nuisance certainly, and elicit many nervous execrations on them and on the eyes they dazzle; but the sun is sloping fast to the west, and they will soon see the last of him. No such luck with those noisy nightingales and —— —— thrushes and blackbirds that make themselves so much at home as gravely to embarrass the conversation of the lords of the creation. Twigs and birdlime! what makes it more aggravating is to think of them half-crowns and five shillings hopping about among the —— branches just beyond a cove's reach, and beer only fourpence a quart too, and —— hard to come by at that. As it is, the tramp is reduced to charily sprinkling his parched gullet with water from the cool brook that goes rippling past at his feet. It is certainly not for purposes of ablution that he courts the vicinity of water.

We may boast of the tramp as one of those peculiar institutions that are the special pride of England; and England is the genuine tramp's paradise. In countries unhappily subjected to personal rule, or haunted still by its tyrannical traditions, the

myrmidons of power are much too fond of making
free with the liberties of the roving subject. Un-
pleasant perquisitions are instituted into papers, passes,
amateur tickets-of-leave, and promiscuous vouchers of
respectability. Vagrants of unimpeachable respectability are apt to be arbitrarily taken care of in the
interests of society and their own, with small regard
to their individual likings or opinions, and the coinci-
dence of a brood of chickens disappearing from a
neighbouring poultry-yard may provide compulsory
State accommodation for the houseless wanderers
scattered through half a dozen parishes. Germany
ought to be a pleasant country to tramp, but vagrancy
in the Fatherland is much of a class privilege, and
seldom goes lower than the gangs of *Handelsbürschen*—
the young artisans on their promotion. In Holland
the people are too busy, too little tolerant of inactivity ;
there is work for every one, and it is impossible to
shirk it in a country where there are no hills, and
nothing higher than an occasional tulip-bed, to screen
the skulker from observation. In Belgium there is
literally no elbow-room for the stroller to turn in.
His case is as hard as that of the negro in Barbadoes,
forbidden by the monopoly of the sugar patch to squat
at his employer's cost, like his happier brother of
Jamaica. Even if he turned up some pleasant valley
by the banks of Meuse or the skirts of Ardennes, one
of the rare bits of impracticable soil abandoned to
woodland, he would be warned back by the ring of
the hammer from some sequestered foundry. Fancy

tramping over the broad grain plains of Artois or French Flanders, or between those interminable lines of poplars along those white, powdery imperial ways that radiate from the capital to its utmost boundaries; or imagine burrowing in the noonday heat among the lizards on the bare glaring face of a Provence hill. It might be a pleasanter lot certainly than that of the pilgrim on the torrid clay plains of the Castiles, or among the savage sierras of the South, where the bitter wind cuts you of a summer night like an Albacete knife-blade. Moreover in both peninsulas, Italian and Iberian, the tramp life would flicker down, and speedily expire in inanition. Mendicity and relief are thoroughly decentralised in both countries, and there are far too many undeserving local objects for a stranger to have much chance of making a lucrative quest. The stiletto or cuchillo indeed would promptly bring such unfair foreign competition to a sudden, and probably a violent, end.

In England the competition is the chief drawback to the profession. Otherwise it has so many attractions that it is hard to see why it should not be more overstocked than it is. You are absolutely your own master, free to wander whither you will, and make what plans you please for the morrow, not chained by the leg to some dismal den you pay to kennel in. You escape rent and taxes. You have no landlords' agents watching your outgoings or incomings, and keeping by deputy a keen eye on the solitary table you too rarely have occasion to use. You enjoy in its wildest charm the liberty which is the birthright of every Briton, although he is so often robbed of it. You preserve not only freedom of movement, but to a great extent freedom of action too. The police may want you ever so much, but they don't know where to put their hands on you when they do; and with a fair start, and so many an earth open, it is your own fault if you are caught by the slow-working pack of the county constabulary. You live at free quarters, and as you beg, bully, or steal your way, this triple variety of occupation gives a constant zest to your life. In their soul-stirring appeals to charity, many of our tramps take very high rank as self-taught actors, and our provincial managers, and some metropolitan ones, might advantageously recruit their troops from among them. There is an admirable versatility in the way in which the prosperous tourist of the slum droops suddenly in the languor of over-mastering famine at a vision of beneficent and unprotected petticoats; the whole robust person seems to crumple up under the pressure of a crushing sorrow and a blank despair, while the appealing whine is rendered with profound feeling certainly, but at the same time with excellent taste and judgment, not at all overdone. The ludicrous, perhaps, sometimes trenches on the painful, and you may be more revolted than gratified when, sharply coming round a corner to the sound of strokes falling on a donkey, or of blows or oaths levelled at a wife, the excited operator subsides into unconscious repose, to rouse himself suddenly to eloquent entreaty. But in point of art the dramatic effect is exceedingly good, and shows how native genius may answer the appeal of self-interest in circumstances and natures apparently the most unpromising. As for the bullying, that is scarcely art in any sense of the word; it is nature pure and simple. Given a lonely farmhouse in hay harvest, when the men are at work out of earshot, and a woman left on solitary guard. Tired and footsore, the dejected tramp drags himself with respectful limp towards the hospitable door. All the time—and he gives himself plenty of it—his small grey eyes are rummaging out every nook and corner of the place like a terrier on the quest, to satisfy himself that everything is really as deserted as it seems. To hear his knock you would fancy he has dragged himself to the door to die, and indeed the respectable female who opens finds him propping himself painfully and despondingly against the door-post. It is but common humanity to invite him to a seat on the kitchen settle, although it may not be common sense to explain repentantly the distrustful delay in receiving him. But there was no one else in the house, and these simple words revive him more than all the proffered attentions of the Good Samaritan who speaks them. The tramp is on his legs at once, master of the situation; imposing contributions in a voice of suppressed thunder, with the appropriate gestures he has practised a thousand times before on the ladies of his family. These are the sunny hours of the trade, when you enjoy the honours and profits of war in the midst of a peaceful country, and taste the pleasures that tempt men to filibustering without any of their accompanying dangers—without appreciable dangers at least. Of course if the law chanced to lay its clutches upon you, and further to take unhandsome advantage of your doubtful antecedents, your summer plans might be unhappily marred, and you might be forced into disagreeable exertion in the holidays. But if the tramp lets himself be caught, he must in fairness confess he deserves all the disagreeables in store for him. Reinvigorated with meat and drink, with wallet replenished as well as the knot in his necktie that serves for *portemonnaie*, his footsoreness cured by enchantment, he strides away full four miles an hour into space, and busy men working against time to secure their crops are scarcely likely to lay themselves down on his impalpable trail. Then with the evening comes the jovial orgy, the social cup, the unclean song, the stimulating slanging match, and the pleasant fight, at long odds, where foul blows are freely exchanged, and the victors literally trample on the fallen.

In England the winter comes hard upon the professional tramp. But it is not his habit to take thought for the morrow, and moreover experience tells him that he can somehow tide through the cold. So far as he is concerned our much-abused weather has a worse name than it deserves. Wet he has got well accustomed to, and severe snowstorms and prolonged frosts are become the exceptions rather than the rule. Besides, if the worst comes to the worst, he can fall back on quarters provided by the counties. Should he be a shrewd fellow, he learns that spells of enforced work send him back with renewed zest to his irregularities; and he may agree with that sage member of the class whom we remember to have forgathered with in the pages of Dickens, that hours and the diet " which is regular, mind you, freshens a cove up a bit and does him good." Then in the spring, summer, and autumn —that is to say, for nearly nine months in the year— from March to November—he is in his glory. To do him justice, he is no mollycoddle. If he shrivels himself up and puts on a piteous face in a bitter wind in March or a drenching day in November, it is only to move your compassion, and invite you to the exercise of melting charity. Should you chance to catch a sight of him while you are invisible to his quick, restless eyes, you may see him stumping along with loose coat flying back *à la* Mark Tapley, occasionally stopping short in the middle of a stentorian whistle to blow on the blue hands he draws out of his ragged breeches pockets. It may be as good as a scene in a farce should he become aware of you in the midst of the hilarity you have intruded upon. Ten to one he loses his presence of mind, and forgetting that he is proclaiming himself a shameless impostor, makes up at a moment's notice for an ideal of abject misery. It is but occasionally that, taken so unfairly by surprise, he may show the highest qualities of his calling, and, recognising instantaneously that disguise is absurd, may carry himself past you with surly defiance.

The Tramp. By George Morrow.

When the weather is really tolerably fine, that jovial bearing of his is anything but forced. The world is all before him where to choose, and he is in no hurry about making his way through it. He has only to avoid those inhospitable localities he has marked with a black spot on the map which he carries in his mind, where mendicity associations have introduced the ungenerous practice of scattering tickets to be bestowed in shape of alms. Nowhere, indeed, in our wealthy and charitable country, need he have any apprehension of being pinched by hunger. Bread may be had almost anywhere for the asking, and he turns up his nose at hunches from the loaf, and even looks askance at fragments of cold meat. He stows away about his person everything that can be bartered for beer, and chucks contemptuously into the nearest hedgerow the superfluity of those broken victuals that he has crammed into his pockets on principle. The tramp, in fact, lives exceedingly well; and if you consider his upbringing, and the circumstances of his existence, many a rich gourmand might envy him. Slumbers *al fresco*, early hours, and gentle exercise not overdone, are perpetually putting an edge on his appetite. As a boy, and before he could fend for himself, he was in the receipt of many more kicks than halfpence, and was kept on something shorter than half-commons. Had he married and become the father of a growing family like honest Hodge, whom he eyes superciliously as Hodge digs in the ditch or hacks at the hedgerows with his billhook, he would have had a load of household cares on his shoulders by this time, and been thankful for a bit of bacon once in the week. As it is, all through the pleasant season his wandering life is a perpetual picnic. It is probable that he is no great admirer of sylvan beauties, preferring the bench before the ale-house door, where he can listen to the echo of the laughter from the bar and the trolling of the skittle-balls in the alley, to the murmur of half-hidden brooks and the soft cooing of the wood-pigeons. Yet even in taking his ease at his inn he seems to be guided by some rude instinct of the picturesque; at all events, he has the good taste to look for shade, and that cool freshness of the green which weighs gently on the sinking eyelids. Sun-tanned and weather-beaten, ragged and dust-stained, with his open shirt-bosom and his hobnailed bluchers, he might sit out the central figure in some village group by a modern English imitator of the Dutch masters. There is the signboard swinging in rusty chains from the great gnarled bough of the old chestnut over the way; and underneath it the long water-trough, where the horses cast loose from the brewer's dray are "distending their leathern sides with water." Overpowered by heat and grateful weariness rather than by strong drink—though if he is temperate it is on constraint rather than on principle—his heavy head is nodding on his hirsute chest, and his clasp-knife, which has been making play with the bread and beef, has slipped from his relaxing grasp to fall rattling on the gravel at his feet.

We should be inclined to define the tramp proper as

a penniless bachelor with a light pair of breeches, who burdens himself at the outside with no more luggage than can be tied up in the corners of a ragged coloured pocket-handkerchief. But after all, the genus is wide enough to comprise the gipsy, or pseudo-gipsy, who is invested with some halo of romance. It is true that the gipsy who has a wife, or a plurality of wives, transports his family and belongings on wheels. But for himself, as it is his habit to go on foot, plodding along in advance of his caravan and flourishing his cudgel of knotted oak, he tramps it, to all intents and purposes. He is by no means scrupulous as to how he lays in his supplies ; he makes no hypocritical profession of keeping his hands from picking and stealing. On the contrary, he takes an honest pride in the dexterity with which he " conveys." All the members of his miscellaneous household, from the failing grand-dame to the toddling brat, keep their eyes on the country they are travelling, with a view to foraging for the family kettle. It is only in the last resort that he extends his patronage to the village ale-house, where his room is regarded as more welcome than his company. He picks out his camping-place in the most picturesque situations, where there are wood and water, grass and shade. Or he pulls up in some sequestered dingle, in a dip of the common not far from the road, where he might lie *perdu* to the sight of the passengers were he not betrayed by the swirl of the smoke from his fire. He is as familiar with the face of the country as a sergeant of engineers on the Ordnance Survey ; and you may see him heading for the well-known resting-place with deliberate purpose. As you are taking your stroll abroad towards eventide you hear the sharp report of a whip and the heavy rattle of wheels. Then you may distinguish the weather-stained tilt of the leading van emerging from among the foliage in the winding lane. In due course the leisurely procession passes you. Matrons, saving their legs, seated upon piles of dilapidated household stuff; babies fast asleep, curled up in bundles of weather-stained rags; spare, sun-dried men, and lithe hobbledehoy lads, lolloping along by the waggon-wheels in the wake of their sturdy leader; boys of the tinge of half-ripened blackberries, staring out with glittering black eyes through the thatch of their tangled elf-locks; buxom girls of Egyptian type, in scanty draperies of variegated colours.

Should you follow them in deed or in fancy to their halting-place, you can hardly help envying the freedom of their bivouac. Every one knows his work, and does it; and all is made ready with swift dexterity. The vans are drawn aside out of the wind; the ragged-shouldered, pot-bellied horses are loosed, and hobbled, and turned out to graze; the low tents are stretched over the poles and hoops; the fires are kindled where there is a natural draught, and the kettles are swung from their hooks over the heaps of crackling sticks. Even in wind and wet the hardy nomads make out wonderfully well, and the venturesome traveller in savage parts might take many a lesson from their camp arrangements; but in a summer evening, when the sloping sunbeams fall dancing through the branches on the grass, and each gentle breath of air comes scented with fragrant perfume, their felicity would appear to be perfect. No need to pry too closely into sanitary details, and possibly it is just as well that you do not understand their speech. To tell the truth, the boisterousness of their spirits is somewhat out of tone with the peaceful charm of their surroundings. But looking on from some little distance at the scene, where good digestion is waiting on hungry appetite, you may easily look longingly at their sylvan independence. They know nothing of the refinements they dispense with. Cracked earthenware and clasp-knives and horn spoons are made to do duty for plate and crystal. But then they have none of that dreary waiting in drawing-rooms while tardy arrivals come dropping in ; no getting up in white-chokered stiffness of demeanour and tight-fitting suits of sombre black, to settle themselves in a sweltering summer atmosphere in a billowy surge of skirts whose appearance of coolness is delusive ; no having to discharge the duties of small-talk by an unconscionable neighbour ; no ringing the laborious changes on the jangling themes of fashion, "high life" and high-lived company, pictures, taste, Shakespeare, and the latest concert. They know nothing of the hardships that press so painfully on well-to-do society, of sitting down in the daily course of heavy living, after late luncheon and afternoon tea, to the same irrepressible *entrées* and joints that haunt one in a train of familiar nightmares. In unreasonable and jaundiced revolt against social rites and ceremonial observances—for your liver is touched and your nerves are unstrung—you contrast the Boccaccio-like licence of the tinker's banquet, within those flowing tapestries of rustling leaves, on those velvety carpets of grass and wild thyme, and under the blue canopies of heaven, with even the bachelor freedom of the club dining-hall that looks out on the shadier pavement of Pall Mall—to say nothing of the smothering City chop-house, with its unctuous vapours of cuts from the joint. Feather-beds and curtains have their charms, no doubt, in a climate so chilly as our own; but when you have passed the vigorous freshness of maturity, you begin to find out that they are unfavourable to flirtations with sleep after the long crush of the crowded drawing-room—even after a bout of whist and sherry in soda in the more ample space of the club smoking-room. And you dream that sleep would come stealing to your arms unbidden, could you but throw yourself down under those strips of dirty canvas, to be lulled by the hooting of the owls and the droning rattle of the night-jars.

CHAPTER X

The Amateur Tramp in England

VAGABONDAGE is a term of opprobrium and contempt, and yet there is a meaning in the word that has a charm for respectable people. Kinglake has expressed the thing admirably in "Eothen"; there come times to most of us who are worth anything at all, when the restraints of society chafe beyond endurance. Our nature has passionate longings to refresh itself by a relapse into the habits of our primitive progenitors. We cannot precisely cast away our clothes, and a loose covering of skins for summer wear would fret our over-sensitive epidermis; the acorns of the golden age would vex our artificial digestions, and we should pull exceedingly wry faces over draughts from the limpid stream. But a little playing at that free-and-easy existence, modified by some appliances of luxuries in the rough, is a very actual joy for the time, that leaves delightful though disturbing reminiscences behind it. Many a care-harassed spirit will keep longing for the wings of the dove; but failing these, a stout pair of legs, a sound stomach, and an easy-going temper, are found to be very tolerable substitutes. Rapid motion and swift change of scene are always exhilarating in any shape. Johnson, whose powerful but ungainly frame was scarcely cut out for steady toe-and-heel work, remarked complacently while being hurried along in a post-chaise, that life had few better things to offer. Scott, when condemned by breaking health to jog along Tweedside on "a canny-trotting pony," reverted with melancholy mingled with pleasure to "the grand gallops he had had among these braes" when thinking of his "Marmion." And many a man has subscribed since then to the dicta of the Fleet Street philosopher and the Great Magician of the North. The revival of coaching days in the Four-in-hand and Coaching Clubs is a tribute to the pleasures of the box-seat behind the fiery-footed team that was being sprung by some workman over the level; and what can be more exhilarating for the moment than the brush after the hounds, when the scent is being carried breast-high, and the melodious pack may be covered with a blanket! But on the road and in the hunting field alike came the inevitable seasons of reaction and depression—cramped legs and tingling fingers, checks and catastrophes where excitement comes to a sudden collapse, dismal rides homeward in the damp and the darkness, when the fires of the day have died down and are smouldering in the dulness of their ashes. Perhaps it is only on his own sturdy legs, with each muscle and fibre in springy motion, that man feels master of his animal spirits, and can assert his absolute independence

THE AMATEUR TRAMP IN ENGLAND 135

of will. There is nothing like walking for getting rid of the blue-devils, or to brace you for a wrestle with more formidable fiends, to whom these blue-devils are mere *diaboli minores*. But it is no idea of such earnest grapple as that last which prompts our pen at this present writing. We speak of pedestrians in the prime of their powers, who, as yet, should have had no more than the share of worry that may be mercifully sent as a blessing in disguise, to put them in training against veritable calamities—of the exercise that comes as near unadulterated happiness as any you are likely to find on earth.

Most people who may chance to read this book have had their fates shaped out for them more or less. Either they have been born to the happy independence which has its responsibilities as well as its pleasures, and have been educated more or less successfully to the decent discharge of their duties ; or they have been brought up to the enjoyment of certain luxuries which can only be assured them by the practice of a profession. In either case they have been broken into some sort of harness, although occasionally they may kick over the traces. Had it happened to them to have been born in humble circumstances—had their wants been more simple, and their aspirations limited to the day—they might never have betaken themselves to regular employment, but have blossomed into full-blown tramps.

Well, it has not been our fate to be born gipsies ; and, like the poet, the gipsy or the tramp *nascitur, non fit*. But if vagabondage can never be our pursuit, we may still fall back upon it as a distraction. Even a single good pedestrian stretch, when nothing better is to be done, may act like enchantment on jaded spirits. What we suppose you to be seeking is temporary relief from the wearing strain of work or society; and then, if you are out of condition—and that, as we presume, may be taken for granted—the mere effort of keeping up conversation with a companion may make all the difference between refreshment and the reverse. We would not insult you by the suggestion that you cannot find entertainment in your own thoughts, although there are people who seem to shrink from their personal company, as if they had a horror of having too much of a most undesirable acquaintance. In reality, the natural thoughts that come unforced; the dreamy languor of mind that listlessly disengages itself over trifles; those simple every-day sights and sounds that may strike you spellbound in sudden admiration; the associations you cannot take the trouble to trace, reviving the brightness of boyish memories—all these things in an interval of sorely-needed repose, are among the most subtle forms of intellectual indulgence.

And as it happens, of the mighty cities of the world there most assuredly is no better head-quarters for the pedestrian than London. Among the European capitals it stands almost unrivalled in that respect. Near Paris, the charming *coteaux* on the Seine, with the ornamental villas in their blooming little gardens, strike you as distinctly suburban, when seen from

THE AMATEUR TRAMP IN ENGLAND 137

some distance—and the impression is confirmed on closer acquaintance. At Copenhagen, as at Frankfort, there is a monotony of beauty, with a sense of confinement, in the magnificent beech forests, whose shades you may seek at no great distance. So there are dreariness and dulness of a different kind in the ruin-strewn desolation of the Roman Campagna; or you must depend for variety on distant views of the hills, or on lights that are apt to be distressingly glaring. Most capitals, like Rome, are situated on plains, although without Rome's natural and archæological advantages. Near Vienna there are most charming valleys running up among the spurs of the neighbouring mountains; but, as a rule, you can only approach them painfully by tram-car, to find yourself in so many paradises of the Cockney, redolent of the fumes of beer and sausages, and resonant of the brass bands that are discoursing popular music. While at Constantinople, the foreground of its matchless views is enveloped in clouds of penetrating dust, and enlivened by the gloomy groves of cypresses that shade the resting-places of the true believer; and the environs of Naples are all dust, clay, or chalk, according to the time of year; and Madrid is a purgatory either of ice or fire, breathed upon from the chilly blow-pipes of the Guadarrama.

London, on the other hand, because it is the biggest city in the world, is brought into most intimate connection with the surrounding country by the countless lines of rail that radiate from central stations.

And what a country! Possibly you may say that it is not very picturesque beyond Shooter's Hill, or over Plumstead marshes; but elsewhere you can hardly go wrong. Even Essex deserves a higher reputation for beauty than it bears, although long encroachment has been making wild work with the oak-clumps and the bramble-brakes of Epping Forest. There is much that is pretty in Middlesex and Hertfordshire, between the Chase of Enfield and the spires of Harrow-on-the-Hill, without going so far afield as Hatfield. Of course the river above Teddington Lock unrolls a rarely bewitching panorama; while as to Kent and Surrey on the south, they boast the most enchanting scenery of the English lowlands. What is strange, too, is the rural, the almost desolate, aspect of districts whence you can distinguish the dome of St. Paul's, and which are enveloped in the folds of the city fogs, when the wind chances to set in that direction. On the other hand, fashion has occupied some of the most seducing positions on the suburban heights, gradually spreading and annexing the environs. The gipsies that were wont to haunt Norwood and Chiselhurst in the memories of comparatively youthful men, have seen their sequestered retreats cut up into building lots. Rows of brand-new villas, detached and semi-detached, have enveloped the oak-glades in the park at Knole; and a township of structures, more or less fantastic and substantial, has been run up among the fir-trees at Weybridge and Claremont. Yet there are other spots, scarcely less attractive, that somehow have been shunned alike by the railroad and the land-jobber, though it would seem, in the mania for sleeping in the country, that wealthy city people, from the banker to the shopkeeper, would have settled down upon them everywhere like gold-laden locusts.

No ; the lucky Londoner can hardly go far wrong in his choice of a country walk. A more or less moderate expense lands him at some eligible starting-point ; and thence he can wander away at his own sweet will, sure to find himself when he has had nearly enough of it, within easy reach of a station, from which he may comfortably return. Nor would we carry our love of solitude or retirement to extremes. A modest hostelry, of good reputation, adds a singular charm to the loveliest landscapes ; and we should be inclined to shape our course for the day by our knowledge of the bearings of the " Hart " or the " Lion." Desultory disquisition and purposeless dawdling are of the very essence of this our literary ramble ; so we may be forgiven if we pause to say a word on the insinuating charms of the suburban hostelry. In point of architecture and situation, these establishments are various enough ; but it is seldom that they have not a certain air of comfort, and bright, hearty hospitality. The cheerful stucco of the façade is by no means to be objected to in a climate where the glare of the sun is rarely oppressive. Moreover, there is sure to be abundance of shade : the spreading boughs from an adjacent copse throw their limbs over the roofs of the stable yard ; and opposite there stands the great elm tree, which shelters the sign-post and the creaking sign. Or, in place of the elm, may be a glorious horse-chestnut—we have more than one of these at this moment in our eye—with its fragrant load of snowy blossom in the season ; and beyond the dusty road, an enclosure of close-shaven lawn ; and beyond the lawn and the bowling-green, a stream that is dear to angling guests, although their perseverance may be unfrequently rewarded. Or, in place of the large white house, with the big bow-windows of its dining-parlours looking out upon the great horse-trough, a little mansion, in modern Elizabethan, may have broken out all over in fantastic angles and gables. In either case, within doors is the cool bar, with the presiding naiad of the ale-barrels embowered in geraniums and fuchsias—a bar that in sultry summer weather might shake the self-denial of the most ascetic of teetotallers ; and there is the roomy cupboard in the passage, with its doors of glass, through which you may admire a choice selection of cold joints, and salads, and cucumbers, and cheeses, and pastry, and fruit-tarts. You may make a very good English dinner in these places ; and a good English dinner is no bad thing, since it is within the scope of the commonplace cook, who would come to shame and confusion among foreign-fangled *entrées*. Are there not the primest of rounds and sirloins reared in those rich meadows hard by, though the beasts that carried them may barely hold their own with the best bullocks of Aberdeenshire ? And there are saddles of mutton from the neighbouring downs, albeit a trifle big in the bone and coarse in the grain; and there is the clucking of fattened poultry to be heard from the yard round the corner, with the cooing of the flock of pigeons that is laid under contribution for the pies. The spring-cart of the fishmonger from the nearest town pulls up punctually at the door every morning, with the offer of anything from soles to salmon. The bitter beer, it may be hoped, is all that can be desired, if the house be not the property of some short-sighted brewer; for most of its patrons are either connoisseurs or profess to be. And the pleasures of a draught from a frothing tankard deserve some dozen of pages to themselves, had we the space to spare and the inspiration to pen them. As for the cellar of wines, perhaps the less said the better, except that they are no worse, and considerably cheaper, than those to be met with in crack hotels, and that they may very easily be dispensed with at the substantial repast to which you sit down. Many a time a chance visit to one of those houses has led to repeated sojourns later, especially if there be an old-fashioned garden with summer-houses, which you may turn into smoking divans at the hours of digestion.

But to come back to that walk of ours, which, by the by, is yet to be begun. We give up our ticket at a station, where all is still enough at present, since as yet it is early in the day, and the City men are away at their business. Late in the afternoon there will be a crowd of carriages, from the barouche and the brougham, through victorias and dog-carts, down to the humble pony-chaise. Now you walk past the pleasant residences of these gentlemen, slumbering languidly in the summer heat. The gravel is kept to perfection; the grass is rolled to the smoothness of a well-starched shirt-front; under the cool foliage there is a blush of roses or a glow of geraniums, according to the month. There is just breeze enough to set the tree-shadows flickering on the lawns, and to rustle the tendrils of the creepers that cling to the columns of the verandas. The broad bay-windows are yawning in the twilight under cover of the striped sun-blinds, giving glimpses of great vases of flowers upon tables loaded with books and newspapers; while the discords of the daughters of the houses at piano-practice within, chime in agreeably rather than otherwise. Here and there may be the signs of deplorable taste: Chinese pagodas, Italian belvederes, and fantastic selections of modern statuary that fall a trifle short of the glories of the Vatican. But there is little that might not be easily remodelled or replaced; and, on the whole, there are few of those "desirable residences" where a man might not be contented to "hang up his hat."

Another turn in the road and another change of the scene. You are in the street of the little village that is the nucleus of this settlement of the Newcomes. There are wide gravel footpaths on either side of the broad causeway, and smart brick residences, with knockers, and brass plates that bear the superscriptions of local attorneys and doctors; and cottages behind low wooden railings in their narrow patches of garden. The whole is interspersed with lilacs and laburnums, and though the bloom may be over, the verdure remains: and outside the village is the Gothic church, newly raised by liberal contributions, with a spire of portentous height, emblematic of transcendent High Church aspirations. A mile or two further, and you are leaving villas and *cottages ornées* behind. You are among country seats that have been built generations before, although many of them have changed hands of late years, as we may judge by the additions that have been recently made. The ground is rolling prettily; there are clumps of trees in the swelling park-land, where colonies of rooks are cawing cheerily, or would be cawing if your walk were early in the spring. A profusion of money has been lavished on landscape-gardening, with more or less taste and discretion: there are masses of laurel and rhododendrons and azaleas enfolding labyrinths of winding paths; and if there be a bit of a brook its bed has been widened and its waters have been carried down over tiny waterfalls, among the ferneries and artificial rockeries. The properties hereabouts are not very big, yet you get among farms and tempting field-paths which cut great angles off the dusty high-road. Some of these farmhouses seem the very places for the well-to-do hermit who has a fancy for cutting his profession or trade, and spending his declining years in losing money in agriculture. It is true that if he were to take them on repairing lease, he must make up his mind to considerable outlay. It is their age that lends enchantment to their view; and doubtless their internal arrangements are rather quaint than commodious. The venerable brick tints blend harmoniously with the dark foliage of the embosoming trees. The lozenged windows, half hidden in trailing roses, let in less light and air than may be altogether desirable. The ivy that has clambered over the roof and settled helplessly down upon it in ponderous masses must be one vast museum of entomology, and distil clouds of damp like a patent condenser. But one must pay in some shape or other for the picturesque ; and it is certain that if the tenant had the soul of an artist, it would be gladdened through the finest months of the year.

The ground rises more and more, and again the country changes its character. You are getting up towards the ridge of the downs, whose hog-back has been looming against your horizon. The soil is poorer and the farms more scattered, and the oaks and beeches and elms are giving place to heather and fir woods. Wherever the sunbeams can thread their way, they are lighting up aisles of golden columns ; and the heat draws forth the fragrance of the resin that is oozing in bubbly and trickling streams. So far as the scents go, you might be on the banks of the Adour, and for solitude you might be in the glades of Rothiemurchus or on the dreary moor of Rannoch. Yet London Stone is within a score of miles, and you paid but half-a-crown for your railway ticket. But those Surrey woods have this speciality, that their beauties are embraced in a reasonable compass, and you may count on coming out on the other side, if only you persevere long enough.

THE AMATEUR TRAMP IN ENGLAND 145

For, blinking owl-like in the unaccustomed light, it dawns upon you that you are on the skirts of an open common. Brakes of holly, bound with bramble and wild clematis, are scattered about here and there, tufted with the wool of the sheep, who are amicably grazing among the rabbits. The rabbits have mined it with their burrows here and there, and a horseman must keep a bright look-out and a firm bridle-hand; but what a magnificent place it is for a gallop. Were it not for these foot-traps, towards sunset, or in the cool of the early morning, you might come across a string of thoroughbreds from the neighbouring training stable. A dip into a little valley, with a stream in the bottom, and then up again and still upwards. Now you are breasting the steep slopes of the downs, and the breaths of air that stirred fitfully below have swelled into a gentle breeze. You look back on a burnished panorama of wheat crops and grass fields lying against the black masses of the woods, and flecked with the shadows of those fleecy clouds that are floating aimlessly across the azure sky. And what a view there is in all directions from the summit! On the one side, the fair fertility of the weald, that stretches in meadows and corn-land, in orchards and hop-gardens, to that blue line of gentle eminences seen faintly through the heat-haze in the distance; on the other, the broad valley of the Thames, with the battlements and keeps of Windsor on the sky-line. One way, were the smoke canopy to thin and lift, you might distinguish the square towers of Westminster and the dome and cross and ball of St. Paul's ; while all around you gradually recognise the heights that are the glory and landmarks of their respective localities. Strictly speaking, we should press you into continuing the walk, for we have many miles to go, and much that is beautiful to admire, before we have brought our work to an end, or honourably earned our dinner. But we would rather part company before you are thoroughly bored, and prefer to change the scene to Scotland.

CHAPTER XI

The Amateur Tramp in Scotland

AND whither shall we bend our wandering steps in the rare embarrassment of half-savage riches in the shaggy land of the mountain and the flood ? Shall we take our walk on the Border or in the Highlands ; or if in the Highlands, shall it be in the west or in the north, in the midlands, or among the highest of the Grampians? In the Highlands, we say decidedly, for reasons we need hardly pause to condescend upon ; and to avoid inviting invidious comparisons, we shall leave identification to the reader's imagination. In the Highlands, and especially on the western coast, there is always an element of climatic uncertainty which you are inclined to regard as a blessing when the chances have turned up in your favour. The night before the barometer was tending down, and the questionable clouds that shrouded the sunset had cast their perceptible shadows on the faces of your fellow-tourists. When, in the words of the Queen of the May, you bade the boots call you early in the morning, anxiety belied your ill-assumed confidence. And when his heavy knuckles interrupted your slumbers he had nothing very satisfactory to say. The clouds of the evening sky were a joke to the morning grimness. You looked out from your window on curtains of vapour that shrouded alike the loch and the mountain. There was nothing reassuring in the feeling of the wind, that fanned your forehead like the forerunner of rain, and vexed your ear with a watery sough. But a man must trust something to fate, and inaction in the Highlands is immeasurably depressing. You take heart of grace and start. You hear the bell of the early steamer chiming somewhere out of blank space like a fog-signal. For anything you can see, setting temperature out of the question, you might as well be in the innermost recesses of a double-heated Turkish bath. But you have lost your road before, and as yet it is not easy to mistake it; so you set the stout heart to the stey brae, and boldly burn your bridges behind you. And you receive your rich reward, even sooner than you had dared to hope. There are light rifts overhead that quickly widen and brighten. When the sun has once unlocked the wheels of his chariot he swiftly follows up his advantage. The vapoury veils have not a chance with him; they shrivel up into drifting shreds before his blaze, and float away into cool corners and nooks. The whole resplendent prospect to the seaward lies extended all of a sudden at your feet, seen through a limpid transparency that throws everything into sharp-edged relief. The gleaming crescent of the breaking surf and the rippling waters of the loch beyond it; the

Grouse fighting on the Moors. *By* F. C. Turner.

APOLLO
REMOLDS

braes of heather and the hills of grass, with the fleecy flocks that lie huddled together on them ; the steamers whistling at the wharf behind, with the unlucky passengers embarking, who are to be doomed to supine inactivity ; the brown sails of the fishing-boats scarcely swelling to the light cat's-paws ; the flights of stooping sea-fowl ; the low verdant islands in the middle distance ; the clear outlines of the rocky peaks, whose base is battered by the breakers of the Atlantic.

But your road leads to the landward, and there is pleasure enough in the sights and sensations that beckon you along it. The oak copses are glistening in showers of fog-drops. The birds are twittering merrily to the promise of the brilliant day ; now and then a hare hops out upon your path, or you have a flying glance at the white stern of a roe, as he bounds gracefully into the thicker cover. Beyond the copses you emerge on the moors, where you hear the shrill cry of the grousecock, and the plaintive wail of the wary curlew. The moors reach away from you on either side in brown rolling stretches of heather, cut up here and there by black peat-hags. There is not a human being or a habitation, for the moment, within sight or hearing ; your bed and the boots and your southern fellowtourists seem to be left long leagues and days behind you. If ever you care for communing with yourself quietly, with the mellowing lights of heaven falling softly on your past and your future, now is one of those rare opportunities that come too seldom in the course of your pilgrimage. Ha ! what is that ? A sea-eagle, as we live, winging his flight towards the loch, and sharp-set for his breakfast; and the sight is far rarer than it should be, now that he is so ruthlessly shot down by the keepers, while fancy prices are given for his eggs. It may be true that the eagle's moral qualities have been absurdly idealised by the poets. He is a fierce and truculent savage, and, like all savages, a glutton to boot; and he assuredly shows to anything but advantage when, after having gorged himself on a heavy meal, he crumples up into a shapeless ball of feathers, resigning himself to the slow labours of digestion. But when you come across him of a glorious morning like this, soaring in the strength of his magnificent pinions, he is as the warlike Osmanli amidst the joys of battle to the same individual in peace-time in the sensuous seclusion of his harem.

Leaving him behind, and his heathery hunting-grounds, you cross the ridge and clear the plateau to descend the watershed on the other side. You may safely leave the road if you please, for the road, that has been most scientifically engineered, tediously descends by easy gradients, losing itself and alternately reappearing among the copsewood. Still, you may be the better of a guide; and here you have one, vociferous indeed, yet not importunate. In these dark peat-bogs, under coverings of emerald duckweed, are the troubled sources of the translucent stream which waters the pastures of the strath below you. But before it runs so smooth and shallow, stringing a succession of silvery lochs on its meandering course, it has to tumble a couple of thousand feet or so, with little elbow-room to do it in. Down it goes, through a series of gorges, leaping in foaming little cascades, roaring with all its tiny force in scores of tempestuous miniature cataracts, catching its breath in swirling pools before it breaks forth again upon its headlong career. Unless you could leap and light on your feet like the chamois, or wear wings on your double-soled walking-boots, *à la* Mercury, it would be sheer matter of impossibility to keep close company with it throughout. But, by dint of scrambling and slipping, cutting off precipitous corners, and swinging yourself downwards by bending boughs, you make shift somehow to rejoin it in the rocky cleft at the bottom. The path you have found or forced is but seldom trodden, and the pair of ravens who have their nesting-place in the rocky recess greet your intrusion with discordant croaks, that are meant unmistakably for malignant execrations. The sun rarely touches these depths, except when he takes a flying shot through the hill-tops some time late in the afternoon; and it is an agreeable change from their sombre shadows into the light of the widening valley below. Thence your path, though it sometimes rises, on the whole leads downwards in an easy descent. Now it winds through groups of Scotch firs, more or less shattered and storm-beaten, throwing out their distorted limbs over jungles of luxuriant bracken. Now it runs by the shores of silent lakelets, their surface seldom broken by the oar, and reflecting in their glassy mirror their fringe of weeping birches. Here and there the oppression of the solitude is relieved by a shooting-box or a shepherd's cottage, and in either case the sporting dogs or the collies are sure to awaken the echoes with a shrill chorus of clamorous baying ; or mayhap you may come on a lonely kirk, with the single-storied manse within a stone's throw ; and a tiny school and a humble schoolmaster's house, and a hovel that may be tenanted by the minister's man. How on earth the most fervent piety, or the most impassioned eloquence, can evoke even the phantom of a decent congregation, is a mystery you cannot profess to fathom. The prolific Celts that once peopled the valley have long since been swept away to give place to the sheep and the deer. You saw the grass-grown foundation of one of their deserted hamlets scarring the turf of the little knoll that was lapped on three sides in a loop of the stream. But the present population of these parts has no notion of distance ; and in many a winding hill-valley that runs up among the roots of the hills are the huts of shepherds and keepers and gillies, whose existence one never suspects till it is betrayed by the peat-reek from the chimneys.

By this time, however, you must have had nearly enough of it, though you did have an opportunity of breaking your fast at midday on oat-cakes and ewe-milk cheese, bottled ale and a caulker of whisky, following up the meal with a pipe and a siesta, basking on the balmy bank of the river. So that as you pass the last of the milestones with a perceptible limp, you welcome the chimneys of your place of destination, where you have prudently timed yourself to anticipate the advent of the cross-country mail and the tourist-laden steamers.

There are people who turn up their noses at Scotland as a touring country, which of course is absurd. Perhaps the chief objection to it, as it appears to us, besides the preponderating type of tourist, who is not to be ignored, and the climate, which often is not to be defended, is the tantalising character of your most romantic walks. The grouse rise whirring from the heather around you, skimming the knolls in their swift flight, and dropping provokingly ahead ; the black game may be seen towards dusk gathering in clusters on the boughs of the fir trees ; the stately hart, sending his hinds before him, goes trotting leisurely over the forest-steeps, to show his antlered profile on the sky-line before vanishing from view. The salmon are leaping in their favourite pools, and the lively little trout on the feed in the lochs are rippling the surface in widening circles. Deer and game-birds seem to show by their indifferent familiarity that they know you are there upon sufferance and impotent to harm them. A simple wayfarer, without gun, rifle, or rod among your belongings, you are apt half to forget the beauty of those mountain preserves while walking through them with hands that are innocent of bloodshed ; and you are envying the inmates of the shooting-boxes and the lodges, whom you see abroad with their rods, their dogs, and their gillies. In your walks on the Continent, on the other hand, you are not often tempted in that way. There may be game in abundance in some of those great forests—forests that are really set thick with trees in place of being bare hillsides, *lucus a non lucendo*—but it is relatively rarely that you get a glimpse of it. And the sportsmen you come across, with their tasselled game-bags and fringed gaiters, with their short guns slung to their shoulders, and their long-backed badger-hounds following at their heels, seem to belong to distinct varieties of your species, and to have got themselves up artistically for scenes in " Der Freyschütz." As for those ranges of the High Alps, &c., that are thrown open to the admiration and pedestrian achievements of the public, in these the sport is mythical. We believe in the presence of troops of chamois in the Royal Bavarian preserves that cast the shadows of their precipitous terraces over the stillness of the Königsee, and of *moufflons* in the Piedmontese solitudes that are kept sacred to his Majesty of Italy. Nay, we have had our attention called to shifting specks on the Pyrenean snow-slopes that, as we were confidently informed, were izzards; and in Switzerland we have eaten overpoweringly savoury meat that was served as chamois-venison, and suggested goat. But in the absence of all sporting distractions, save the occasional whistle of the marmot from among the beds of Alpine roses and the boulder-strewn rocks, you can resign yourself absolutely to the enjoyment of the changing and dissolving views, and revel in the grandeur of the glaciers and snow-fields.

CHAPTER XII

Fishing in River, Stream, and Loch

LET those abuse the practice of field-sports who will, it is a question of the feelings, not of reasoning. We believe that Providence knew what it was about when it implanted an ardent devotion to the chase in the bosoms of most lovers of the country. The passion of hunting up wild things, and following them in their haunts in woodland, hedgerow, and rush-grown pool, is never more intense than in innocent childhood; though it is confirmed into a rooted habit of life with the scientific successes of youth and manhood. It would be hard upon us if, in a more advanced state of civilisation, we had to renounce the recreations of the virtuous savage.

And although we cannot see ourselves as others see us, or judge ourselves as our posterity will judge us, it is our opinion that in indulgence in various sports we Englishmen of this present generation must have nearly hit off the happy mean. Some of our tolerated amusements may still be open to objections; but, generally speaking, a healthy sentiment draws the line between "field-sports," properly so called, and their bastard kindred, where the victim had no chance and his pluck was cruelly *exploitée* by his persecutors.

Say the fox has a *mauvais quart d'heure* after the exhilarating edge has been taken off his first burst of excitement, and he finds that he is really racing for his life. Up to that time, and with the exception of an occasional breather, the sly and jovial freebooter has been living on the fat of the land. Of what a sum of sorrows has he not been the cause in the course of his maraudings on the neighbouring poultry-yards and rabbit-burrows! How many melancholy bereavements have been laid to his door! His nocturnal trail has been strewn with tattered plumage, and there is a very Gehenna of bleaching bones round the earths where he relaxes towards the gloaming among his ravenous cubs. At last the hour of retribution has come—and who shall say that he has not been working for his fate? Had it not been for the *gourmandise* that had sleeked his coat and thickened his wind, he might have carried off his brush undraggled with all the honours of the chase. As it is, the pace and scent have been so good that his sufferings are at an end before he has well realised them. He has died the death that would have been desired by his human counterparts—our Scotch Highland caterans and Border reivers—and has breathed his last in the throbbings of mad excitement, in place of wasting away in slow inanition when his strength has failed and his jaws are fangless. We have far more sympathy for the harmless hare, tossed over in the teeth of the remorseless greyhounds. But there too, after all, the end came quick; and up to the moment when she was seen squatting in her form, her hours had been gliding by in blissful unconsciousness of the tragedy in which she was so soon to play the leading part. While, on the other hand, the rattling gallops after the hounds, the long days on the breezy down among the coursers, have spared more pain to many gentlemen of the field than any amount of physic or mineral waters. Who can say how many latent diseases have been indefinitely stayed off, if not eradicated? We know that that gallant veteran, who groaned heavily in spirit in the early morning as he painfully raised his rheumatic limb towards the stirrup, swung himself from the saddle in the afternoon a different creature, after the "sharp sweating in his clothes." While as for fishing, to come back to our *moutons*, the "cruelty" in fishing scarcely deserves consideration. We do not go so far as to say, with some enthusiasts, that a fish is the livelier for the hook he carries away, and that it tickles his palate at meal-times like pickles or Worcester sauce. But we are persuaded that the inconvenience it causes him must be infinitesimal, since the smart no more interferes with his appetite than the burn of a *chili* on the palate of an epicure. Every angler must remember cases in his personal experience when the fish he has played, having broken his line, has come to a change of flies on the second time of asking, as if ten minutes' tumbling on the hook against the stream had merely put a keener edge on his voracity.

So we cast considerations of morbid sentimentality to the winds, and write of angling from the sportsman's point of view. A contemplative recreation, some people love to call it. Well, a contemplative recreation it is ; nor is it a slight charm about it when the fish are shy to be wooed, and you are wandering through the woodlands by the rippling water, that you may abandon yourself to reflection in the interludes of working, and draw profitable inspirations from the beauties of nature. Always supposing, that is to say, that you do not let your wits go a-wool-gathering from your immediate business ; for you should make each cast as if the odds were in favour of a rise—and moonstruck abstraction is fatal to heavy baskets. But there are anglers and anglers, as there are streams and streams, from the swift-rushing Spey or the treacherous Findhorn, to the waters of the Midland shires, that go softly over bottoms of mud between borders of willows. A contemplative recreation, you say ! We put it to any man who boasts himself a good all-round sportsman. What are the moments of most thrilling excitement he ever experienced in his life ? He has felt the beating of his heart come suddenly to a stand-still as he crawled upon the antlers of a "stag of ten" showing over the heather hillock in the corry, when the gusty breezes threatened to betray him, and he was listening fearfully for the warning crow of the grouse-cock. He has felt his blood at the boiling-point in bitter January, as he laid the broad pastures behind him in the grass counties, and went clearing the ox-fences and crashing through the bull-finches, as the pack that might have been covered with a waggon-tilt were carrying the burning scent heart-high. For aught we know, he may have stood face to face with the crouching tiger; or he may have slipped "by the skin of his teeth" through the hug of a "grizzly." But in these last situations the sensations though sharp enough, must be short, and we should fancy that the horror predominates over pleasure in them. While in the struggle with the salmon in the rapid stream, the prolonged and pleasurable excitement after the first moment of rapturous assurance, goes on growing in intensity through minutes that may extend themselves into hours. There may be the piquancy, too, of some dash of danger in the reckless gymnastics you may be forced to perform between the depths of the pools and the cliffs that overhang them; while faculties already strained to the uttermost are wrought on by alternations of fear and hope, till the contest comes to an end in one way or another.

Take a single reminiscence among the many that memory lightly recalls. It was on the first day of one of your fishing seasons, when, hurrying away from work, worries, and late hours in town, you had gone to the Highlands, brimming over with expectation, and in the spirits of a schoolboy broken loose for the holidays.

Had your spirits been less exuberant, they might have been dashed by the news that welcomed you to your lonely lodge in the wilderness. The river was running low after a portentous period of drought. Some of the surest pools were scarcely worth the trouble of casting over; and through the limpid waters of the soft-murmuring stream you could almost "prospect" the gravelly bottom for yourself, and see that the favourite "seats" of the fish were untenanted. The best rods had done little or nothing for a fortnight or more; even your opposite neighbour The M'Closkey, renowned far and wide among the heroes of the angle, had renounced his efforts in despair, and gone in for solitary drinking. But after all, nothing venture, nothing have: you had not travelled so far northwards for nothing, and the mere sight of the familiar water sufficed to set your fancy on the alert. Whether your skill and perseverance be rewarded or no, it is pleasure breathing the fresh air from the hills, and feeling your muscles extend themselves to the play of the rod, as you stretch your shoulders in the loose-sitting shooting-coat. Whatever the condition of the water, the day is all that can be desired: in the meantime there is a canopy of dull, grey clouds, though there may be a threatening of sunshine to disperse them later; and the breathings of the south-west wind have brought a light ripple over the pools. Sticking chiefly to the stiller but deeper water, you make your casts with a conscientiousness that does you credit. Persistence, and a patient faith in the rise that may come to you at any

FISHING IN RIVER, STREAM, AND LOCH 161

moment, are the tests of the good and fortunate fisherman. But no doubt it is uphill work, that hoping on against discouragement ; and you begin, in spite of yourself, to take some interest in surrounding objects, and a trifle less in the fly you are playing more mechanically among the eddies and the back-water. But here you are arrived at the famous " Fairy's Pool," and compelled to pay closer attention ; for the drooping birches that strike their roots through the clefts in the rock throw their shadows over your fly-bedecked wideawake, and you must cast a moderately long line underhanded. You are drawing the fly with a gentle twitch in artistic zigzags, behind that jutting black point of rock, where you know there is a favourite " seat " of the salmon. There is a swirl and a surging wave in the pool ; the reel spins round in double-quick time, and the line runs out to the whirring music. However long that fish may have been in the river, he is clean as if he were fresh from the sea. You could see the shimmer of the silver scales, as, bending himself like a drawn bow in a mighty splash, he vanished again in the depths from which you disturbed him. Salmon-fishing a contemplative amusement, indeed !—there is small time for contemplation. Nothing will ever bring that fish to bank but the instincts of long scientific experience, with prompt and decisive strategy. He is bent upon " breaking " you, and you are bound to humour him while you hold him fast ; and humouring him is no such easy matter with the slippery foothold, the lack of arm-room, and the canopy of drooping birchen boughs. Yet the triumph of tasting blood, in the circumstances, at your very first venture on the water! And already there is a spectator of your prowess on the opposite shore, in the person of the head-keeper of your neighbour's shootings.

Duncan is moved with envy, and sneeringly critical; and by way of calming your nerves, when so much depends on coolness, your own attendant has forgotten his self-restraint, and is shouting out unheeded counsels. As to the fish, to all appearance he is quite capable of taking care of himself. He made his rush in most serious earnest, and it is to be hoped that he is securely hooked. But your fly is small, and the casting-line fine, both having been chosen in consideration of the lowness of the river. A slack in the line, a slight friction on the stones on the rugged bottom, and all may be lost, honour included. And your antagonist would appear to be as wily as he is powerful. After that first movement of natural irritation, and the rush that tested the strength of your hold, he has dived calmly into the depths, where he has gone to working quietly at extrication. To your gentle tightening of the strain, he opposes a sturdy, passive resistance. "Keep those reel-steps of yours till you next take the floor to the pipes, Donald, and favour him with a stone judiciously thrown." Ha! he may be a sagacious fish, but he is by no means a sullen one. He had hoped to get rid of his silent sorrow without having to shift his defensible quarters; but now, as you mean fighting, you shall have it. He makes a shoot like a submerged

FISHING IN RIVER, STREAM, AND LOCH 163

torpedo, straight at your boots. As the hobnails slip about on the moss-grown boulder, your heart jumps towards your throat, and you feel for a moment that all must be over. But when persistency in his strategy might have saved him, he changes it; and you can straighten the rod that was hampered by the trees, and haul in the line through the rings in a handful. For out he goes again to mid-stream, turning the silvery wheel in showers of waterworks, while in each of his swift revolutions you seem to shave a catastrophe. He is bent apparently on going back to the sea; he makes a resolute dart for the channel, where the pool, breaking into a stream, flows swiftly down the incline of a shelving staircase. There is nothing for it but to let him go or to follow. A contemplative amusement! There is little time for meditation, though you never needed more the inspiration of thought. You are plunging to mid-thigh in the rushing water, seeking a doubtful foothold where you may—doing your best with your heavy rod with one hand, while clinging to the slippery rocks with the other; struggling forward somehow with the shoulders uppermost, and breathing hard all the time, like a hunted otter. Were you ever conscious of a more blissful sensation of relief than when, safely landed on the smooth sward lower down, you have a reach of comparatively uncheckered water before you with shelving gravel in that tiny bay? If line and hook will only hold there should be but one conclusion now to the hard-fought battle, and it is on that strip of yellow beach you mean to land him. A gallant fish he is, and makes more than one desperate rally, but he can by no means avoid his destiny. Answering to steady, irresistible persuasion, he is being manœuvred in easy beauty curves towards the bank, with an occasional wallop of unavailing remonstrance; and Donald, bending over the stream in an attitude of sanguinary expectation, has driven home the clip behind his shoulder. " 'Deed, sir, she's a fine fush, whatever," is his remark, as he stoops to relieve " her " lovingly of the hook. And then he calls your attention to how near a thing it was. For the hook has worked a fissure in the lip, and merely holds by the skin ; and the line has been frayed below the shank to something like threads of gossamer. For a spirit so courageous, what end could have been more becoming? so that there is but the faintest tinge of compassion to dash the exhilaration of the triumph.

So much for the excitements of the sport ; but there are anglers and anglers, as we observed before, and we may turn by way of contrast to scenes of calmer enjoyment, when the name of the " gentle craft " becomes more appropriate. For one man who has killed salmon in the Scottish and Scandinavian rivers, there are hundreds of skilful brothers of the angle who have never cast a fly save in streams we might call Cockney. Masters of their branch of the craft they often are, and almost invariably passionate enthusiasts. No men are better versed in the times and the seasons: no men have more inexhaustible stores of patience; have a more intimate acquaintance with local entomology,

SALMON FISHING. *By* LANCELOT SPEED.

UNIV. OF
CALIFORNIA

FISHING IN RIVER, STREAM, AND LOCH

natural and artificial; can handle the rod and line more deftly; and are more fertile in ingenious devices to bring suspicious victims to their lure. Yet such men are often tied fast by professional pursuits, and have seldom *carte blanche* for fishing in good water. When they do go on a visit to some friend in the country, or get a day's permission in some carefully-preserved stretch of stream, how they do enjoy and make the most of it!—all the more, however, if they are at home in the neighbourhood, and have marked the great fish feeding placidly of an evening on the insects that tumble in from the banks and the tree-roots.

It is no easy matter anywhere to beguile those sated epicures, and in popular streams that are free for a trifle to all comers, it is the next thing to an impossibility. We used to know one particular river trout who went far towards making the fortune of a large hotel in a village some twenty miles from London. It was very much a repetition of Lord Lytton's story of John Burley and his one-eyed perch in "My Novel." True, the situation of the hotel was charming; with a mighty horse-chestnut before the door, coming out towards the middle of spring in a flush of pink and white blossom, and overhanging a picturesque old bridge, and a strip of miniature meadow enamelled with cowslips. But the most generous patrons of the establishment, of a Sunday, were the admirers of that corpulent trout whose fame had spread far and near. The good genius of the flourishing house, he was always at home in the limited domains, and yet nobody knew exactly where to have him. Now he was under this stone, now behind that other one ; and again he would be lazily flipping his fins among the roots of the alder over the way. So the banks were planted thickly with respectable gentlemen of various conditions, though all of the City. Some were in the full swing of business through the week ; others had retired to suburban villas, and were killing time, on a competency. Those were usually attired in glossy broadcloth ; these in tweeds of fantastic patterns. Each had an elaborate apparatus of rods, &c., with a formidable basket, though the door of the inn was almost within arm's length. Jealousy was out of the question ; for though all of them professed to be sanguine in the extreme, nobody in his heart believed in a capture. On the contrary, they struck up close friendship on the strength of their common failures ; they formed themselves into informal clubs for luncheon and dining purposes ; they called for bottle after bottle of fruity port, and bathed, metaphorically speaking, in brimmers of brandy and soda-water. Some of them took a rather unfair advantage, lingering on till the middle of the week ; and while nobody lost by that ungenerous assiduity, the landlord gained enormously. It was a dark day for him when that trout mysteriously disappeared : some people said it was owing to the machinations of a poaching ostler, who had been dismissed at the request of a keeper in the neighbourhood. Yet for long the suburban fishermen came back, hoping against hope, whipping the water indefatigably as ever ; and even after the conviction of their loss became irresistible, the tradition of that trout continued to draw through a couple of seasons while it was gradually fading.

That was of course an extreme case, so far as the odds against the fisherman were concerned. We may picture him rather on a soft May day, when he is turned loose upon the private fishing in one of the beautiful English parks. The day is cloudy, and there is a gentle westerly breeze ; and all nature is rejoicing after some recent showers. Our friend is early afoot ; and the dews and the light rain-drops lie thick upon grass and bracken. He steers straight for the stream by a side path under the trees, the fallow deer scarcely taking the trouble to trot out of his way. The rooks are clamouring and circling round the elms overhead, and jackdaws and starlings are almost as vociferous, as they flutter in and out of the holes in the hawthorn boles. The rabbits, scared from the finish of the morning meal, go scuttling into their burrows in the banks, and thrushes, blackbirds, and finches, when they are not singing, are busied over nest-building and domestic duties. In the balmy fragrance of a morning like that, the mere sense of life and movement is enjoyable ; but though the angler may be a lover of nature in proper time and place, now his gratitude for the pleasures she bestows upon him is unconscious. His eyes and his thoughts are fixed on those clumps of alder that mark the course of the winding stream. He will have more leisure to appreciate the beauties of nature when the fishes shall leave off feeding towards high noon. In the meantime, his hopes rise high as he catches sight of the river. Both in fulness and colour it seems in prime condition. His hands tremble with pleasurable excitement as he puts his rod together—not a very long one, and somewhat stiff. The tapering horsehair is a masterpiece of delicate twisting; the tough casting-line, of a tinge the colour of the water, is a miracle of fineness; the flies, tempered of well-proved material, are something in size between midges and mosquitoes. Having taken a general survey of the scene of operations, he goes stealthily to his work, as if he were stalking deer. Standing well back from the bank, so that no line of his shadow may fall on the water, he makes his quick casts up the stream, letting the flies drop down like thistle-down. He never cares to dwell on the cast or play his flies; for he knows well that if the trout do not come at the first offer it is seldom worth while to press it. Very frequently it is a most difficult and delicate bit of work to touch the surface at the likely-looking spot where experience tells him his friends should be at home. Sometimes, to make assurance of lightness doubly sure, he pitches the fly against some hanging stump, letting it drop naturally back in a gentle ricochet, just as its living prototype might be supposed to do. And even if the trout be in a taking humour, and if weather and water be all that can be desired, he may have to labour on long enough without having his patience rewarded. There is no accounting in any circumstances for the caprices of fish ; though in a stream like this, meandering through wormy, beetley, and fly-haunted meadow-land, their coyness is not difficult to account for. But then, on the other hand, they may waken up of a sudden to a voracity that is at least equally inexplicable. Then the alderman-like fish will make a plunge at the line, with the snap of a bull-dog and the greed of starvation ; and though you must make hay while the sun shines—or, more strictly speaking, while it is not shining—you may fill your basket first. For after having played and killed and lost, with a fair proportion of cases of "hanging up" upon the willow-boughs, and breaking the line on submerged snags, the clouds are rolled aside in a burst of sunshine. Then it will be the wisdom of the angler to adjourn for luncheon, subsequently flirting with the beauties of nature through the afternoon, in anticipation of fresh successes in the evening. And after a light and early breakfast, and with the appetite for which you have been honestly toiling, the sight of those speckled prizes of yours may be the best of sauces for the meal ; though, for ourselves, we should care but little to see them served at it, since low-country trout are apt, both in savour and complexion, to remind one unpleasantly of their native mud.

It is very different with the firm-fleshed fish you take from the chilly waters of lochs in the north, or from the bright gravelly bottoms of the swift-rushing streams— fish that gladden alike the eye of the artist and the soul of the *gourmet*. The vivid tinges of colouring range from delicate pink, through blushing carmine, to flaming rose-colour. No need to seek the flavouring in the cruets—*vide* Mrs. Poyser. Serve simply, like crimped and curdy salmon, in the water in which the fish has been boiled ; add at the utmost a touch of vinegar, and possibly the faintest *soupçon* of ketchup, to elicit without stifling the native essences. Nor is it the mere reminiscences of *gourmandise* that warm the imagination in recalling the simple but exquisite banquets at which these trout may have figured. Pink, firm flesh means glorious scenery, and a strength of play out of all proportion to the size. Sometimes you have the strength and the size combined, as in the fierce rush of the *salmo ferox* of Loch Awe when it pleases the savage tyrant of the waters to come upon the feed, somewhere between the depths and the shallows. But then you are prepared for the best or the worst ; the minnow is attached to tackle of unimpeachable strength ; it is a case of " pull devil, pull baker," and science is in some measure in suspension when the prey has been fairly hooked. We talk rather of killing what are pigmies by comparison, but who afford very fair sport nevertheless, and with briefer intervals of wearisome expectation ; pigmies, that is to say, perhaps running on the average from three-quarters of a pound to a couple of pounds.

For ourselves, we never greatly cared for loch-fishing. There is something depressing in being cramped between thwarts and benches, that reminds one of those

FISHING IN RIVER, STREAM, AND LOCH 171

sufferings at sea you may have read of, in the boats of the *Bounty* or on the rafts of the *Medusa*. So there is in casting over the surface of a sheet of water where the topography of the lower regions must be as a sealed-up chart to everybody except the fisherman who acts as the pilot. And yet it may be agreeable enough by way of variety. We have pleasant memories of cruises in the bays of Loch Awe, in the days when it was far less fished than at present, and where the long odds were against your finding the fishing-ground pre-occupied, even if you did not get up overnight and stand out to sea in the darkness. We have pleasant memories, too, of expeditions to mountain lakelets in the countries of Rob Roy and Roderick Dhu; or to localities more remote from the tread of the tourist, in the less hospitable wilds of Inverness-shire and Ross-shire. Half the fun of those rough-and-ready trips often lay in the preliminary excitement as to how you were to find the means of getting afloat. Throwing the longest line to any purpose from the shores was made impracticable by the fringes of rushes that sheltered the broods of wild duck and water-hen. The crazy craft you found to launch often sorely wanted coopering, and you embarked yourself with your piscatory belongings on the off-chance of a swim and a shipwreck.

We used to envy the luxurious independence of a friend who drove about in a boat of his own, mounted break-fashion upon wheels, the light carriage being constructed of tough hickory-wood, warranted to stand any amount of trackless jolting. Until, on one occasion, being caught by a gust down a gully, the break-boat and its contents came to a sudden capsize; and the proud owner, being saved, with the sacrifice of his property, by a dangerous swimming-bout across the loch before the storm, condemned his craft forthwith. We do not say that these carriage-boats may not be constructed so as to be safe and reasonably commodious. St. John made his tour in Sutherlandshire in one of them. We merely record a fact which disenchanted us of any special hankering after them. And to return to our loch-fishing, some of our most agreeable memories associate themselves with long days upon Loch Leven. Now the loch is *exploitée* by fishing-clubs, who put forth in fleets each day through the season. Then there were but a couple of boats available on the water, one of these belonging to the proprietor, and the other to the "tacksman" of his fishings. Perhaps the pike were less persistently netted down than they might have been; but the trout must have been all the heavier on that account; and surely they were less shy than they have since become. We know that, wind and weather permitting, we used to make highly satisfactory baskets. And at the risk of being called dog-in-the-mangerish, we maintain that it was a pleasure to have the pick of the expanse before you. The whole circuit of the loch is classic ground, and you might steep your soul in romantic associations while relaxing from your labours on the most exciting of the fishing-ground. Now you were within easy hail of the old castle, on the very spot where the boat with muffled oars stole in under cover of the night to rescue Queen Mary and her ladies. There Roland Græme—or the little Douglas—consigned the castle keys to the keeping of the kelpies; and thence you looked across to the picturesque village, where the page, having broken away from the Chamberlain, met Seyton at the mountebank's, among the frolics of the fair. Now you were at anchor off the islet of St. Serf; and now you were drifting beneath the brow of Benarty; while scarcely a height in the sub-Highland landscape around you but had been touched by the wand of the Wizard of the North. And if a man have a soul above so many pound weight by the weighing-machine, the romance of such associations goes for much in loch-fishing.

There is the romance of scenery too, which is often the romance of desolation, when the trout, though many, are so small as to be a mere pretext for the excursion—as when you follow up some mountain-burn flowing down through the moors—possibly tumbling in cascades over stony staircases, or growling and murmuring between the banks it has mined, under leafy arcades of tangled vegetation. Colquhoun, in "The Moor and Loch," will tell you how you have often to scramble up its course upon hands and knees—how, here and there, where you find tolerable footing and some shoulder-room, you must still make your casts have doubled up, with the shortest and stiffest of rods, and a mere fag-end of casting-line. Very probably, though you have rather a distaste for bait-fishing, you had better discard the fly for the worm. But the yellow-bellied little fellows come leaping up so keenly, in flashes of brightness, through the brown of the peat-coloured fluid, that you are ceaselessly occupied in pulling them out. It is a relief, no doubt, to straighten your back on some tiny patch of verdant sward; but when you have got your breath again, and the aching has died out of your muscles, you are only too eager to go back to the work. Then there is "guddling"—that delight of one's happy boyhood—a passion which, like that of birds'-nesting, sticks to us in maturer manhood. A useful art is guddling on occasions. More than once have we eked out the meagre commissariat of some out-of-the-way inn by stripping off coat and shoes and stockings and going to work in the adjacent brook. You mark the trout shoot under the stone in mid-stream, and there you circumvent him with a hand on either side—tickling him gently, if he eludes all but your finger-tips, till you persuade him to subside, in a hypnotised intoxication, into your clutch; or you have thrust your arm into the winding hole under the bank, at the risk of provoking the bite of a water-rat, and find you have introduced yourself to a happy family of fishes, which you draw forth successively in assorted sizes. That is charming sport for a warm summer-day—when the silvery stream has shrunk down in its stony bed, and the coolness of the water is an agreeable relief from the oppressive temperature of the thundery atmosphere. Or you may be tempted to go "pot-hunting" in another form. You have shot the moors, towards the beginning of September, somewhat hard; or the weather has been wet and windy, and the birds are packing and shy. By way of variety, you may go otter-fishing in some of the mountain lakelets, and a dish of fish of any kind will be by no means unwelcome. A poaching piece of mechanism that otter is: yet if it were more freely used it would be all the better; for the small trout multiply marvellously, though it is hard to tell how they feed and fatten; and if they must sometimes suffer from hunger, they enjoy absolute immunity from pike. The tarn lies high among mists and clouds, and far above the level of the sweet hill-pastures, among the stone-strewn slopes of the straggling brown heather. Insects of any kind are scarce; you seldom hear the hum of the bee, and never see the flutter of the butterfly. As you adjust the otter and unroll the lines, you hear nothing but the twitter of some moorland bird, the crow of the grouse-cock, or the croak of the raven. You set your board afloat before the breeze, among the cold shadows cast by the clouds on the dark-brown ripple of the wavelets. But as the long trail of flies drags slowly out, the whole finny population awakens to the sense of the unwonted excitement. The phenomenon of a flight of flies, all of them most inviting, stirs it up by shoals in jealous rivalry. There is a line of popples and bursting bubbles on the broken water; tiny heads come to the surface, and seem to knock together; there are conglomerations and disturbances here and there. When you haul in, which you may do very speedily, you find you have made what in point of numbers may be almost called a miraculous draught of fishes. Hardly a hook but has attached its greedy place-hunter; and time after time you may send out your snares with the full assurance of equal success.

CHAPTER XIII

Some Writers on the Gentle Craft

BUT we must leave those recollections which tempt us into lingering, and turn to the experiences of more eminent fishing authorities. And writing on fishing in " Blackwood," one goes back almost involuntarily to old Christopher North. The Professor was an expert and an enthusiast—a philosopher, a practical naturalist, and a poet to boot. Some of the brightest passages in his " Recreations " are those connected with his fishing achievements ; and never in the well-timed " daffing " of the " Noctes " does the old man show to much greater advantage than when bending the long-bow in his merrier moods, provoked thereto by the lively imagination of the Shepherd. Take the " Recreations " ; and there we have an admirable bit from " Our Parish," in which old Christopher becomes little Kit again, and goes back, in poetic descriptions of the moorland landscapes, to his early initiation in the mysteries of a craft to which he took like a Newfoundland puppy to the " Brother Loch."

"But few were the days 'good for the Brother Loch.' Perch rarely failed you, for by perseverance you were sure to fall in with one circumnatatory school or other, and to do murderous work among them with the mauk, from the schoolmaster himself inclusive down to the little booby of the lowest form. Not so with trout. We have angled ten hours a day for half a week (during the vacance) without ever getting a single rise, nor could even that be called bad sport, for we lived in momentary expectation, mingled with fear, of a monster. Better far from sunrise to sunset never to move a fin, than oh! me miserable! to hook a huge hero with shoulders like a hog—play him till he comes floating side up close to the shore, and then to feel the fleckless fly leave his lip and begin gamboling in the air, while he wallops away back into his native element, and sinks utterly and for evermore into the dark profound. Life loses at such a moment all that makes life desirable —yet strange! the wretch lives on—and has not the heart to drown himself, and he wrings his hands and curses his lot and the day he was born. But, thank Heaven, that ghastly fit of fancy is gone by, and we imagine one of those dark, scowling, gusty, almost tempestuous days, 'prime for the Brother Loch.' No glare or glitter on the water, no reflection of fleecy clouds, but a black-blue undulating swell, at times turbulent—with now and then a breaking wave—that was the weather in which the giants fed, showing their backs like dolphins within a fathom of the shore, and sucking in the red heckle among your very feet."

Talking of giants and monsters, we have a laughable companion picture in the "Noctes," where the Shepherd, posing as a border Baron Munchausen, tells in the richest Doric, and with a marvellous wealth of imagery, how he hooked and killed his "three stane salmon," following him like an otter between land and water in a cork jacket, and finally "gripping" and landing him in his teeth. And the actual incidents of the struggle are made so true to realities that we almost forget we are listening to a rhapsody of the fancy.

SOME WRITERS ON THE GENTLE CRAFT 179

The sporting Shepherd is in even greater force at a meeting of the worthies of the "Noctes," at the appropriate "anglers' retreat" of Tibby Shiel's on St. Mary's Loch. The meeting came off, by the way, in late autumn, which made his piscatory feats the more wonderful. Answering North's inquiry as to what he had been doing, the Shepherd begins his matter-of-fact narrative with a charming affectation of modesty. "No muckle. I left Altrive after breakfast—about nine—and the Douglas burn looking gey tempting, I tried it with the black gnat, and sune creeled some four or five dizzen—the maist o' them sma'—few exceeding a pund." Tiring of trouting, he had changed his trout-cast for a salmon-fly, and left the Douglas burn for the Yarrow. "I was jist wattin my flee near the edge when a new-run fish, strong as a white horse, rushed at it, and then out o' the water wi' a spring higher than my head." That incident ends, after sundry thrilling vicissitudes in landing the heaviest fish that was ever killed in the Yarrow, when the fortunate captor turns for a change to the loch, and tries the otter. Result—two dozen, the one half the size of herring, the other half the size of haddocks, with one grey trout as big as a cod. Next, he pays a parenthetical visit to some night lines, pulling up pike and eel alternately, "wi' maist unerrin' regularity of succession," till he could have fancied that "a' the fishy life the water had contained was now wallopin' and wrigglin' in the sudden sunshine of unexpected day."

Experiences like those have never occurred to anybody save men of the Shepherd's poetic fancy, though there are well-authenticated facts on record which sound almost as extraordinary even to the initiated, as when the present Lord Lovat killed in the river of Beauly no fewer than 156 fish in five successive days. And so we leave the realms of the literature of fancy for those of sober fact, albeit not altogether untinged by romance; as in that delightful volume of Scrope's, "The Days and Nights of Salmon-fishing." As accomplished an artist with the rod as the rifle, no keener hand ever pursued the noble sport in serene indifference to weather, wettings, and the bitter caprices of the northern climate. A glance over the illustrations is a pleasure in itself, and eminently suggestive besides; for Scrope had enlisted the services of no smaller men than Wilkie, the two Landseers, and Edward Cooke. Their drawings are a panoramic epitome of sport on the border river—for Scrope confines himself entirely to the Tweed; and they embrace all forms of fishing, legitimate, illegitimate, and commercial, with rod, and net, and leister. Here we have a boatful of men "burning the water," their faces and forms lighted up by the ruddy glow of their fire; there you have a group by Wilkie working the drag-net, enthusiasm and the keenest eagerness of expectation expressed in each speaking body and limb, down to the bulging back sinews in their sturdy calves. There a party has pulled ashore after a catch, and the mighty salmon is being scrupulously weighed; and again the angler, after a doubtful fight, under difficulties, sees his line about to be "cut." In the background of all the views is scenery characteristic of the river—a beetling crag, crowned by the ruins of its shattered keep; a snug fishing-box, showing its smoking chimney-stacks over a bank of wood; or an amphitheatre of bare, bluff hills, broken with patches of furze, and backed up by some well-known group like the trinity of the Eildons. And the people whose acquaintance we make are just as characteristic as the scenes they figure in. Not to speak of the nobles and lairds, who doubtless deserved the praises they receive from the best of good fellows and even better sportsmen, there are the peasant worthies, who might have led happy but inglorious lives had they not been immortalised in the memoirs of the author of "Waverley." There are Tom Purdie and Rob Kerse, who often kept the author company, and of the former of them he tells sundry capital stories. It is one great charm of the angler's life, the forming fast friendships with men of this kind, when differences of station and education have been forgotten in the indulgence of common tastes and the interchange of common sympathies. Among the many friends Scrope made on the border river was the immortal patron of the Purdies himself. The fifth chapter begins with an eloquent tribute of affectionate admiration to the Tweed, as he knew it before Scott had made it famous, though it was endeared already to the salmon-fisher and the artist. And then he goes on, in a passage that has a melancholy interest still, though doubtless the interest was fresher when it was written some half-century ago :—

"Since that time I have seen the cottage of Abbotsford, with its rustic porch, lying peacefully in the haugh between the blue hills, and have listened to the wild rush of the Tweed as it hurried beneath it. As time progressed and as hopes arose, I have seen that cottage converted into a picturesque mansion, with every luxury and comfort attached to it, and have partaken of its hospitality; the unproductive hills I have viewed covered with thriving plantations, and the whole aspect of the county civilised without losing its romantic character. But amidst all these revolutions I have never perceived any change in the mind of him who made them, 'the choice and master-spirit of the age.' There he dwelt in the hearts of the people, diffusing life and happiness around him; he made a home beside the border river, in a country and a nation that have derived benefit from his presence and consequence from his genius."

Figuring in the fictitious character of Harry Otter, Scrope relates a humorous adventure that must have had its counterpart in the lives of most angling novices. He tells how, having turned out with a spick-and-span new rod, exquisite in workmanship and resplendent in varnish, he crowned sundry highly satisfactory exploits by landing a 5-lb. grilse, and that with fragile trout tackle. How, swelling inwardly with intense self-satisfaction, he met a native who might have sat to a painter for Wat Tinlinn, and whose rod, with its makeshift appurtenances, were at least as uncouth as himself. How, condescending graciously to this rough brother of the craft, he was provoked by the *nil admirari* manner to tantalise him with a display of his booty. And how the borderer, "premeesing" carelessly that he could "speecify" that he had no had muckle luck, made the practical retort to his southern interlocutor of producing a couple of seemingly interminable salmon from the bag that had been half-concealed behind his broad shoulders. That is the sort of irritating adventure that may happen to you, to the latest day of your life. Luck, of course, may always have much to do with success, and you try to lay that soothing unction to your vanity. Moreover, a local man must know his native water, and be more familiar with the flies, and all the rest of it. Nevertheless, there is no getting over the fact that both luck and skill must be handicapped by his clumsy apparatus, and that if your indifferently equipped acquaintance has fairly beaten you, it has been in spite of his having been heavily overweighted in that respect. And talking of equipment, one thing strikes us in these pictures in Scrope. A better sportsman never lived, yet he is got up in costume that would stamp a man now as the most unmistakable of Cockneys. He fishes the Tweed in a curly-brimmed beaver, in a flowing frock-coat and gracefully-cut white pantaloons descending on highly polished single-soled boots—in a dress, in short, which would have become a man who was no great dandy as he took his stroll along the shady side of Pall Mall. We must say that in dressing for our field-sports we are become wiser in our generation; and that coarse home-spun jackets and baggy knickerbockers, deer-stalking wide-awake, and hobnailed boots, are more graceful " in that connection," as they are undoubtedly more suitable. Mr. Scrope's hat must surely have gone flying over his shoulder at each gust of wind that swept down the river; and a driving shower must have soaked him to the skin, unless he were prepared to envelop himself at the shortest notice in wrappings carried by his attendant. Though the sportsman should be made neither of sugar or salt, speedy saturation on a nipping day in spring seems to us to be a very gratuitous infliction; nor do we see the wisdom of laying in rheumatics and remorse by way of distractions for our declining years.

If Scrope confines his reminiscences to the Tweed, Mr. Colquhoun, in his excursions to river and loch, carries us over the length and breadth of Scotland. "Excursion," indeed, is scarcely the word to use, for he has probably rented more shootings and fishings in a greater number of the Scotch counties, in the course of a most active life, than any man living. The publication of a fifth edition of "The Moor and the Loch," by the way, is a proof the more of its well-deserved popularity. And we are glad to think that a suggestion of our own, in a former article on that delightful book, may have had its share in inducing the author to prefix to this new edition a very interesting bit of autobiography. It abounds in lively anecdotes of his school-days and early life, especially after joining his regiment—the gallant 33rd —then quartered in the wilds of Connaught. The story is everywhere impressed with the author's vigorous individuality; and the Connaught of those unsettled times was by no means an enviable place of residence for a nervous man. Of course, Colquhoun liked it. Yet the young Scot, though generally popular with a peasantry and gentry who delighted in sport, has to tell of more than one hair-breadth escape, when duels were affairs of every-day occurrence, and soldiers were likely to be shot at on account of the colour of their cloth. We may say of young Colquhoun,

> "Alike to him . . .
> . . . the brand, the bridle, and the oar";

as he was as much at home in a boat as in the saddle, and has more than one memorable feat in sea-racing to tell of, when he and his elder brother were pulling in company. But so far as fishing goes, his autobiographical recollections are scattered broadcast over the pages he has consecrated to that branch of sport. We trace him through Lowlands and Highlands, from fishing quarter to fishing quarter and stream to stream; from the Stinchar in Ayrshire to the Dee in Aberdeen, and the smaller rivers of the more northerly Highland counties; and as for the lochs, he seems to have tried, in his time, most of those that have more than local reputation. A pleasanter companion no man need desire; and those stirring exploits of his, which he so vividly records, have been photographed on a singularly retentive memory. But the comprehensiveness and clearness with which he handles his favourite subjects give his volumes a very practical value. As for comprehensiveness, the angler will find hints that may help him in each and all of the localities he is likely to visit, and through every season of the year; while for clearness and simplicity, Mr. Colquhoun is as little given to multiply rules and instructions pharisaically as to embarrass himself with an over-elaborate apparatus. Two or three coils of flies wound round his hat, and composed, of course, like French salad, "after the season," and according to his ample knowledge and experience, serve his turn for any day's angling. He is none of your brilliant theorists and connoisseurs, who have collected, to their own extreme confusion, whole libraries of fishing-books, stuffed with fur, feathers, and tinsel; while you are perpetually coming, in his pages, upon one of those practical maxims that may spare infinite disappointment to the sensible novice, and set him up with the best second-hand experience. Those passages might be extracted with advantage, and codified, in the shape of a summary, in the Appendix; and we may select a few of them, by way of example. Angling, says Mr. Colquhoun, though not precisely in these words, is emphatically a science that must be cultivated by thought and observation, and practised by the exercise of careful induction.

"It is the exact perception of the seats of fish, and where they may shift about, according to the varying moods of the river, that constitutes half the science of angling. As the late eminent Dr. Munro used to say of medicine, 'It is but shrewd guessing after all.' Nevertheless, as in physic, the shrewdest guesser is the best physician; so in angling, the shrewdest guesser, if not *always* the ablest, will go far to be the most successful fisher. . . . As to upstream trouting, many will reject it on account of the perpetual casting it entails. There is this in its favour though, that, in trout-fishing, the more casts the more rises. All good trouters are aware of this, and never put off time by leading their hooks, except in lochs and the still deeps of streams. . . . When the fly is dropped in the *centre of the ring, the instant after the trout has belled up*, it is ten times more likely to rise again than if the fly touched the water at ever so short a distance. . . . Another hint to the young angler is to mind what he is about when he approaches the still deeps of the river. Many are apt to pass them by altogether. . . . Perhaps the best test of a finished performer is the manner in which he fishes these dead, deep places, especially if there is little wind ; for they generally harbour the largest and best-fed fish, which are, of course, the most suspicious and difficult to rise."

Fond as Mr. Colquhoun is of trout-fishing, he maintains, what few salmon-fishers will dispute, that there is no comparison between its more tranquil pleasures and the excitement of the nobler sport. It is "only the germ of salmon-fishing," he says ; and he advises its devotees to "get out of this nursery-fishing and to become salmon-anglers if they can." Of course, the more costly voyage to Corinth is not within the means of everybody ; and while all people who have the leisure can compass an occasional week's trouting, a man, to make sure of satisfactory sport with salmon, must have either money or more fortunate friends. As for trouting, Mr. Colquhoun comforts those who seldom have access to well-protected water by pointing out that they will become far more accomplished workmen by fishing ordinary rivers than those that are profusely stocked. He has remarked that men who shoot habitually in preserves are not to be compared, as steady shots, with others who have been in the habit of making wild bags. "The one blazes thoughtlessly away, committing, time after time, the same errors; while the other carefully notes every miss, and endeavours to correct it next opportunity. There is also no doubt that both the angler and the shooter who have to work and *think* for their sport acquire a self-command and nerve only to be obtained in this school."

Among the liveliest of Mr. Colquhoun's cheery reminiscences are those that associate themselves with his summer quarters on the Lyon in Perthshire; and for a picture of fishing under extreme difficulties, there is nothing better than a description of his to which we have already referred, of working one of those Highland burns that come brawling down over the rocks beneath a tangle of underwood. But perhaps the most dramatic adventure he has put on record is the fight of one of his sons with a heavy salmon, hooked late in the day in a pool of the Stinchar. The action began with a "vindictive plunge" on to the hook, which augured ill for the ultimate success of the fisherman. For—

"To my dismay, I now saw that my son had chosen, by mistake, the lightest reel line in my possession, only intended for sea-trout or grilse, in the clearest water of July! Its length, however, was one hundred yards; and having perfect confidence in the skill of the fisherman, I resolved not to flurry him with a warning, but to wait in patience until the prize was either lost or won.

"The fish neither dashed round the pool in terror, nor refused to move in sullen indifference, but with a degree of calm dignity steered along the opposite bank, giving fitfully a revengeful toss which made my heart flutter. Higher, higher, he rowed himself, till he arrived within a few yards of the overhanging trees. If he resolved to pass this barrier, I knew well the alternative was either a broken line to the angler, or a jump to the shoulders in the rapid current. At this crisis the fish was turned by wary coaxing, and brought cautiously down to the deep water where he had been hooked. A new danger was here threatened, for the eddy tree appeared provokingly near, and it was likely the huge fish might strike across the river, twisting the line round its branches. Again he was foiled by the coolness of his tormentor, and the up-stream march was resumed."

The daylight darkened into the gloaming, but happily there were no clouds on the sky, and "to our delight, the glorious red harvest moon rose 'broad' over the brow of the Ayrshire hills." The villagers hearing of the sport going forward, rushed down from their cottages to look on at the fun; and young Mr. Colquhoun went on playing his fish for the benefit of a "gallery" of excited peasants, by the brilliant light of "Macfarlane's lantern."

"It was nearly ten o'clock at night before the noble fellow began to show symptoms of yielding. 'Bring a lantern, Sandy, as he can never be gaffed by moonlight.' Sandy was soon ready, and eager with light and steel. The salmon, however, though nearly spent, refused to come within reach of his weapon, and kept lashing the water into foam on the opposite shore. Quick as thought, Sandy dashed across the black stream and reached the fish before he sank. Then poising the lantern for a second, up to his waist in the water, he struck his victim with deadly determination—a pause ensued—the light hissed in the river and was extinguished. Then followed a severe unseen struggle under the darkened bank, when Sandy [plucky fellow that he was], with a grip like a bull-dog, dripping from head to foot, crawled from the deep, shouting, 'I hae him noo!'"

The weight of the fish was 25 lbs.; and as he was

the finest fish killed with the rod that season on the Stinchar, the angler's patience and skill were amply rewarded.

Many admirable books have been written on fishing, with not a few songs, ballads, and idyls, good and bad, indifferent and execrable. The marvel is, that we have no more of them, considering how naturally a man with a turn for literature seeks sympathies among the reading public in a pursuit that has grown into a passion with himself. We have no idea of running over a roll of names, since we should infallibly make invidious omissions ; but there is one that has made its appearance recently, which we would notice before reeling up our article, as being not only among the latest, but among the best of its class. "My Life as an Angler," by William Henderson, with its admirable illustrations, seems scarcely to have received the welcome it deserved. Many of the views on the Tweed and the Northumbrian and Durham waters recall some of the most picturesque features of the scenery that has been immortalised in Border warfare, and in the fiery old Border ballads. Great part of that country, moreover, like Tweedside and Coquetdale, has been made classic in the lays of the poets of the angle. Nor less attractive are the charming little head-pieces and tail-pieces to the chapters, which blend graceful fancy with realistic truth, while they have much of that characteristic and humorous individuality which distinguished the tiny masterpieces of Bewick. Mr. Henderson, who is now in his sixty-second year,

SOME WRITERS ON THE GENTLE CRAFT 191

was one of those boys who were born fishermen. " Of all the signs of the Zodiac," as he observes in his opening sentence, "undoubtedly 'the fish with glittering scales' ruled my horoscope." And all through his life, whatever the importunate " distractions " of graver business, he always returned in his ample intervals of leisure with redoubled ardour to his early passion. Like Kit North, he goes back with affectionate enthusiasm to the circumstances of his first becoming possessor of a rod, and the capture of his first fish. How many of his readers could tell stories almost similar—stories defining themselves down to their most minute details, as they take shape and substance from the mists of memory. Prowling along the river-bank in search of minnows, "I came," he says, "upon two boys apparently possessing a joint-interest in a fishing-rod, which was projected over a willow-bush. Youth is a period of freemasonry, and I was soon on good terms with the strangers, who proudly exhibited the results of their sport—three small eels strung upon a willow twig." A not ignoble envy, and the contemplation of the magnificent booty, stirred his small soul to its depths ; and so he wheedled a fond mother out of eighteenpence, which he invested in the purchase of a two-piece rod. Nor was it long after that ere he " blooded " the much-valued acquisition, though more by good-luck than skilful management. While playing leap-frog with some companions, they had baited their rods, and stuck them over the stream. The cry arose of a sudden, " There's a bite at

Henderson's." "A rush to the river, an anxious pause, a gentle uplifting of the rod, a loud scream of wonder, and backwards I ran, far into the dusty road, dragging a trout, whose weight was at least a pound." Breaking ground, or rather water, with such a monster, was surely an amazing piece of good fortune. The first of our own early prizes must have run ten or a baker's dozen to the pound; and we well remember how the first really satisfactory rise we had set us whipping a bit of stagnant and brackish back-water in the estuary of a northern salmon-river, through the brightest and most unlikely hours of a long summer afternoon. We had had ocular evidence that a "whopper" had been there, and we were determined to bring him up to the hook again if indomitable perseverance could do it. That by the way. As for the far more lucky Master Henderson, in his case, as in our own, the boy became father to the man. As he had whooped and danced like an Indian on the warpath over the triumphs of his maiden rod and line, so in riper years he settled down into the earnest enthusiasm which made matter for this volume which has taken our fancy. We know the city and county of Durham pretty well—archæologically; we know the county of Northumberland very well—piscatorially; and it is delightful to revisit many a favourite haunt with a guide so intensely sympathetic as Mr. Henderson. The very names in his pages are eminently suggestive in one way or another. The first trout of his was taken on the Brancepeth Road, near the romantic towers and park of the old fortress of the Nevilles. He remembers when there were great trout in the Wear under "the Bishop's Corn-mill"—that was before the river of St. Cuthbert had been poisoned by mining industry—and one of the first expeditions he describes was to "the beautifully situated village of Rothbury," and the fascinating pools of romantic Coquet, where it swirls past the ruins of Brinkburn Priory. Setting aside considerations of county patriotism, and the pleasant memories of auld lang syne, we do not wonder at Mr. Henderson's strong attachment to the streams of the "north countree." Even on casual visitors, with their wild variety of feature and changing play of expression, they invariably exercise a lasting fascination ; and the liking that may have originated in legend and song ripens into affection with personal knowledge. There is the Coquet flowing downwards from Brinkburn through haughs and corn-fields, between hanging copses, and banks of the flowering furze and broom, to the amphitheatre of woods by the hermitage of Warkworth, and the sweep that is dominated by the keep of the Percys ; and the Alne, that runs from the brown moorlands, and steals past the ruins of its abbey, over shelving ledges of rock, under sombre bowers of foliage, through the deer-park and home-park and fragrant shrubberies of his Grace of Northumberland. As you throw the fly, you look back over your shoulder at the battlements of his castle, with their sentinels of stone. You come on grey farm-steadings in sequestered nooks, only accessible by fords or stepping-stones ; and upon mills that, if you may judge by the colouring of their massive walls, must have had their wheels turned by those rushes almost from time immemorial. Not a ford, or pass, or bridge but has been the scene of sharp fighting in the old raiding days ; and at least two Scottish monarchs came to sorrow with their hosts almost within an arrow-flight of Alnwick Castle. The very monks, who owed comparative immunity as much to the secluded situation of their convents as to their sanctity, are said to have been betrayed on more than one occasion by the bells they had tolled prematurely in gratitude for their deliverance from the sacriligious invader.

Mr. Henderson proceeds to tell how, after confining his sport for several years to the Wear and the Coquet, he went on to wander farther afield, to " the Glen, with its picturesque Bell of Yeavering ; the Tweed, dear to the angler as to the poet ; the Till, so deadly, for all it flows so still ; the Bowmont, slowly stealing through its peaceful vale ; the Eden, tumbling from the rocks of Newton Don—spot blessed alike by fishermen and lovers true ; the Breamish, scene of, ah ! how many happy hours enshrined in my memory! the Cale, flowing beneath the Dragon's Lair ; and the Whiteadder, which, from its long trailing in snake-like coils, first gained its loathsome name." It was in the autumn of 1839—an era in his life—that he first began his acquaintance with the Tweed. It is sadly tantalising to hear of the terms on which a sportsman might get the best of fishing in these unsophisticated days, in the very water which is now the most "fashionable." Mr. Henderson, on his arrival, sought out Adam Johnston, who then rented the fishings of Dryburgh and Bemerside. Even then it surprised him to find Adam's charges so moderate. "A day's fishing, including boatman and use of boat, was only 5s. At the present time a rent of £200 a year, and all attendant expenses, are paid for the water which I was then free to roam over at will." Half a dozen years later, with some congenial spirits, he originated a small club, which took the Edenmouth salmon-fishings on a five years' lease. And these Edenmouth fishings included "the farfamed Sprouston Dub, the gem not only of the water but of the Tweed itself." Thenceforth his sojourns on the Tweed were long and frequent, if not regular ; and many are the good days' sport recorded ; though, to do him justice, he is most honestly frank in commemorating his failures as well as his successes.

The book must be to a certain extent tantalising—since good fishing in these parts is far harder to come by than when Mr. Henderson was in the heyday of his youth and vigour. Now that railways have been multiplied and high-roads improved, the great landowners are necessarily become stricter in their preserving, and more chary in giving strangers permission to fish. While farther to the south, in the Durham coal-fields, the miner has been playing the mischief with the limpid streams. Nevertheless we believe that the fishing tourist will still find himself sufficiently rewarded, more especially if he goes decently accredited ;

and though he may have to look on and long at the pools of the Tweed, and omit the best of the Glen or the Coquet from his pilgrimage, he will, notwithstanding, find angling excitements enough ; and he has always the glorious landscapes to fall back upon. For we have written to little purpose if we have not shown that angling may be nearly as often your pretext as your object ; and keenly as he may appreciate the triumphs of his sport, the true fisherman can make himself tolerably happy even when fortune has proved persistently unpropitious.

CHAPTER XIV

August on the Moors: A Shooting Lodge

GIVE us the August moors for the ideal of an earthly Paradise. The moors and the hills, a perpetual twelfth, with the flush of vigorous excitement or early youth, fresh as the waking breeze that lifts the skirts of the mist-mantle still enveloping the drowsy mountain tops; with spirits buoyant as the air that sends the light pulses of your heart bounding along at the double; with hopes of autumn sport bright as the glittering dewdrops sown broadcast over grass and heather. Most refined ideal of the earthly Paradise, as it can shape itself to the mental eye in exaggerated anticipation of realities, for it sends you to familiar communing with all that is sweet and sublime in nature. Sin and death must enter, of course, for the Paradise is earthly, and in a sense sensual. They must enter as they enter its counterpart of the Far West, the happy hunting-grounds of the Indian savage. The difference is, that there they reign, while here they subordinate themselves on sufferance. While the brave dreams his eternal joy in an interminable round of insatiate slaughter, gallops his spectre-steed, and bends his phantom bow, without wasting the spirit of a sigh on the dull monotony of his shadowy prairies, death merely recurs incidentally in episodes, in the heaven of the Highland sportsman. True, armed with breech-loader for fangs or beak, he fulfills his allotted part in the universal scheme of destruction. Around him, eagles, ravens, hawks, grouse, foxes, wild cats, and promiscuous "vermin" are all preying on their kind. But he asserts the superiority of his God-like nature over rapacious carnivoræ and voracious insectivoræ that perish, by the thoughts that throb to the inmost fibres of his nobler nature, by an exuberant intensity of grateful enjoyment, that places him in charity with the very gor-cock that finds its way with mocking crow through his bloodless No. 6.

Moors and hills, we said to begin with, because we talk of mountain-sport and not of slaughter. There is nothing to remind one of Hurlingham in what we mean—no steady rattle, remorseless as the harsh grind of the mitrailleuse—no lawn strewed with dead and dying doves in their blood-soaked plumage—nothing to recall the hot corner in a home cover, when inquisitive hares pay the penalty of their confidence as they prick their ears trustfully among the knickerbockers, and hand-fed pheasants meet the usual fate of pets as they come to untimely ends. We do not even speak of the long level stretch of flat, where the heather grows in rich swathes, as if it had been carefully top-dressed in model-farm fashion; where, except for an

A SHOOTING LODGE 199

occasional moss-pot, you might walk blindfold for miles without a trip or a stumble ; where gout itself may do a fair day's work, and timid corpulence shoot quietly from the well-stuffed saddle, as from the bath-chair or perambulator for the matter of that. These are the moors that contribute such bloody butcher-bills early in the season to the columns of the local press ; and they have their uses in their way, for they send Leadenhall grouse down to reasonable prices. These are the moors where you can saunter straight ahead without straining your back-sinews or bringing your breathing to a standstill when your shaking frame has breasted a bluff something less than sheerly perpendicular. As you potter forward, you find work in abundance for the spare breech-loaders the henchmen carry at your heels, and your dogs scarcely get well into their range for the constant coveys that taint each rood of the heather.

For a fortnight or three weeks the slaughter is superb for those who revel in it, and by that time the compensatory tenderness of nature has put the survivors of the massacre up to a thing or two. Your scared birds seek safety in society, set their sentinels, take their siestas with one eye open, feed with their shattered nerves on the alert, and rise in packs a couple of rifle-shots off at the vision of the human form. Unless you care to charge your panniers with mountain-hares, nothing more than an occasional outlying cock taken napping will repay the most indomitable perseverance, and perseverance is not the *forte* of the thick-winded gentlemen who shoot for the spit, the poulterer's stall, and the paragraph.

Very different is it with our favourite moor. It lies well-nigh lost in the wild heart of the mountains, although a beaten high-road does skirt its pathless solitudes. In these days of political miracle and perpetual surprise, even in stagnant holiday-time, the hermit must compromise with civilization. But it is five-and-forty miles from the nearest railway-station, and there is no danger of confounding the scream of the hunting eagle with the distant whistle of the panting engine. From the blue summits of its high land you catch glimpses of the distant Atlantic down loch-bottomed glens, sacred to the red deer; too distant, though, to distinguish the smoke of the tourist-laden steamer from the light wreaths of the rain-clouds that are always floating in the west on the sunniest of summer days. Not that you don't have quite as much of the tourist as your misanthrophy cares to see. You buy your mutton from your neighbour the innkeeper; but the "machine" that daily drops your beef and other foreign delicacies at your gates, lumbers along the road, heavily laden with excursionists. Luckily, as yet, the guide-books have not damned your selfish solitude to fame. No embarrassed chieftain, who saw his way to filling his sporran at the cost of the banished dynasty, ever set up his standard in the peaceful glens, nor was its easy-principled, light-fingered population ever annihilated wholesale in sweeping and summary vengeance. It may come to be another thing altogether, should the practical romancers, who draw the prospectus of the proposed railway, get to sight or hearing of the waterfall that at present roars out of earshot of all but heedless shepherds, or learn that there are sculptured stones in the lowly graveyard attached to the ruined chapel by the holy well. Meanwhile, let us live in the present, and be thankful. After us the deluge ; and it will be all the same when grouse have been proscribed and game-laws abolished ; when the English Commune has enclosed the commons in the name of the people, and reclaimed the moors to the profit of the proletariat.

In keeping with the rough shooting, the shooting-box is a rough one. No sacrifices made to the soft, and few, indeed, to the beautiful. With its low, flat roof, it cowers down out of the way of the elements that sweep the gorge in winter—and sometimes in summer too—as if the wild huntsman was racing his devil-bred pack through the chimneys. Chimney-pots there are none, of course. In the days when occupants held to these vanities, they used to set down the valley in a steady rush, to be picked up by wreckers lower down, as driftwood is swept round the Bay of Mexico on the Gulf Stream. Yet, though it bows its head, it squares its broad shoulders and sturdy strength, like a man who jams down his hat ere he sets his teeth to the tempest. It wears a waterproof against the wind-driven flood ; and, although there are two good feet of stone in the weather-wall, it is cased carefully in tight-fitting pine-shingles. Within, a relatively spacious hall—that serves as cloak-room, gun-room, parcel-delivery office, &c.—leads to the more spacious sitting-room, whose double windows, with their storm-gallery, command the lake. To the left, kitchen and offices; to the right, the fir-panelled packing-cases, where you accommodate your wardrobe on pegs in the wall, and stow yourself of nights in a compromise between the bunk of the forecastle and the box-bed of the shieling. If your toilette is performed in a series of adroit gymnastics between the bath and the table, the want of elbow-room within is compensated by the sense of space and freedom without. The breeze, faintly fragrant with the peat-reek and heather-bloom, that comes breathing in at the open window, was playing the moment before with the heaving or tumbling waters—plucking a second or two before that at the stunted grass and the lichens that thatch, *tant bien que mal*, the rocky scalps of the mountain-lake wall.

The place can be repelling enough, when the little garden is packed with snow in a December storm from palisade to palisade; when the wreathes are heaped high against the dimmed windows, tumbling in on the floor by shovelfuls when you succeed in forcing the frozen sashes; when it is a work of doubt and danger travelling through the blinding drift for the twenty yards that divide you from the keeper's cottage; when your vain attempt to visit the yet nearer kennel lands you in the peat-stack at the opposite angle of the lodge. It can be sufficiently *triste* even in an unpropitious August, when the rain, tumbling out of opened sluices, drops impenetrable curtains between the steaming window-panes and the outer world. And sometimes it feels eerie enough of a night in late September, when you are reading yourself to sleep by a flickering candle, to the sad symphony of winds sighing and moaning in the stunted fir-plantation, like scores of Æolian harps gone melancholy mad. But see it of a sunny afternoon on the eleventh, when you have travelled straight by crowded limited mail from the smoky, sulphureous purgatory of St. James's, where you have been doing society for months past, fevered in the frame, fagged in the stomach, and, as you begin shrewdly to suspect, slightly touched in the liver. You have been breathing in laughing-gas for the last few hours, as you dragged up by heather, and bracken, and hill-locked meadow, through pine-woods and feathering glades of natural birch, as you crossed and recrossed the silver stream that laughed you a welcome as it came leaping down the strath from the lake that filters it beneath your windows. You are half beside yourself with the bright intoxication that is untroubled by any sinister shadow of the inevitable reaction, with just sense sufficient of yesterday's weariness and boredom to make you hail the idea of a peaceful sojourn in this Eden. There stands your unpretending home, blooming in the bright paint of its gay spring hues, smiling cheerily at you as if an infallible barometer were screwed fast at set-fair, as if summer sunshine were eternal, and there had been no such thing as winter wear and tear. The peat smoke curling up cosily out of the kitchen chimney, dissipating itself deliberately in dissolving rings in the flickering, stirless air, appeals at once to the poetry and prose of your nature, and with blessed assurance of dinner calms the jaded appetite that is ravening like a famished bear after the dulling influences of the London season.

See the place that evening when the pleasant memories of many a past season came crowding round you—memories from which time has evaporated the bitter, and only left the sweet—as you issue forth, cigar in mouth, when a temperate measure of claret has washed down your mountain mutton—temperate, that is, for the high latitude you are landed in, for circumstances alter cases, and the frugal hermit of the Tartar steppes or the Highland hills might be the glutton and drunkard of a club in Pall Mall. After all, the pleasure of the evening, profoundly all-pervading as it is, is more than anything else the anticipation of the coming morning. If only the mounting glass do not belie its promise; if only the weather-sage keeper or the hoary shepherd have not said what they know will please, to rise convicted in the morning as lying oracles. Not likely, or those gorgeous clouds that are fading into gloom on the mountain seaboard of the Atlantic must be liars too; and as for the martens, if there is any truth in omens drawn from the flight of birds, the morrow will be a day to mark with a white stone in the weather calendar.

CHAPTER XV

August on the Moors: The Morning Start

OF course for the man who means to make a heavy bag on scientific principles and extreme economy of exertion it is short-sighted policy to be up and about with the "skriegh of day." The sluggard may ask for a little more sleep with a clear conscience, muttering as he turns himself over about the more haste and the worse speed. To say nothing of the scent and the birds, mortal flesh and blood, especially when wretchedly out of condition, can't work from an August dawn to a sunset dinner, and shoot as steadily at the end as at the beginning. So if you go in for the bag and the bare sport, you may just as well be out during the orthodox hours when other Christians of your hemisphere are pursuing their business or their pleasure. But then there are the associations that hurry you back in spirit to that twelfth of auld lang syne when you were a boy. The freshness of that early morning air is so exhilarating that you scarcely sadden yourself with thinking of the torpor of feeling that has grown on you these many years. It is something to quaff the elixir of life and renew the boyish enthusiasm of your youth on a single morning in the three hundred and sixty-five. You are hardly less excited than those couples of young setters who are positively moaning and trembling with delirious joy as they crouch and wriggle in their couples. A carelessly indifferent appetite for breakfast, although perhaps on second thoughts the dinner of yesterday may have something to do with that. No matter. There is an ambulatory larder in the ample panniers slung to the shaggy pony, and if we should chance to climb, as may well happen, to where even those sure-footed limbs of his dare hardly follow us, his burden can always be transferred to the broad shoulders of the gillies. Meanwhile, if you can't buttress your back with a substantial meal, there is no difficulty about disposing of that brimming tumbler, and you silence any scruples of your slightly morbid liver by dashing the creaming milk with Glenlivat or old Jamaica. There is music in the snap of the locks of your breech-loader—such music as you have not listened to for some months or more; and yet since you listened to it last you may have lolled in many an opera-stall, and yawned critical approval of sublime symphonies at many a classical concert. But, looking after it tenderly, you part with your gun to a brawny member of your Gaelic tail. You know, by long experience, the hills you are condemned to mount before you begin your beat—hills that would try the steel and whipcord of the red deer, to say nothing of those flaccid calves of yours.

So you grasp a staff in the meantime, and the sporting procession *s'ébranle*, the old keeper marching modestly half a foot or so in rear of your right flank, "cracking" cheerily of old times and memorable days, talking sanguinely of present prospects, although another hour must bring his promises to the test. Four summers now since there has been a touch of disease or a tainted feather in the place, and in the seven-and-twenty years he has been here he never recollects such a breeding season nor so few barren birds. Behind you and your friend come a couple and a half of gillies, one of them retained permanently on the strength of the sporting establishment, the others amphibious jacks-of-all-trades, recruited for the season. Members of the Ross-shire militia; tillers on an occasion of the barren acres that surround the paternal croft; every season ploughing the heaving sea with the herring fleet; now, as we perceive, taking to the hill-side as to the manner born—and so they have been. Poachers on temptation very likely, although, to do them justice, the canny Donalds and Duncans prefer getting their living and their little luxuries by honest work. Yet more than once have one or the other tumbled over the lordly red deer with half a handful of swan-shot, in the grey light of the dawn or the gloaming, as the monarch of the wilds came to seek his tithes in the scanty harvest of the crofter. Donald, Dougald, and Duncan each lead a couple of straining setters in leash, sustaining up hill and down dale without the slightest effort an animated Gaelic conversation in guttural undertone. Yet by this time, so steep is the hill-face, that the panniers containing your larder and cellar are slipping back on the pony's cat-like crupper, and the boy at his head has left that accomplished mountaineer to zigzag upwards over the slippery heather-roots after his own way and devices.

Tantalising work, having to plod forward toward the point where you have arranged to begin the beat, that you may give the dogs what wind there is of their quarry. Yet you cannot afford to throw away a chance in that way, for, judging by the signs of the weather, there is all the promise of a sweltering day. "'Deed, sir," says the keeper, "you'll better be settling to take your lunch by the well at Crohallion. We'll all of us be wanting the best of wa-a-te-r-r by that time, I'm thinking." Meantime, the merry crow of each outlying grouse-cock, as he dashes away upon the wing, rings like a challenge in your ears, long after he has carried himself and his note over the hill shoulder; and now and again you pause with irresolute foot uplifted in the air, as the young brood that have lain like stones flash up panic-driven round your boots, to stream through the air like scattering fireworks.

Luckily you are gifted with a soul for scenery, and, with all your impatience, fill pleasantly enough the pauses that the labouring ascent makes matter of simple necessity. Although you have to climb even higher yet, what a wealth of broken landscape lies beneath the airy Pisgah you have reached already. The shooting-lodge diminished to the size of one of the boxes you left by the kennel-doors to pack those spoils of the day you mean to barter for dinners in future seasons; the rippling lake, toned by the distance into a glassy mirror; the thread of silver stream meandering through the purple heather; the fleecy patches where the sheep fleck the valley and dot the hillsides; the sunlight falling full on the wrinkled chest of the opposite mountain, with the morning clouds fluttering in tatters from its crest and flanks. Higher still, and you look over intervening ridges into distant glens, down giant vistas into a remote jumble of forest, flood, and fell. You are high enough, in all conscience, now; up in the zone of grey stone and barren turf; and, indeed, you have to dip sharp again down the other water-shed before you draw a long sigh of gratitude and anticipation by your starting-point. *Finis coronat opus.* At last the end, or rather the beginning of the end, crowns the work. The dogs know it well —old Don and Carlo, at least, who are led forward to the front. As for the young ones, they must yelp down their disappointment as they may, confine themselves to the simple *rôle* of spectators, and make the most, for the present, of the aggravating pleasures of hope.

The couples are slipped by the side of a mountain brook, where the brown water breaks round the mighty boulders that have tumbled into it; where the rush of the floods has mined the banks at each rapid turn that follows the sharp bend of the mountains, and where the rank heather droops its purple fringe over a succession of gravel-floored caverns. A rush, a scramble, a shower of spray and pebbles, and from one of these emerges a mighty ram in mortal panic, scaring, as he tops the banks, a half dozen of the ladies of his family, who have been leisurely picking their morning meal, buried in a bracken-bed over their curling horns. Whir-r-r-r! Up rises a covey among the bounding feet of the fugitives, the old birds having the advantage of their offspring by a full dozen of seconds. For yourself, you had been bending over the peat-stained stream, filling the leather drinking-cup. You have just time to toss it aside as you snatch at your gun. Fortunately the keeper had been slipping in the cartridges. All the same, in the surprise and agitation, you make a clean miss of the single bird that sweeps round your shoulder from the left—miss him with the first barrel at least, for the messengers from your second do overtake him just in time.

Rather a questionable beginning, but, after all, it was only a bit of bad luck, and the covey was strong on the wing and wonderfully well grown: hard to tell the young birds from the old ones. And while you are yet speaking, there you are again: and this time with every prospect of a shot in orthodox first-day-of-the-season fashion. Carlo, dropping on that knoll, as if he had been shot, only there is abundance of life in his eye, as he gently turns his head among the heather sprays to make sure you are awake and mean action. Don's stern feathering in a quiver of nervous excitement, as he backs upon the very spot where the vision

THE SETTER ON THE GROUSE MOOR. *By* A. COOPER, R.A.

CRITICAL OF
JUDGMENT

of Carlo has struck him motionless, precisely as he was scrambling over that moss-grown stone in an attitude that nothing but his native grace can redeem from awkwardness. You pick your way towards Carlo, rising the knoll cautiously, your gun pitched well forward. But there is no especial need for over-care ; the sheep flushed the last lot, it is true, but this balmy morning the birds will sit like brooding-hens. At last the tenseness of the situation becomes too much for the nerves of the old cock, who knows something of dogs and breech-loaders from vivid recollections of luckier seasons. Till now his eye has been half-fascinated by Carlo's, but at last the spell is broken, and he is up and away, leaving his wife to look after the chickens, with the confirmed selfishness of a family man demoralised by bachelor habits. His cheery crow of triumph is premature. You give him law enough, and then drop him with a heavy thud on the heather, in all the delicate consideration for his plumage that the circumstances admit of. Nor does his widow survive a score of seconds to lament her lord, and before the last pair of interesting orphans have collected their faculties sufficiently to leave the scene of the bloody drama, you have charged with a fresh pair of cartridges and taken a couple of pot-shots. Superb the old birds are, with the ruddy pencillings of their delicate breasts and wings, and those white-feathered knickerbockers which nature has so thoughtfully drawn over their rough boots. And so you go on till the sun beats down with concentrated heat, and the wind drops ; until scarcely an air is stirring in the simmering hollows, and your breath comes short, and molten lead seems running down your aching arms into your gun-stock and barrels, and the rank heather-stems, that reach to mid-thigh, cling to your failing legs like coiling serpents, and the tired ankles in your heavy-soled boots go slipping and twisting about on the smooth moss-bedded blocks. There is a certain sinking sense of vacuity in your inner man beside, spite of the biscuits and spirit-laced water you have been indulging in at intervals, and the birds are getting decidedly the better of you at your game of hide-and-seek, as they generally contrive to do towards noon of a hot summer day. So, although what should be an excellent stretch of ground lies between you and the trysting-place for luncheon, you resolve to make a short-cut of it, and bid the panting dogs be coupled up forthwith.

CHAPTER XVI

August on the Moors: The Day's Work

THE diamond of the moors bubbles up in a secluded nook that you see nothing of until you stumble right in. Sheltered under the hanging shoulder of the mountain, from the precipice above you surmise nothing of the peaceful sanctuary beneath your feet. The very winds that search each cranny of the Highland corries might be puzzled to find their way to it ; and the worst chance of discovery lies in the streamlet that trickles down from the fountain turning traitor, and the streamlet keeps a quiet tongue in its head as it steals down in the groove it has worn beneath the hanging bracken. In the daytime the place is tranquil enough ; the slumbering silence broken only by the low twitter of the whinchat or the piping of the water-ousel. In the night it might be otherwise were mortal ever there to listen, and, doubtless, you would hear the sad cry of the martin cat and wild cat from the loose-heaped, bracken-thatched boulders where they kennel with the mountain foxes. At present, when you make your way in, the only occupants are a hoary-headed raven, hopping about most perfectly at home, as if he were the tutelary genius of the cool shades, and a couple of wild-eyed ewes with crumpled horns. The raven rises heavily with vindictive croak, and flaps his deliberate flight resentfully upwards with hanging head and drooping legs, as if he gloried in his enchanted privileges, and mocked at anything short of silver shot. The sheep make a frantic dash at the outlet, meet your formidable party face to face, stand wildly at bay for a second or two in the very extremity of agitation and terror, and then escalade the precipitous sides in avalanches of gravel, and a style that would do credit to chamois or *moufflons*. Once within, the very gillies draw grateful breaths of happiness, not alone at the change from sun to shade, but in mute acknowledgment of beauties that find their way to the feelings, through water-proofed suits of homespun, and skins tanned by exposure to every variation of weather. That silent tribute paid to sentiment, the next thought is of the practical. "Just pass the baskets this way, Donald." Donald is already busy disengaging them from the pony, who has scrambled somehow up the treacherous staircase, scenting his way with those keen nostrils of his past the ugly dangers of the sunken stream.

The baskets are unpacked, and the contents spread on the green turf table-cloth, that serves you for couch as well. You make your breakfast-lunch reclining classically, after the manner of the ancients, round materials for a meal that are equally solid and simple. Slices of cold beef and bread—nothing of the abominable sandwich, with its dyspeptic memories of

THE DAY'S WORK

hustling crowds at railway-counters, laden with fly-blown pastry, flowing with fiery Hamburg wines. After to-day you may add a cold grouse or two; on the twelfth you must dispense with that luxury. You feel like the Ancient Mariner travestied in mountaineer —" Game, game around you everywhere, and not a scrap to eat." Never mind, you manage to rough it somehow, with a tolerable local imitation of a Yorkshire pie, with cheese and oatcakes, and such manly fare. Your meal is somewhere half-way between a breakfast given by Lucullus, and one of those Spartan spreads whose frugal *menus* were settled by the statutes of Lycurgus. With the appetite you find, after getting your breath again, and sending a lightly-laced mouthful of chilling water hissing over your glowing palate, the repast approaches nearer the former extreme than the latter. Nor has the department of the cellar been unattended to. Dugald, officiating as chief butler, has already, with a certain careful contempt, deposited in the cooling wave the flasks that speak of shadeless vineyards on the glowing gravel slopes of the Gironde. With infinite love and tenderness he has immersed by their side the more sturdy green glass bottle that contains the sacred usquebaugh—the Highlandman's genuine water of life. There are metal flasks of it besides ; but that is a point on which prudence counsels stinting your liberality. The honest members of your tail walk steady enough as a rule, and you may trust them absolutely in most things ; but you can scarcely complain of their tripping if you set the snare for them with your own hands. They are mortals, after all, and if you tempt them beyond mortal strength, small blame to them if they succumb.

You have eaten and drunk, and chassed your claret. Pipes are ablaze, and the pungent clouds that wreath themselves so picturesquely round the group are playing the very mischief with the appetites of the midges, who, up to a minute before, had it all their own way. The wiry Donald, who is risen like a giant refreshed—although, indeed, the latent energy of his frame scarcely needed refreshment—is already busy over the game-panniers.

"That's right, Donald : now for the bag."

Fifteen and a half brace, a mallard to boot, a couple of snipe, and a mountain hare or two. We could have knocked over dozens of the last, had it been worth while overburdening the unlucky pony. A very fair morning's work up to eleven for a man who shoots and doesn't slaughter ; but how some of the millionaire aristocrats in the Perthshire and Aberdeenshire flats would turn up their noses ! Superb plumage the birds are in, even the young ones springy as india-rubber and plump as quails in season. After all, for man, beast, or bird, there is nothing like the mountain air, always bracing when it does not bite.

That tribute paid to the susceptibilities of the keeper, who holds himself personally responsible for the plumage and condition of his birds, you think of imitating the undepraved instincts of the dogs, and recruiting nature with a siesta. Already Ponto and

Carlo are deep in the dreamless sleep so sweetly earned by honest labour; while the young ones, who have been more excited than fagged, lie tumbled promiscuous in a hairy heap, ranging through worlds where there are no dog-calls nor dog-whips; standing birds in dreamland, and very possibly running in and mouthing them. You sink back, with eyes contemplating through the warm flicker of the sunny air the light fleecy clouds becalmed here and there against the deep blue of the heavens. Nothing between you and them to remind you your Eden is earthly after all, but a troop of these bothersome midges hovering at a wary distance, and a speck something larger than they, and seemingly a good deal farther off. It may be your acquaintance the raven you turned out so unceremoniously; it may be the golden eagle, the secular bird of the mountain, who has had his eyrie on the cliffs above from time immemorial. In any case it does not greatly signify, and you have no idea of taking the trouble of thinking the matter out. Already your eyelids grow too heavy for the strings that should hold them in suspense, and midges, eagle, everything, melt back into a field of vision that removes itself dreamily beyond the ken of the bodily eye. Another minute or two and you are gone to your dogs; have wandered after them at least, away from the world that was so all-engrossing to all of you, when you made your lively start that morning from the kennels.

Nothing like a siesta in the circumstances. You waken from it another man, all languor gone from mind and body, or little left of it but a slight stiffness in the lower extremities; and half an hour of leisurely exercise will soon loosen the knots your sinews have been gathering themselves in. Besides, there is a bit of a breeze sprung up, and the scent is fresher, and the sport likely to be excellent; altogether, the afternoon promises at least as well as the morning. Nor is the promise belied, and you are tempted to linger. The sun is sloping to the west as you reach the black moss that lies in the water-shed between the valley you have been shooting along and the valley you are returning to. You strike the sinuous path that threads its treacherous flow—a path very much resembling that by which Bunyan's pilgrim picked his way through the Valley of the Shadow of Death. You have had somewhat ugly walking for some time back: among moss-holes with treacherous coverings of green, when a single false step may make it a case of over the ankle, over the ears. But here it is altogether a different thing. The slimy soil of the quaking bog may settle under your heavy boots at any moment, and you may find your resting-place fifty feet beneath the surface, lying peacefully until future generations of improvers disinter you, looking much as you look to-day, a little browner perhaps, thanks to the antiseptic properties of the peat. So rarely is the spot visited—for the shepherd need seldom come where no sheep would dream of straying after pasture—that the instincts of the wary red deer tell him he may sleep secure when the odds are so long against surprise. As a case in point, we actually catch a pair of them napping. Two sleek hinds spring out of a moss-bog within half gun-shot, but, as it would be idle cruelty mangling them with No. 6, they are quit for the fright. Their light bounds lift them safely along where no human foot dare follow, their ruddy hides smeared to the ears with the jet-black mud they have been lying in. A sporting who-oop from the gillie nearest, and they change their canter for a startled gallop, and, taking each obstacle as it comes in their frantic stride, are away at their fleetest for the wild sanctuary of their forest.

There are gorgeous evening lights on the rocky peaks and the heathery summits, although the valley depths are disappearing in the evening gloom, as we turn the shoulder above the shooting-box, and in the calm satisfaction of a well-spent day drawing to a pleasant close, work our way in zigzags down upon the orifices of the chimneys. We shoot conscientiously still; although from time to time, as Shot or Sancho conspicuously come to a stand on the heights above, and compel us to retrace our steps, there is something like a plaintive murmur in the depths of our hearts in response to the appeal of aching back-sinews. But what is pleasure without the alternation of hardship, if not of pain? the dreary monotony of a magnificent summer without a cloud or a shower? and the countless steps you have made since you left that door at early dawn, to return to it some fifteen hours later, have all been leading on to the moment when, after bath and deliberate toilette, you draw your chairs to a table where the sparkling wax-lights are reflecting themselves in plate and crystal and amber wine. How the talk flows as the evening goes on! If you don't hurry your memory it leisurely brings you back each incident of the day in most minute detail—a panorama of sharp-cut impressions—and photographs everything on your mental retina, down to the very stones and heather-tussocks where you dropped your grouse; the shallow reach of water that winged bird splashed through to seek a vain concealment among the overhanging heather-roots; the black sedge-fringed pool by the grey boulder where you flushed the unsuspecting mallard; and then the well-won repose, as you nestle snugly in the blankets; for after the sunny day the air that comes in through the casements feels something more than cool as it fans cheeks still flushed with exertion—and that glorious header in the morning, when you leap into the lake and life, to emerge dripping as a water-god in the vigour of his immortal strength.

Not that the life of the moors has nothing but its sunny side: very far from it indeed. The heather would never grow so rank, nor the grass in the corries so green, if floods did not come like familiar things to the barren soil that teems in the luxuriance of its wild vegetation. How it does pour when the weather makes up its mind to it: Holland would be swamped in its rivers and the ocean waves, if it had but a single season of the weather of the western Highlands. Luckily Providence arranges a perfect system of natural

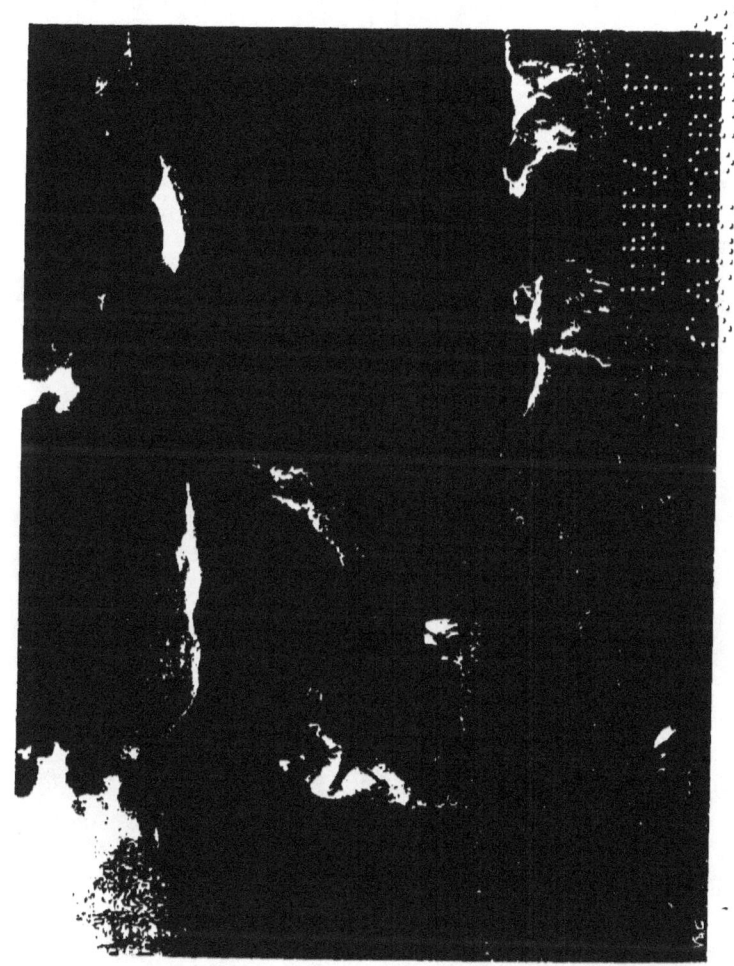

Grouse shooting. *By* Abraham Cooper.

drainage, and as, save in the mosses, there is not a yard of absolutely level land in a circumference of fifty miles, the rain is off on its way to the sea as fast as it touches the land. One lovely evening as you turn homewards from your sport, you see grim clouds with all manner of sinister browns and sepias dashed into their colouring banking up over the Atlantic. If that is not sufficient for you, if you disbelieve the ominous shakes of the keeper's head, reluctant experience must yield conviction to the winged heralds of the coming storm. The huge white sea-gulls come floating up the glens with plaintive cries. The swallows are skimming through the waving grass in your paddock—in early seasons you get in your rough hay-crop somewhere towards the middle of October ; and as for the mercury in the weather-glass, it has vanished clean out of sight in the bulb. Next morning you can scarcely hear the heavy drip from the storm-gallery for the deadening plash without. Not a vision of the lake, although you can hear it grinding on its gravel bank within a few feet of your windows ; the only life you distinguish among the waste of waters is the ponies, that in vain search for shelter and companionship, and with streaming hides are leaning miserably against the gables. So it goes on day after day, until you have a profound sympathy with the uneasy impatience of Noah, when he raised the window-sash and started the raven on its mission. You have the *Times*, it is true, the *Pall Mall* and the *Saturday*, and some of the magazines ; a choice selection of green and yellow novels you have read before; such light popular literature, in short, as is suitable to men determined beforehand on being idle. It is wearisome, there is no doubt; and if desperation drive you beyond the watery walls of your prison, you are washed back again in spite of yourself. But with firm faith, even then, in the doctrine of compensations, you feel all your *ennui* will be repaid you, in the burst of joy with which your bounding heart greets the first outbreak of the returning sun. He has to make a hard fight of it, it is true; and before the weather settles back to serenity, you have one or two off-days, when you know it to be idle to risk your gun-locks in the chase through plashing water and pools, over sloppy, slippery mountain-sides after birds as wild as hawks. But *toujours* grouse might become as tiresome as *toujours* partridge, and not the least pleasant of your recollections link themselves to these off-days when venturing abroad in water-proofing you shake off the sense of confinement as you inhale the freshened air. You turn out to drag the lake for trout and pike. What lights on loch and fresh-washed mountain, as the suns falls on the glistening patches of green; on the red seams where a yard or two of landslip has just descended into the water, on the hundreds of rain-rills throwing themselves from cliff to cliff in tiny cascades, till taking the final plunge they waste themselves in "dustfalls," like the Staubach, on the driving breeze. The men, glad to find themselves again on the element that comes so natural to them, stretch their sinews and brawny arms to the oar after their long confinement to the kennels. The cobble spins over the rocking waves almost too rapidly for the chances of sport, as the brown net runs swiftly out from the stern and the black corks rise bobbing merrily on the track. And when they have put the girdle round the bay, how like children they strip off boots and stockings to dash in bare-legged and drag the net to the land! What excitement over the silvery scales gleaming in the shallow water among the tarry meshes! The heavier trout are tossed up walloping on the bank, while the long-jawed pike grunt out their savage souls, previous to being stuffed with odoriferous herbs and embalmed in claret sauce. Nor is it bad fun when the birds are a little wild after broken weather—they scorn to pack for protection in these wilder hills—sending the otter afloat on a mountain tarn, and watching the stirring of the water in its wake, as the little fishes fling themselves by dozens on to the dragging flies. Ptarmigan-shooting repays you, if you care to scale the very highest of your mountain peaks, feast your lungs on the very purest of the mountain air, and your eyes on the very finest of the mountain prospects. And in its own way, a mountain fox-hunt is nearly as good a thing as a fast burst with the Quorn, although the find, the run, and the kill take place in a few acres of country like the *débris* of a score of pyramids of the largest size, just blown sky-high by a portentous explosion of subterranean gases. Were the weather more to be reckoned on, autumn on the moors would be too perfect happiness for mortal man, and could you only arrange the weather for your own convenience, it would not be in human nature to return contented to your lot in lowland life. As it is, you may be sure it is your own fault if you were not happy as mortal can reasonably hope to be, and you must be unreasonable if you ask anything more.

CHAPTER XVII

"The Moor and the Loch" : *the Nestor of Scottish Sportsmen*

"THE Moor and the Loch." Seldom has such infinite suggestion been so happily compressed in a title. It awakens a whole world of memories : it presents a shifting panorama of Scottish scenes and sport. We see the broad extent of blooming heather, backed up by the brown ranges of mountain or by the peaks sapped by the weather and shivered by the storms, standing out sharp and clear against the distant sky-line. We see lakes like Loch Lomond, winding round bay and headland, in the shadows of the mighty Ben and embosoming an archipelago of islands. We see lakes like Loch Awe or Loch Leven embosoming historic strongholds, where the garrisons like the ospreys on their isolated pillar-rocks could only be reached by swimming or reduced by starvation. We follow the great chain of the Central Glen Albyn, with many a silent nook and solitary pool gently washing the shelving beach when stirred by the breeze and mirroring each tremor of the weeping birches. Or we are in the more stern severity of such lonely moorland waters as Erricht or Rannoch, or in the sublimity of the land-locked sea-lochs that indent the genial Western Coast, or breach the bleak and barren precipices of the misty Western Islands. In tranquillity or storm, everywhere we hear the rushing of many waters after rain, or the roar of brawling cataracts. Fed by the myriads of burns and mountain rills, these inland lochs are the natural reservoirs filtering brown floods to the crystal streams which swell into the famous rivers, which, as Scott said, the Caledonian regards with feelings approaching to reverence. And all are swarming with fish, strong, subtle, and vigorous, from the clean-run salmon sheathed in his sea-lice to the *salmo ferox* of Loch Awe and the lively trout of Loch Leven. So as the old associations revive, the poetry of imagination is translated into action, and many an epic or idyll of the rod falls into the picturesque and appropriate setting. We remember how playing the heavy grilse in a slippery gorge had nearly landed the angler in a watery grave, and we feel again those pangs of bitterest anguish when the phenomenal monster, lured for once from unknown depths, broke away as the boatman fancying him already in the scales, bent over to clique him in the shoulder. And we hear other sounds besides the fall of the cataract or the scream of the eagle. The report of the gun breaks the stillness of the moors, and the crack of the rifle reverberates in the forests, till the last faint echo dies away in the distance. We hear the pack of keen little beagles following hot and fast on the trail of the roe, and the scratch lot of rough hounds swimming and diving on the track of the otter, gurgling and yelping between water and wind. Our fancy has run away with us, and it is time to rein up. For everywhere and in all things Mr. Colquhoun has anticipated us: he has emphasised and illustrated each possible situation with the graphic touch of a Landseer and the knowledge and experience that are all his own.

Nearly sixty years of sport by flood and fell, in field and forest have left him the Nestor of Scottish sportsmen. What changes these sixty years have witnessed! We know not to what we may look forward in the future. We may take to acclimating the reindeer of Scandinavia in the Shetlands, the elk in the Blackmount, and the izzard in Torridon or Applecross. We may stock our coverts with the golden pheasant and the bantam-like jungle-fowl, and lay down the spawn of the sturgeon in the breeding-ponds of the Highlands and the Border. But it is only too certain that no future writer can rival Mr. Colquhoun in reminiscences of the characteristic Scotland of the olden time. No doubt we have witnessed many improvements. We have reclaimed an infinity of unproductive wastes; and financially, the national income has benefited. Socially, too, we have made marvellous progress, and have left our grandfathers leagues behind, while we can only blush for their ruder progenitors. But from the artistic and æsthetic point of view, many of these material "improvements" must remain at least an open question ; and looking at them as a sportsman, they are simply deplorable. We have always inclined to subscribe to the sweeping condemnation by St. John's old Donald, when he missed the geese from the Morayshire lochs and the snipe from the bogs, and saw the semi-domesticated partridge steadily creeping up on the grouse-ground.

Not that there is unmingled melancholy in the retrospect, and *laudatores temporis acti* as we may be, we hope we regard with suitable gratitude the modern inventions in firearms and sporting equipments. Sixty years ago we fancy that the venerable flint-locked single-barrel was still in fashion. The author of the Oakleigh shooting code, writing many, many years ago, concedes certain merits to that exploded weapon. He says that it made steady and deadly shots, because knowing that you had but a single chance, you were constrained to dwell on your aim. Those flints and single-barrels may have been sure, but they were abominably slow. The woodcock would have dipped under the bough and twisted away behind the tree-trunks while your fingers were fumbling with the lock and the charge was in course of kindling. The rabbit jerking across the ride, or the grouse-cock topping the crest of the brae, would have laughed at the beard of the baffled shooter. No ; the single-barrel was emphatically the weapon of the old school, and, as a rule, must have bred a race of potterers who would prematurely develop into fogies. A vast stride was made in advance with the introduction of double-barrels and percussion-locks. Then Joe Manton and his less famous rival Stevens attained, according to their lights, to the perfection of finished workmanship. Curtis and Harvey followed with their lively "diamond-grain," and Eley with his waterproof caps and wired cartridges. Given tolerable weather, and but a fair sprinkling of wild game, and the shooter had good reason to be satisfied with the readiness of his new-fangled tools. But there are occasionally dripping days to the north of the Border, and then to what misery and provocation that laborious muzzle-loading used to lead! The wads in your open pocket grew saturated, and bulged when thrust into the barrels. The powder half choked the damp measure in the mouth of the flask. The slender ramrod bent and sometimes broke when you were cramming down the reluctant charge in a series of frantic contortions; and it was a godsend when it was replaced by the more substantial loading-rod. Above all, the best barrels would hang fire, and then you were placed *hors de combat* till you had cleaned the touch-hole and replenished it with dry powder in the drip of the driving rain. That, with the nuisance of seeing birds getting up about you, before you had reloaded and were ready to drop them, might have been admirable discipline for the patience which should be one of the fundamental virtues of the sportsman. But too often the temper flashed up when the powder refused to burn, sending you on your way sulking and shooting wildly; and altogether there was great reason for thankfulness in the introduction of the swift and simple breech-loader.

Having said so much in favour of modern innovations, we can go back to our grumbling with an easier conscience. Sixty years ago there was genuine wild sport, and a man of moderate means and agreeable manners was made welcome to more shooting than he could overtake, and could pick and choose among his many invitations. There were no professional agents in Perth and Inverness to negotiate fabulous rents for the moors and the forests. Indeed, strictly speaking, there were no deer-forests at all, if the idea of a forest implies solitude and a sanctuary. The smoke curled up in the remotest straths from the straw-bound chimneys of the hovels and hamlets that were teeming with human and canine life. There were herds of black cattle ranging the hills, and groups of sheep grazing in the corries, and hoary patriarchs and witch-like old women were out with their "shelties" cutting the peat or fetching it from the neighbouring bogs. Here and there in some out-of-the-way den among the rocks, that might have sheltered caterans in more lawless times, one of the "sma' stills" was in cheerful activity. The red deer had to shift as they best could, and to run their chance with the other *fera naturæ*. Duncan, though he might have a profound reverence for the chief, would make many a quiet stalk on his deer in the gloaming; and Dugald would lie in ambush for them in his patch of oats, ready to empty his charge of buck-shot point-blank into the shoulders of the marauders. The deer did not multiply as they do now. They were always on the watch as they snatched at the herbage, and lay down to sleep with one eye open. They were hounded about by yelping collies, and got the wind of roving Highland laddies, till they became preternaturally wild and restless. But then there were "harts of grease" which attained enormous size and carried portentous heads with wide-spreading antlers that made them notorious over the range of the surrounding districts. To circumvent one of these suspicious veterans, you had to be versed like Donald Caird in "the wiles of dun-deer stalking"; and the stalk was made more difficult by a *cordon* of feathered sentinels who were always on the look-out to give the quarry the alarm. There was no systematic killing down of the grouse who keep their eye on each movement of the stalker, and rise with their warning note at the moment when he is counting his chickens. It is not so many years ago since St. John described how he spent three days on the hills of Morayshire in pursuit of "the muckle hart of Benmore." Now the regular forests are so many patrolled sanctuaries where all profane intrusion is forbidden. The land has trebled and quadrupled in value, though the grazing rents have been sacrificed. The deer have increased till the forests are over-stocked, and slaughtering them has become comparatively a certainty; but though well-laden ponies may follow you home when you are hurrying back to the lodge for the dinner-hour, yet the heads and the haunches are seldom what they used to be.

Sixty years ago there was good rough shooting on many a half-moorland estate that carries nothing now but partridges and a hare or two. No doubt, had we the good luck to be the laird, we might console ourselves by a reference to the rent-roll. But not being the laird, but merely his guest, we find few things more depressing than revisiting one of the favourite shooting-haunts of our youth in these days of accumulating mortgagees and scientific farming. The yellow oats are waving over the purple hillsides where the moorcock used to crow so cheerily of an August morning. There is a superb growth of swedes in the sunny hollow where the black-game lay like stones among the bracken and the cotton grass on that memorable Twentieth when we made a massacre of the innocents. The bog has been drained where we used to spring the snipe, as we threaded our way among the weed-covered moss-pots; and the old mill-pond has been dammed and embanked where we flushed the wild-duck in the rushy back-water. It is but poor compensation for the loss of that sensational variety that we can half fill a capacious pannier with partridges; or that the covers where we went rabbit-shooting, in season and out of season, are now strictly preserved for the coop-fed pheasants. And, to leave the land for the water, it is worse still with the fishing. A downfall of rain in the droughts of summer used to secure safe sport for many days to come. The superfluous moisture trickled slowly through myriads of tiny runs into the burns that filled the streams that went to swell the brimming river in their turn. After the first rush of the flood, the water, as it gradually rose and subsided again, was in grand and growing order. Now the stream comes down in a sudden spate, and falls even more quickly than it has swollen. The rushes have disappeared from the haughs and hills under an admirable system of scientific furrow-draining; and you may see the river shrinking visibly to those silvery rills that meander among the pebbles in crystal translucency. The most finished of artists need hardly put up his rod to try his luck in the sparkle of the sunshine; and even an invisible midge on a gossamer casting-line would scarcely move the monsters that are lolloping in the pools.

That is of the less consequence to many of us, that there is so little good fishing to be had for love. The laird has let his stretches of water, only reserving himself an occasional day or two in the pools that lie most convenient to his residence; and the eminent banker in town, who is his tenant, may be said to do his fishing from his offices in Lombard Street. A telegram warns him of the coming condition of the river, and he jumps into a hansom for the night-train from King's Cross, to turn up on the following morning on the platform at Perth or Berwick. These railways have not only run up the rents, but they have wrought a revolution in everything. When you had to make your way into the remote glens of the Highlands by coach, cart, or "machine," you were a welcome and an honoured guest with the Celtic innkeepers and boatmen. Strangers were as few and far between as cocks in September. You had the best parlour and bedroom placed at your disposal; the fattest fowl was killed for you forthwith—for you were sure to find next to nothing in the larder—and a flask of the mellowest Glenlivet came forth from the recesses of the cellar. Now, unless you send warning a week beforehand, you may count on being turned away from the door. One of the parlours is made to do duty for a "coffee-room," and you must be content with a table hustled away in the corner. The house is crowded from ground-floor to garret with Saxons from the Stock Exchange or the Inns of Court, who have run down for a ten days' fishing holiday. Capital fellows they may be in ordinary circumstances, but the sentiments of jealous repulsion are mutual. These first comers have the best of it, for they have the most skilful of the boatmen in their pay. With an *et tu Brute* expression of countenance, you learn that the most trusted of your former allies have sold themselves and their services for Southern gold; nor will they show much scruple as to lying on occasion, if you appeal to their old friendship through the medium of the cigar-case or the whisky-bottle. We will suppose you are lucky enough to find a boat for next day with somebody to pull you about in it. You make a start in the smallest of the small hours, and are rowed round to your favourite bay. A piratical craft is already in occupation, skulking to and fro under shadow of the birches ; and the gentleman in the home-spun Norfolk jacket who scowled at you over his bedroom candle is trolling away for his life, as if your favourite fishing-ground belonged to him. You feel inclined to forswear the land of your sires, and to seek a solitary wigwam in some vast wilderness on the lonely banks of the St. John River or the Saguenay.

Sixty—forty—nay, twenty years ago the lochs and tarns were the favourite resorts of migratory waterfowl. The many admirers of St. John and his "Sport in Moray" will remember his fascinating pictures of the flight of the wild swans as they flew trumpeting into Findhorn Bay ; of his circumventing the flocks of wary grey geese who had set their sentinels and settled down to feed among the ditches ; of his expeditions in the frosts to the Loch of Spynie. We chance to know little of the neighbourhood of Elgin, or of Invererne, where that most genial of sportsmen and naturalists had made his home for so many years ; but we suspect that there, as everywhere else, things have greatly changed for the worse since his time. We lament the disappearance of the noble birds of prey and the picturesque ground "vermin" that come in so characteristically in the foreground of Mr. Colquhoun's mountain landscapes. Organised corps of keepers and gillies have been waging indiscriminate war against eagles and peregrine falcons ; extravagant rewards have been set upon their heads ; fancy prices are offered for their eggs, till each daring shepherd lad is tempted to risk his neck, scrambling down to their eyries among almost inaccessible precipices. The mountain-fox still holds his own among the cairns and the rifts of the rocks on the summits of the loftier hills; but the wild cat and the marten have well-nigh disappeared. Even the badger and the otter have been dying out in the Lowlands, though happily there is still sport for the shaggy water-hounds in the quiet pools and among the cataracts of many a woodland stream. It is true that we have gains to set against the losses. The graceful roes have increased with the spreading plantations, though very greatly to the injury of the woods; and the capercailzie, introduced by the late Lord Breadalbane, has spread far and wide through the pine-forests of Perthshire. And Mr. Colquhoun can tell how, when shooting as a boy on the Arrochar hills, he made acquaintance with one of the forerunners of these alpine hares which swarm now in Glenfalloch and Glen Fruin, and indeed, breed rabbit-like or rat-like all over the Highlands.

Few are so fortunate as the author of "The Moor and the Loch" in having been brought up in a sylvan paradise. The picturesque domains of his ancient family stretch along the banks of Loch Lomond; within easy reach of their mansion of Rossdhu were the remains of their forests of the Lennox and Ben Cruachan; and between it and the many arms of the sea that wind up into the western coast from the Atlantic is a jumble of hill and wood and heather. Long ago, on a memorable occasion, we ourselves shot along the broken banks that look across to that lovely inland archipelago. Though we set more store in those days by shooting than scenery, we could have been comparatively indifferent to the contents of the bag in admiring the endless beauties of the prospect. But though the shooting was rough and the ground but half preserved, the bag contained a little of most things, for there was a touch of the softer richness of the Lowlands relieving the savagery of the Highland landscape. Sixty years ago young Colquhoun could follow the keepers over the broad rolling stretches of the grouse-moor into the recesses of the hills ranged by the red deer. There were black game in the hanging coverts and roe in the thickets of bramble and bracken. There was abundance of low-country shooting on the lower ground, and whatever there may have been then, now there is a fair sprinkling of pheasants. There were trout in the loch and salmon in the streams that have been poisoned since by chemical works and manufacturies; while in the sea-lakes and out of the season, there was always the rougher fishing which seems to have an indefinable charm of its own. No wonder that such a sportsman had become catholic in his tastes, for as Laidlaw remarked of Walter Scott, after the excursions in Liddesdale, "he was making himself all the time" to be the author of a Scottish sporting encyclopædia.

CHAPTER XVIII

Among the Wild Fowl

IN these chapters, which recall the picturesque reminiscences of the Nestor of Scottish sportsmen, our humble experiences are interspersed with his own. But to some of the more irregular sports in which he specially delights we were never addicted. There is wild-fowl shooting, for example. It must become an absorbing passion with a man if he means to follow it perseveringly with pleasure and success. The keenest enthusiast on record is Colonel Hawker, whose ponderous volumes are chiefly devoted to that pursuit. The colonel was something of a valetudinarian, something of an epicure, and he was suffering besides from old wounds received in Wellington's campaigns. Yet no weather deterred him, no hardship daunted him, and he bivouacked in bitter winter on the beach of Pool Harbour in a cottage with the accommodations of a squatter's log hut. As the wild-fowler is bound to suffer himself, he cannot be expected to be over sensitive as to the sufferings of his victims. Yet surely, over the claret or cigar, he must have his moments of remorse, when he thinks of the cripples never picked up and of the fugitives doomed to die in lingering torments after a raking discharge from the scattering swivel-gun. In the punt or the boat a man may wrap himself up warmly and so bid tolerable defiance to the cold. But ambushing himself among the sand-hills or stalking on foot, he dare not encumber himself with body or foot hamper. Waterproof boots interfere with the silent celerity of the stalk, and heavy dress with the agility which may have to be displayed at a moment's notice. We are told that the warmest wear should be a duffel shooting-jacket, and that only an excess of frost can justify a double pair of stockings. In the heat of youth and the height of excitement, he may plunge into the water after the winged birds like his own shaggy retriever, and for the sake of a leash or so of teal or mallards, risk racking agonies of rheumatism in the future. In any case the seasoned wild-fowl shooter should possess extraordinary stamina and be an exceptionally warm-blooded animal to boot. Our own experience is that steady shooting must in any circumstances greatly depend on bodily comfort, and if sick or sorry, soaking or chilled, the aim must inevitably be proportionately affected. When you begin by missing, you are most likely to go on missing ; and when you have been having stray shots at wide intervals, you are apt to break down on unexpected opportunities. Insensibly you become distracted and indifferent in spite of yourself, and have to think about pulling yourself together at the moment when you should be "all there." Now the wild-fowler, above all men, must be devoted in his pursuit to the entire oblivion of adventitious circumstances. It needs no ordinary concentration of energy to watch and wait, with each faculty on the stretch, when the extremities are immersed in an icy puddle; when the frost is knitting your moustache to your beard, and congealing the tear-drops that gather beneath your eyelashes; or when the wind is whistling through that duffel shooting-coat of yours and chilling the very marrow in your aching bones. When the chance comes to ordinary men under such highly trying conditions, it is long odds that they fail to make the best of it. And we know few things more trying in this world of disappointment than missing the purpose of your privations and your patience, when Providence has brought it for a second or so within your grasp.

There is even more science in stalking ducks than deer. From the nature of the broken ground in a forest, you have a fair chance of making your approach under cover; but the ducks are almost sure to have settled on a sheet of water in the flat. You may walk up almost within arm's-length of outlying birds in the hags of a peat-moss; but when the ducks are gathered into flocks, no creatures are more suspicious or more watchful. They have an extraordinarily keen sense of sight, and they never cease to be on the alert. They are a much less conspicuous object to the sportsman than the sportsman is to

AMONG THE WILD FOWL

them, as they sit floating on the rippling water, which they closely resemble in colour. Their hearing, too, is at least as sharp as their sight—a reason for not wearing substantial fishing-boots. Mr. Colquhoun's directions for stalking them are invaluable; but then it takes an expert to carry the instructions into practice, and an expert with the instincts of an Indian. You have no friendly keeper at your elbow, as in the deer-forest, to guide you passively in your sinuous approaches, and whisper instructions when your intelligence is at fault. To begin with, you must take the bearings of the birds by conspicuous landmarks upon the shore, with others farther to the inland, and then, having suppressed yourself as promptly as possible, you wind round upon the latter by a cautious detour.

Akin to wild-fowling is seal-shooting—the deerstalking of the seas; and while you meet with many men who will tell you they have killed seals, comparatively few have the conscience to take oath to having bagged them. According to popular notions, the seal is a miracle of tough vitality—almost as hard to kill as his amphibious congener the hippopotamus—and he is said to have a provoking habit of sinking to the bottom with his death-wound, vindictively entangling his corpse in the sea-weed. We incline to the belief that the notion is a fallacy, and may be partly explained by indifferent shooting. Experts have assured us that if you hold straight for the fatal spot, the seal will float and may be gaffed like a salmon. Unlike the wild-fowling, which has generally to be pursued at unholy hours and in the most unpropitious weather, seal-shooting may be enjoyed in calm and sunshine. Nor can anything be much more enchanting than a leisurely boat-stalk among the islands and the weed-strewn reefs of some land-locked estuary, when the rosy dawn is tinging the eastern hill-tops, or when the sun in a radiant kaleidoscope of colours is slowly sloping towards the west. But unless you have trusted yourself to practised hands, or are skilled yourself in the amphibious chase, what is apparently the most promising day may prove a blank, so far as even powder-burning is concerned. The persecuted seal —and he plays the mischief with the salmon stake-nets—is suspicious enough in all conscience, and although he goes to the shore or the reef to indulge in a siesta, it is as hard to catch him asleep as the proverbial weasel. Moreover the basking seal is scarcely to be discovered among the tufts of sea-ware, nor is his sprawling form to be easily distinguished from the grey blocks of stone strewing the shingle.

CHAPTER XIX

In Forest and on Hill

WE are reminded by Mr. Colquhoun of the old Highland apothegm, "No man has a right to the hunter's badge who has not killed a red deer, an eagle, a salmon, and a seal." And undoubtedly deer-stalking deserves the place he assigns to it, as much for the sport itself as for the wild picturesqueness of the surroundings. But for its full enjoyment it must be studied as an art, and followed habitually and systematically. The stalker must pay for his own experience, after an ordeal of disappointments and many mortifications. Should you have the offer of a day's stalking once in a way, you must be content to abjure your individuality if you hope to come home with a head. You must place yourself unreservedly in the hands of the professional stalker, whose eyes have been exercised on the hills from his boyhood; who knows the lie of the hidden corries, and has an instinct for the mysterious currents of the wind. But even in these somewhat humiliating circumstances the excitement is so intense that you are unconscious of fatigue and indifferent to danger. What can be more romantically exhilarating than the novel sense of adventure when you are plunging into a wilderness of mountain and valley untrodden for the time being by any feet but your own? There is a glimpse of the savage life brought in contact with advanced civilisation; for happily you have slept in luxurious quarters, and look forward to returning to them to recruit from your fatigues. Except perhaps the hooking and playing of your first salmon, while you remember the slightness of the line by which you were holding the sixteen-pounder, there is nothing to equal the excitement of your first vision of the red deer in his native wilds, with the hope that it may be given you to make him your own. What matters all you may go through in the meantime? You are not shivering off a bleak storm-beaten coast in a biting snow-drift. The season is summer, the weather is glorious, and prolonged immersion in the mountain stream comes refreshingly, rather than otherwise, to your fevered pulses. Far from you be the apprehension of aches and rheumatism: for once you will have lived, even if you are doomed to be crippled. Should the climbing be stiff, you find yourself following your leader by the shortest cut, up the rugged steps of some rocky staircase that would set your head swimming in your more sober moments, when the croak of the raven that you have startled might sound ominous. And then in the final crawl on the rock or the bank of heather that should be screening the antlers from your straining eyes, how marvellously lithe and supple you make yourself as you

Deer disturbed by Grouse. *By* Sydney Steel.

BIBLIOTECA DE ASTE

wriggle yourself through the heather in the convolutions of the serpent. Yet all the time your pulse seems to be beating six to the second, and your whole being is throbbing with suppressed thrills! for you have a sense that nature is conspiring against you. The crow of the solitary cock, the mere twitter of some alarmed moor-bird, a sudden twist in the breeze, the flight of a hawk or a raven—may be so many significant signs that will convey warning of your proximity; and the consciousness of that long and anxious stalk—of the concatenation of outward contingencies that you are in course of surmounting successfully—all conspire to raise excitement beyond control when your hopes are at last on the verge of fruition. We envy and yet we compassionate the novice who lies ensconced at last within easy range, longing to still the fierce beating of his heart and to clear away the gathering film from his eyes. His mentor knows too well to flurry him, and yet the worthy Gael is naturally impatient. Is the grand stalk to go for nothing, as seems only too possible? As yet the deer are feeding in tranquillity, all unconscious of their peril; but it is tempting Providence to hang back too long; and it is a marvel that that lean-looking hind is not sniffing the air suspiciously. But the nerves are steadied in a measure by an almost superhuman strain; the aim is taken and the shot is fired. We would rather drop a curtain over the scene should the hart go off unharmed, or have his gallop merely hastened by a flesh-wound. But should he drop in his tracks, or dash down to the brook in the corrie, there to turn savagely to bay, while he is dyeing the rippling water with his life-blood—what a crowning moment of unadulterated triumph is that !

For those who shoot for the sport and not for the fashion or the larder, Mr. Colquhoun makes the suggestion that the chase of the wild goat might be an excellent substitute for that of the red deer. The one animal is at least as wary as the other, and frequents by choice more break-neck country. Goat-shooting would be within the reach of men of very moderate means, who might cheaply rent the run of a grazing where it is difficult to get up a head of grouse. And there is this advantage besides, that, like the Cockney's famous jack-snipe, a single cautious old billy-goat might amuse his proprietor through many seasons, and carry his silvery beard in peace to the grave after all. We can speak from experience. Year after year it was our privilege to sport over a most savage range of shootings in Ross-shire, which we shall advert to again in speaking of the ptarmigan. In that rocky wilderness were a pair of secular goats, which were said to have haunted the heights from time immemorial. No man, at least, pretended a claim to them ; nor could anything be learned of their origin or antecedents. Frequently of a fine summer morning, lounging on the gravel before the shooting-lodge, we contemplated them through a telescope on the opposite slopes. Often of an evening we made long practice at them, with rifles sighted to fabulous elevations ; and they cast dust upon our beards by mocking at the misspent bullets. More than once, when the grouse were shy, we broke away in impromptu stalks, invariably having our trouble for our pains. They never had young, for the best of reasons. The female must have been some score of years past bearing, and although our acquaintance with them ended a dozen of seasons ago, we can well imagine that they may be still be "to the fore." But more youthful animals might make more hopeful practice than those diabolically wily ancients; although we are sure, from what we have seen of the race, that they would be hard enough of approach in any case. But for the story of a goat-stalk in the most thrillingly romantic circumstances, we must send the reader to "The Moor and the Loch." It came off, some sixty years ago, on Crap-na-Gower, "perhaps the most fascinating spot of the far-famed Loch Lomond." "The island rises perpendicularly out of the loch by an almost inaccessible succession of rocks and shaggy heather, full of deep holes and caverns. Seen at a distance, with its wild goats grazing among the grey rocks and scaurs, shaded here and there by a clump of reverend yews, a finer study for the artist's pencil could not be found."

Scrope has commemorated the annual deer drives in the forest of Athol, which perpetuated the historic traditions of the days when Scottish monarchs on their northern progresses had sylvan welcome from Highland feudatories. The "tinchal" for obvious reasons has fallen into disrepute; there is great disturbance, more noise than steady shooting, and a heavy bill if the maimed and wounded animals which can never be even approximately reckoned up. Quiet deer-shooting in dense woods is a rare experience in these islands, and very few have enjoyed such opportunities of driving coverts for red deer as Mr. Colquhoun dilates on enthusiastically in his recollections of his residence in Mull. There we are reminded rather of the skill and stealthy devices brought into play by the "still-hunter" after elk in Canadian woods. But the bare chance of coming across the wanderers from some neighbouring forest goes far to enhance the excitement of one of those roe battues which Mr. Colquhoun condemns as blundering and unsportsmanlike. That they are generally mismanaged may be very true, chiefly because the covers contain hares, rabbits, and pheasants as well, and partly because few of the head-keepers organising the beats remember that the roe has the scent of his red cousin and is even more wary and timid. So if many are moved, but few are knocked over, and that, sportsmen as we are, we should consider matter for jubilation if the roes were not so terribly destructive. No Scottish creature is so graceful and ornamental, the pity being that their shrinking timidity keeps them invisible through the daytime in the seclusion of the woods. But no creature is more hateful to forester or farmer, whether feeding at dewy daybreak towards harvest time in the nearest oat-field, or delicately nibbling the top shoots in the young plantations pretty nearly all the year round. So from the practical point of view they are justly proscribed, like the hill foxes

IN FOREST AND ON HILL

that take ruthless toll of the lambs. With their habits, in the games of hide-and-seek with the beaters, they have generally much the best of it, and the strategy in the autumnal battues may be lamentable, yet from pleasant associations we own to a fondness for these. For we remember the jovial bachelor party that used to assemble for the annual week in October in the grey old mansion among its wide-stretching woods—woods which might be driven through five hard working days without ever coming to the end of them. We recall those larches and silver firs of portentous girth that reared their clear stems toward the skies in long-drawn lines of russet-coloured columns as they flung the broad shadows of their graceful boughs over the velvety turf by the clear-flowing river in what is locally known as "Paradise." These were the good old days before Radical tenants cared to trouble themselves about the game-laws; when they held their farms at the reasonable rents which made ample allowance for inevitable damages; when the surplus game, instead of going to the local markets, was sent round to the homesteads among the fields where it had fed; and when sundry of the laird's old friends among the farmers came to make up the long line of guns that drew themselves out across the breadth of the cover. But it was a right merry gathering all the same, as might be seen and heard at the meeting for the *al fresco* lunch, when tongues relieved from restraint were recompensing themselves for their previous silence. And then the comparing notes over the events of the day, when, after indulging in the host's admirable claret, his guests had adjourned to the vaulted smoking-room. For there is one undeniable advantage in a roe-hunt—as every man has his solitary station, removed from the jealous eyes of his neighbour, the narration of his personal exploits is an affair between himself and his conscience. He may drop a judicious veil over the misses and give generous scope to the frolics of his fancy.

At the same time, for a quieter kind of pleasure, to say nothing of making surer and more deadly work, there is nothing like shooting roe alone or with a single safe companion. You slip silently and stealthily to your places, sending into the cover the staunch old hound, who is all the better for your purpose if he be stiff in the joints. The first faint hesitating whimper grows into a deep-mouthed bay as the dog gets fairly on the foot of the roe, who are bounding through the bushes ahead of him. You make a rush for the direction in which they are coming round, for the roe has a suicidal habit of running in circles. And then from the crest of some commanding knoll, where your shooting-dress blends with the leaves and the branches, you stand motionless, with pricked ears and half-levelled piece, watching the openings within easy gunshot. Nothing is more noteworthy than the extraordinary stealthiness with which the roe will thread its way through the thickest and most tangled cover. You hear the dog crashing along through the undergrowth, and yet not a sound may have reached you from anywhere nearer, when of a sudden a phantom form flits over a low-hanging branch, and lights softly as a snowflake in the open, looking back and listening intently with flashes of startled curiosity in the gentle hazel eye. Nothing in the animal world is more graceful, and we suspect that the most prosaic of sportsmen must have a qualm when he sees the embodied poetry of the pose collapse under the murderous charge of buck-shot. The snap taken at the flying form that merely shoots into sight to vanish again instantaneously is of course a different thing altogether. Then you think of nothing but the miss or the kill as you rush forward to search the cover, and are too pleased with your quickness to feel a touch of remorse when you come upon the body of the slaughtered beauty. Shooting over a little pack of lively beagles, too, is more exciting, if less destructive, than turning out with a single experienced hound. And we have had better sport than on many a more solemn occasion, when we have merely taken the roe as they came in the course of a mixed day; for they will lie like rabbits till you almost set your foot upon them, under the branches of the scattered trees, on the banks of the beautiful West Highland lakes. The mischief is, that when your main object is woodcock, and one barrel is charged with small shot, while in the other there is a cartridge loaded with B.B., you are apt to make a mistake in the hurry of the moment, if you spring a deer where you were looking out for a bird. And the roe is almost as clever as the woodcock in interposing shot-proof screens between itself and the breech-loader.

The grouse is *par excellence* the game-bird of Scotland, but nothing in the last sixty years has changed its character so entirely as grouse-shooting. Sixty years ago, it is safe to say, no gentleman dreamed of renting a moor. Until then, and for half a generation afterwards, the grouse had to take its chance among the *feræ naturæ* that preyed upon it. The Western Highlands, with their watery climate, have never shown such a profusion of game as the more level moors of the Midlands and north-eastern Shires. Yet it sounds strange nowadays to hear of ten or twelve brace being regarded as a good day's sport for three crack guns on the hills of Luss, Arrochar, and Glenfalloch. But since the tracts of barren waste became marketable the grouse has been artifically fostered. The eagles in many districts have disappeared from their ancient hunting grounds; hawks of all kinds have been indiscriminately trapped and killed down; ravens and hooded crows have made practical acquaintance with the virtues of strychnine, though that is a fatality which few will be disposed to regret; while ground vermin of every sort have been gathered in for the open-air museum, displayed ostentatiously on the gable-end of the mountain kennel. In short, the balance of Nature has not only been disturbed but upset, and there can be no question that Nature avenges herself. Experts may differ as to the origin of the grouse disease, but we believe the most reliable are agreed that it is aggravated if not caused by overcrowding. As for Colquhoun, he lays it down as an axiom that on no moors in Scotland can the birds be increased with impunity beyond a certain point. Over-stocking tends to generate disease, and contagious maladies are not stamped out, as they used to be, when every sickly member of a pack was sure to be struck down by some hawk on the hover, or picked up by the fox or the foumart on the prowl. Nor does the genuine sportsman of the olden time care greatly for what the advertisements style a "first-class" moor. He loves to brings hill-craft and science into play, and to see the dogs he has bred and broken at their business. But where the coveys are lying thick in the summer sunshine any novice who goes out with tolerably straight powder may come home with nearly as many brace as his seniors and betters—and that, it must be confessed, is somewhat aggravating.

Whether the game be plentiful or the reverse, the subject of satisfactory relations with the sheep farmers and their shepherds is all-important for the occupant of shootings. If you cannot have the sheep-walks in your own hands—and that is a counsel of perfection for all but capitalists—make a point, if any way possible, of keeping on terms with the shepherds. There are difficulties of course. The more jealous the keepers are, the more likely are they and the shepherds to strive like the herdsmen of Lot and Abraham ; but after all, it is the shepherds who are masters of the situation. They are out early and late; they stumble across the nests of the sitting hens, and mark the basking-places of the newly-hatched chickens to a nicety. They are for ever followed by lean, frolicsome collies, always eager for a range, a rush in, and a worry. They may gratify a long-standing grudge with one wave of the hand, which will seal the doom of a whole pocketful of "cheepers." So it is absolutely indispensable to endeavour to conciliate them. And though they may be "dour" and bristly when rubbed the wrong way, for the most part they are frank and manly fellows, open to a kindly "crack" and a pouchful of tobacco, and with no sort of objection to an occasional sovereign. Once make them your friends, and they will be ready enough to make amicable arrangements as to gathering their flocks, burning the heather, &c., which are privileges they are pretty free to exercise at their discretion, whatever the covenants and restrictions in their lease.

The solitary form of sport in which Mr. Colquhoun has to own to limited experience is ptarmigan-shooting. Naturally he has bagged ptarmigan repeatedly, but he always had to work for stray specimens. He says he has never shot on the mountains of Ross and Inverness, which are relatively accessible, and where the birds are far more numerous than elsewhere. We have been more fortunate, and can confirm what he says as to the abundance of the birds and the comparative ease of procuring them. In those Ross-shire shootings to which we alluded *apropos* to the wild goats, the lodge stood high upon the stormy watershed between the dips to the North Sea and to the Atlantic. It was not much of a climb from the loftier of the grouse-grounds, across the stony zone of the alpine hares, to the lichen-stained rocks frequented by the ptarmigan; and though the walking was wild enough round slippery and dizzy heights, on a clear and calm day the sport was almost tame. At the outset there was no great difficulty in finding the birds, for they would rise wild. Circling and soaring like carrier-pigeons, they would go sweeping round the jagged angles of the cliffs, or dipping downwards to the heather flats below. But they always come back towards the point from which they started, or at least to the same level, and generally to the same mountain. When you kept following them up, they seemed to grow sullen. The second or third time they would let you approach to within a half or a quarter gunshot. Walking cautiously, and looking closely, the graceful bend of the head and neck would disengage itself from the tints of the cliff with which it harmonised closely in colour. Then you might take a sitting shot if you chose, or give them law with a fair probability of missing them; for, once scared from their perch, they had a knack of disappearing behind it. In these haunts of the ptarmigan, by the way, more than one pair of golden eagles had their eyries; and when caught in the clinging folds of a fog we have felt the sough of the pinion on our cheek as the mighty bird swept over our shoulder, more startled and surprised than the intruder on his solitude.

CHAPTER XX

After Deer

THERE may be excitement enough in hunting the elk in snow-shoes through the depths of Canadian pine woods, with your huge quarry ploughing away before you, belly deep in the yielding snow; still more of it in shooting sambur in the Indian jungles, when each passing rustle in the leaves may mean anything, from a monkey to a "man-eater." But after all it is questionable whether you may not find more of the poetry of sport in a day's stalking at home. If you care for sensations, you may feel your blood flow as fast and your pulse throb as fiercely; and as for roughing it, if you find a luxury in that, you can import as much of hardship as you please into the romance of your sylvan campaign. You have cast your lot say, in one of the islands of the Atlantic, and your lodge stands on the little arm of the sea, that, embayed in sheltering headlands, comes winding up through the woods. There the waves gently lap the shore, while you hear the faint roar of the ocean surf as it tumbles in on the beach without. But the choice of the site was influenced by considerations rather practical than sentimental, and the mansion stands hard by the great water-way paddled over by the coasting steamer that keeps your communications open with your grocer and wine-merchant, and the world in general. Behind, and to right and left, forest and moors stretch away in weary leagues of hill and bog, peat and heather, and in the most distant glens, had you a prejudice in favour of always sleeping sheltered by a roof-tree, the deer might find perpetual sanctuary. The hospitable natives who dwell afar by the shore would gladly welcome you to those turf-built hovels of theirs, where the blue peat reek, after pervading each nook and corner, escapes at last through the hole that does duty as a chimney. But independently of shortcomings in the architectural arrangements, the well-bleached sheets that gape so temptingly for you are generally teeming with vigorous animal life. Should you commit yourself to them and slumber, but brief time will elapse before you awake again to consciousness, and then your fevered and mangled frame seems to have slept in minutes an uneasy sleep of hours. But it is the less needful to throw yourself on native hospitality, or to bivouac under flimsy canvas, that when you go out to play Robinson Crusoe you find classical and appropriate quarters in a comfortable cave. During long ages the Atlantic has been at work fashioning you a dwelling-place, and if Nature has not reared there a minster as stately as on the neighbouring Staffa, it must be remembered that this cavern is devoted to domestic, not to ecclesiastical purposes. The apartment is spacious, the roof is lofty, there is soft carpeting of firm, white sand, and—rare thing in caves—there is an infinitely better system of ventilation, and a far freer draught for your smoke, than in any of the neighbouring cottages. Your fuel and furniture come from the drift-wood that lies tossed up everywhere against the foot of the cliffs; for those troubled seas are dotted thick with black points on the wreck charts. You may picture the fate of the luckless seaman, struggling in the grasp of the waves, when you see how the massive ironwork of the shivered rudder that helps to form your table has been dragged and twisted by the water as if it were a weak strand of wire. Nor, if you resign yourself to melancholy reflection of the sort, are the especial associations of the cavern much fitted to enliven you. For it is the chosen resting-place of the Hebridean dead, whom island piety or superstition fondly consigns to the sacred earth of Columba's blessed isle, and many a queer funeral company has held grim revelry in the "cave of the corpses." But, steeled by use perhaps against impressions like these, our animated after-dinner chat flows on as little disturbed by gloomy fancies as in all probability was the mirth of an Egyptian banquet by the familiar skeleton. And we cast ourselves hopefully on our beds of bracken while the fresh heaped drift-wood crackles on the blazing logs.

The forked flames leap up towards the stalactites on the ceiling, their flickering shadows rise and fall on the cavern walls, while, lulled to rest by the droning of the surf, in a few minutes we have consigned to a temporary oblivion all our hopes and fears for the morrow.

An early waking, a hurried, shuddering plunge into the ocean, a deliberate breakfast, and a more deliberate pipe. It is a regular Hebridean autumn morning. Last evening we and the sun separated on the most pleasant terms, scarcely one fleecy cloud in the sky, everything below responding to his parting smiles. Now a bitter north-west gale is blowing off the ocean, snatching up armfuls of sand and tossing them into your eyes, driving the dirty grey clouds fast over the heavens, and tumbling about the cold grey water in showers of drifting foam. We make our arrangements stolidly, fill our flasks and sling our glasses; but even after we have corrected the rawness of the atmosphere with a modest "morning" of mountain dew, it takes an effort to force out a sentence or screw up a smile. We half envy our rifles the warm seclusion of the waterproof coverings in which we leave them for the present. Roughing it, indeed! We bear it all with a subdued pleasure, and a grim gratification in endurance which does us infinite credit; but we are inclined to pit our Highland hardships against any chance of frost-bite in Canada or sunstroke in the Wynaut jungle. And in spite of the wind that goes roaring past us as we mount a breach in the cliffs and turn inland towards the more sheltered feeding-grounds, heavy masses of mist are hanging from the rocks and wrapping the hills in their dripping folds. Outlying wreaths come rolling down the steeps, and steal ghost-like along the bottoms of the valleys. The gull that floats past overhead looms through the haze large as an albatross; and the mountain hare that jerks himself by easy stages up the hill in front might well pass for a roe, were it not for his characteristic action. And deer there are, and not far to seek; for a roar sounds out of the gloom, and fainter and fainter is bandied backwards and forwards between the mountain echoes. It is also taken up by some rival in flesh and blood, who desires nothing better than to accept the challenge. And just then, as we stop to reconcert our strategy, down drops the wind; and simultaneously, and as if they had been watching their opportunity, the heavens empty themselves out upon us in a succession of falling sheets of water. The sporting council adjourns in undignified haste to the shelter of a convenient rock; whereupon the waterspout ceases abruptly as it commenced, having converted into a brawling young torrent the modest brook that, stealing from pool to pool, came trickling down the mountain side. Then the sun actually comes struggling out, although he looks drenched and watery like everything else around. Much of the mist has been washed away, although there is still a good deal floating about, and we decide to mount to the *col* above by that natural staircase where the stream is tumbling down. Once up there, all wet and half blown, we sink down among the scattered blocks of stone, and from behind a fringe of soaking heather gaze eagerly into the long bare glen below. The damp lies so thick on the telescope glasses that we reject them as useless; but even with the naked eye we can make out a stag as he grazes quietly among some broken knolls at the upper end, where there is always shelter of some kind in the wildest weather. What his size may be it is hard to guess, a matter of the less consequence to us, as we own with a sigh that it is almost impossible to stalk him. Did the brown dwarf of the moors haunt the Hebrides instead of the Cheviots, he could never find cover among the pebbles and stunted heather on that bare hillside, or on the smooth natural meadow through which the stream winds at the bottom. But the wind blows from the deer to us, and, as he is feeding straight away, there may be a distant chance of bringing him to bag, if we only walk straight forward and trust to Fortune and the mist. What they might have done for us it is impossible to say; for an imp of a mountain sheep, wild and wary as the deer himself, comes scrambling out of a hollow, and goes bounding up the steep, clattering down the pebbles behind him as he mounts. The stag accepts the friendly hint, and, taking for granted the danger that he neither smells nor sees, trots leisurely over the ridge, showing to our longing eyes a pair of antlers well worth following as he crosses the sky-line. And so we do follow, the air, breathing fresh in our faces, setting our minds at rest on the score of giving him our wind ; and we find that, scarcely startled as he was, he has gone no farther than the adjacent corry, the wildest and roughest of the wild shooting-ground. Deep in the bottom there is rich green turf, but one side and the other are a jumble of grey, weather-beaten rocks, while through their ragged portals at the farther end the eye rests far below on the leaden rollers of the Atlantic. The stag has found friends, and the half-dozen of smaller deer that are grouped around him serve to set off his own stately form, while a lanky meddlesome hind pricks her sharp ears, and sweeps with her restless glance the broken ground over which we might otherwise have made our approaches. There is but one thing to be done, and that is to pick one's way by the back of that broken ridge to the right, which, if luck should stand our friend, may possibly bring us within some one hundred and twenty yards of the herd. Talk of the chances of a tiger dropping on your shoulders in an Indian covert—more imminent peril waits you here. As you leap from ledge to ledge, a sprained ankle would seem inevitable if you took time to think about it ; and every now and then, as you bound, you land on a spot where, if you do miss your footing, you may realise the hopes of the venerable raven who is croaking sanguinely overhead. It is the path of the chamois or bouquetin hunter ; and, although the abysses of the Alps may be deeper, yet the penalty of a false step is no less certain here than there. But you have

The Stag and his Friends. *By* Sydney Steel.

CATALOGUE OF MEDALS

neither eye nor thought to spare for the depths; and on you go, using your rifle as a balancing-pole, until, all palpitating from your violent work, you stand clinging to the rocks below the jagged pinnacle that marked the end of your stalk. It is a moment of deep suspense. Have the deer heard you as you came scrambling along, or have they taken the raven's warning? You have the resolution to give your beating heart and trembling hand a couple of minutes to calm themselves. One single mouthful of whisky to clear any lingering mists that still float before your eyes, and then you quietly raise yourself to the edge of the ridge overhead. And there is the stag, his neck carelessly stooped as he ruminates in all the placidity of a vigorous body and well-balanced mind. You lay the fatal muzzle well behind his ample shoulder, his keen eye barely catches the flash, when the sound and the ball reach him together. The next second, with gigantic bounds that leave his companions far behind, he is descending the valley. Missed? impossible! You knew you covered him, and almost fancied you heard the thud of the bullet. Yes, the effort was but the last blaze of life. The next moment he stops, staggers, and falls—so much venison, hide, and horn—in a patch of rank bracken; and there is your friend the raven, cheerfully croaking the requiem, as he almost stoops on the carcass. Now the sun bursts out in a flood of light, the ruddy hide of the fallen deer and the ruddier tints of the withered fern seeming to catch fire at the rays. Straggling up by more practicable paths than yours, keepers and gillies chant a chorus of congratulation, and your friends envy you your trophy of branching antlers. In the afternoon you have sun and scenery, and sport as well; but the deer you slew in the mist is the hero not only of the day but of the season.

CHAPTER XXI

The Coverts

COVERT shooting is almost the sole survival of the old-fashioned manner of sport, and even covert shooting, especially in the Southlands, has been inevitably degenerating into the battue. We use the word "degenerating" advisedly, because although the battue is absurdly abused by those who know nothing about it, and though it tests the skill of the marksman like grouse driving or pigeon shooting, yet it cannot compare for the exhilaration of excitement with wilder and more irregular work. For the partridges, even in September, unfortunately no man can go out nowadays with the well-broken couple of pointers and the drilled retriever at heel. In place of wading up to the ankle in hand-shorn stubbles, the fields have been swept clean as a tennis-lawn, and the straggling roots in the broad drills offer no satisfactory shelter. The birds are up and away before the dogs would be within drawing distance. Even with the muirfowl in Yorkshire and on many of the best of the Scotch moors, driving is become the fashion, and with good reason. If birds *will* pack before the season has well begun, they must take the consequences. Moreover, driving incalculably increases the head of game. The old cocks who used to escape scot-free, leaving the poults and cheepers to be butchered, head the flights as was always their custom, and are shot down in place of saving themselves to spoil the next breeding season. No doubt the trimming of the rambling hedgerows and the grubbing of copses and spinneys in agricultural districts where the soil is valuable tend to make the battue a matter of necessity if a gentleman means to offer fair sport to his friends. But even in these districts, and far more elsewhere, the coverts are the glory and beauty of the British Isles. We have no desire to make invidious comparisons, but on the Continent you have the forest rather than the covert. In our idea nothing can possibly be more gloomy than the endless stretches of dark pine in Scandinavia, whether they offer protection from the blazing summer sun or are snow-laden in the winter-time and spangled with icicles. In the glorious beech-woods of Germany you are impressed with a brooding sense of their solemnity, and tread gingerly, as during high mass in a cathedral, upon a crackling carpet of withered leaves. So you feel in looking down the aisles and arching cloisters through the stately columns of the clean-stemmed pines in the valleys of the Schwarzwald, when the bracken beds are shrivelled and collapse to the first frosts. As for the French forests, where there are swamps and impenetrable thickets, they are so vast, and the dwarfed timber is so overcrowded, that herds of wolves breed securely in their recesses, and even experienced rangers lose their bearings in the mist or the dusk.

In the British Isles, on the other hand, all is lifelike and homelike, for everything sylvan is on a more moderate scale. Above all, the kindly damp of the climate makes the vegetation of the undergrowth flourish in rare luxuriance. Shakespeare, Milton, Spenser, Scott, and scores of other poets have sung the rich picturesqueness of the bosky bourns, with their tangled wealth of natural shrubbery. Except among the firs, it is seldom indeed that you get an open view ahead and beneath in the British woods. Nor do we know in which of the three kingdoms the woodland scenes are most enchanting. Look around from any eminence in England, even in the level midlands or the hunting shires. There was a time when the country from the Cheviots to the Channel, from Bamborough Castle to Michael's Mount, was almost unbroken woodland with occasional clearings round town or hamlet. Everywhere the sylvan shreds and patches of that prehistoric period have, latterly at least, been jealously guarded. And now, in this utilitarian age, the "amenities" of romantic woodland are recognised as having a market value, which is the surest guarantee for their preservation. Looking out over the landscapes, you see the gabled roof of the ancient hall, sheltering in the foliage of ancestral woods; the towers and spires of the village churches, surrounded by tall groups of trees and rising above the venerable yews in the churchyards; the chimneys of the farmhouses embosomed like the hall; and the mill lying low in the vale among the beds of willow and alder. Even in the copses of the grassy shires and of the Home Counties you may wander away into a world of romance. We know nothing wilder on the Scotch border or in the Yorkshire dales than some of the valleys in West Kent, although it is true they are on a smaller scale, and the grandeur is Lilliputian. But there are dells with as steep a dip as the Derncleugh of "Guy Mannering," with the brook brawling unseen under matted foliage in the bottom, and but scanty room for a gun on either side; while the man in the middle, as he threads his devious way, can seldom bring the weapon swiftly to his shoulder. But elsewhere and anywhere there may be idyllic surprises in store for you. You come on the meandering streamlet that has hollowed out its banks, under dense canopies of the bramble and wild rose intertwined with the clematis and clinging honeysuckle, where in a gloom that may be said to be visible at noonday you may hear the sullen plunge of the otter, or listen to the frequent plashing of the water-voles as they dive to the vibration of the foot-tread. Or after warning from the faint earth-smell floating in the air, you come out upon the swampy precincts of the sedgy pool, where the water-hens have their favourite nesting-places in the reeds and the pike are said to grow to portentous dimensions. In the New Forest, though horribly spoiled by prosaic plantation, you have still the old forest scenery on a noble scale. There are farmhouses almost as solitary, though far more beautiful, than anything among the charred stumps and snake-fences of a Canadian settlement—where the belled cattle will go astray in the fenceless wilds, and where a wandering herd of shaggy ponies may make irruptions into the old-fashioned flower-garden. There are glades where the gipsies and caravan vagabonds have their immemorial camping-places, and hamlets with their bulging roofs of ragged thatch, peopled by charcoal-burning aborigines, whose ancestors have cursed the devastations of the Conqueror or rejoiced over the corpse of the ruthless Red King.

If we change the scene to the North, the beauties only change their character. In Northumberland, where the woods take naturally to the waters and the sheltered valleys, you have the plantations skirted by the beds of gorse, redolent of perfume in early summer, where the small birds make their nests in safety by thousands, and the foxes have their earths in the thick of the rabbit warrens. Or go to the Scotch Highlands, where the birches feathering down to its brink are mirrored in the shallows of the sleeping loch, and the gleaming white stems rise out of thickets of bracken, bramble, and bilberry, of holly, honeysuckle, and wild rose. Or to the genial shores of West Ireland, warmed by the Gulf Stream, where the myrtles through the mildness of the winter are uninjured, and the arbutus flourishes as in Southern Italy, laden with the luscious red berries that tempt the pheasants. And all these coverts are swarming with animal life, for they are as inviting to migrants and birds of passage as they are safe refuges for the natives. Of course the game must reckon with the exigencies of the shooting season, but that is in conformity with the inexorable laws of nature. And game preserving presses hard on the beasts of prey, and on some others that are unfairly classed as vermin. But that only makes the covert a sanctuary for almost everything harmless and ornamental. The copses are melodious with joyous song in the spring, and as full of animation in the more silent autumn. We pity the man who cannot pass the time agreeably, while kicking his heels at the cold corner of a lingering beat, as the harbingers of the first hares and pheasants pass in review before him, from the chattering jays and clamorous jackdaws down to the screaming blackbird and twittering willow-wren.

It must be admitted that our British coverts hold nothing more formidable than the fox, or possibly a badger, for the wild cat and marten cat are well-nigh extinct even in the most remote districts of the Highlands. You have not the excitement of a wounded lynx dropping on your shoulders from the pine boughs, of being hugged by the unfriendly bear you have cornered, or of startling a sounder of wild pig from their siesta with the chance of being charged and ripped by the old tusker. Nor do we know that that is greatly to be regretted, as it would assuredly upset the admirable arrangements of the battue. Acclimatation of ferocities has been tried and has failed. Gilbert White tells us in one of his letters that General Howe, who was the Crown grantee of Alice Holt Forest, turned out some wild boars and a few buffalo to boot, when the countryfolk rose upon them and destroyed them. The Chillingham wild cattle still perpetuate the fierce breed of ancient Caledonia, so dramatically commemorated in the "Bride of Lammermoor" and the ballad of "Cadyow Castle." They are ugly customers at the best, and not to be lightly approached, of which we once had personal experience when stalking them from motives of curiosity. But there seems to be no reason why covert shooting should not be varied by turning out some of the sporting birds we have only half domesticated. The turkey and the guinea-fowl retain so much of their wild nature that they will always for choice stray far from the farmsteading to make their nests in the roots of a hedge or in some impenetrable patch of bramble. The hens are reported missing, and the disappearance is credited to the foxes, till they turn up again some fine morning with the chicks trooping at their heels. His Majesty George II. was as partial to turkey shooting as any West American pot-hunter. In his time there were flocks of turkeys in Richmond Park, which are said seldom to have numbered fewer than two thousand. They fattened on the acorns and beechmast; they were fed besides from stacks of barley, and the cocks often grew to thirty pounds' weight. There were wild turkeys in Wynnstay Park, we believe, so late as the middle of the present century, and likewise at Lord Ducie's seat in Gloucestershire. At the same time peafowl and guinea-fowl had been breeding and multiplying at Aston Hall and in others of the Warwickshire woods.

But, after all, in our wilder covert shooting—say, on the shores of Loch Fyne or the innumerable sea-arms in Western Scotland—no one need complain of lack of variety. The keeper sends word by a swift-footed gillie to the nearest telegraph office that a flight of woodcock has come in with the November frosts. Responding promptly to the despatch, the guns drive to the ground through all the autumn beauties of a Scotch Riviera, along a winding road now commanding broad views of the ocean sounds and archipelagoes, and now dipping into the depths of the gorge or ravine where the dimness is fitfully illuminated by stray shafts of the flickering sunshine. The difficulty in these back-of-the-world shootings is in recruiting a sufficiency of beaters; for men or even boys—in these high education days—are as hard to come by as for the chamois drives in the highlands of Tyrol and the Salzkammergut. But the numerical inefficiency of the force only increases the excitement, for as the guns are going forward in line with the natives, they do a good deal of the seeking and finding for themselves. The great thing is to take it leisurely and do nothing in a hurry. Indeed, not unfrequently you come on a place where anything but the slowest progress is impossible, and as you force your way through the thicket or make the *détour* to get across the burn, friends and attendants are constrained to wait for you. The walking may be toilsome, but it is singularly picturesque. The rills

THE COVERTS 273

come meandering down from the moors above, in a succession of deep rifts and broken clefts. In the rains they are rushing streams; now they are fast frost-bound, except here and there, where the flow is too swift. The hollies fretted over with the flying snow-showers form so many sheltered bowers to tempt the snipe and the woodcock. The intervening slopes, clothed with the heather and withered bracken, are studded with clumps of holly, fir, and dwarf oak, with a sprinkling of hanging birches and rowan trees, bearing their ruddy fruit. The lower boughs of the spruces are weighed down with the snow and so many natural blankets or *tentes-abris*, to make the roe comfortable in their resting-places. For there the roedeer in the wintry cold appear to lose much of their natural timidity, or rather it takes another form. In place of stealing away ahead at the first sound of the sticks, they crouch in their forms like hares, in the hope that the enemy will pass them. And on these shootings they are almost as numerous as the hares. So you must load with moderate-sized shot and take your chance, for you never know what may get up. You are fording a burn gingerly in fear of a slip, when a woodcock is flushed from beneath one of the hollies. You tread on the trailing bough of a spruce, and up springs a roe from under your boots. The guns close in round some likely-looking scrub of oak and mountain ash, while keepers and beaters struggle in to thresh it out. A rabbit or two come out as you expected, and then, when it seems that all is over, there is the rush of a rocketing cock-pheasant, or perhaps a hen. Lord or lady, it makes little difference : in those solitudes you are not over-particular as to sex. Climbing one of the watercourses to the broad belt of skirting upper plantation, the guns are disposed in it and above it, to do their best. Were you to attempt to walk the lower side systematically, you would topple over into the abyss. That wood is a famous haunt of the black game. As the cock skims the tops of the fir trees in his powerful flight, it is into that abyss he goes crashing when stopped by the charge. For somehow the black game always appeared to head to the seaward, and hard work it often was to retrieve them in the labyrinth of brushwood. On the upper side were the heather hills and the open moors, and more than once the beating has roused outlying red-deer from their lairs. The close of the day's proceedings was almost invariably satisfactory, nor need it be said that the mixed bag made a trophy that would have gladdened the soul of a Weenix.

Talking of woodcock, it is somewhat surprising that killing a cock should still be considered a triumph. No doubt it is partly because woodcock are really wild game—birds of passage, here to-day, and fled to-morrow. Consequently there is a certain romance about bagging them. But it comes chiefly, we believe, from a surviving tradition of the primeval days when the sportsman made awkward play with his single-barrelled flint gun. It was no joke bringing that unwieldy weapon to the present, and the flint ignited

Black Cock and Setter. By A. Cooper, R.A.

CYTOLOGY OF
NEUROSES

the powder so leisurely that sea-fowl had time to dive to the flash. The mystery was as to how the cocks were ever dropped, and we fancy that when they did come down, luck had a good deal to do with it. Let a woodcock get well away, and he will go winding and twisting through the tree-tops like the capercailzie, for both birds are well served by their instinct, and can take uncommonly good care of themselves. You must take a cock when you can, as you snap at a rabbit, and if you shoot quick, as he generally rises in a glade or an opening, the shot should be easy enough, though the charge goes rather ball-like. With their congener the snipe, by the way, it is different. He gets up in the open, and if you coolly wait, after the preliminary jerkings to right and left, which are the eccentric prologue to a steadier performance, he usually shoots out straight before beginning to soar.

It is seldom one finds such roe shooting as in the circumstances we have sketched, but the roe is always a great addition to the battue in the North. A chartered denizen of the wastes and woods, he seeks the deepest solitudes of extensive plantations. Hence he is scarcely the ornament of the landscape he ought to be, for he rarely shows. Strolling quietly about with the gun in the woodland glades, you may occasionally catch the gleam of a white stern vanishing behind a tree trunk. Few creatures are more graceful, and very few more destructive. The roe steals out to feed at night or in the early morning, and there is no prettier sight, except to the unfortunate farmer, than a family party in the high green corn, delicately nibbling the tender blades. Somehow they are less shy in Germany, where you may see them any day of an afternoon grazing with the cattle in the sequestered valleys surrounded by woods. With us, when they keep themselves to themselves in their sylvan retreats, they make frightful havoc of the young saplings. That is the best antidote to sentimentalism with the tender-hearted shooter who is greatly inclined to spare them for their beauty, and feels remorseful when he plunges the hunting-knife in the quivering chest. Nothing keeps one up to the mark at a Scottish battue like the expectation of roe. Instinctive timidity has bred intense suspicion. The sight is as keen as the sense of smell. The crackle of a twig, the striking of a match, or the faint whiff of a cigarette will give timely warning, and like all deer they will rather charge the line of the beaters than face an unknown danger in front. The gun standing motionless at his post has no notice of their approach. The roe moves as if shod in velvet, as indeed he is: silent as the shadow he throws forward in the sunshine, he emerges phantom-like from the screen of twigs, which has never rustled at his passage. The quick eye in its circular glance embraces everything: he has a glimpse of the sportsman, who may be looking the other way, and with one bound into the air, like the South African springbok, he clears the ride and vanishes as he appeared. The roe is on no friendly terms with the fox, who freely takes toll of the young fawns when he finds them, and the fox is another contributor to the excitement of a Scottish field-day. Though there may be no hounds within a couple of counties, at first it goes against the grain of the Southron to shoot him; but as he does more mischief in the preserves than in the poultry yards, he soon comes to be proscribed and outlawed as the marauder he is. If the roe is the incarnation of shrinking timidity, the Scotch fox is the embodiment of audacious impudence. Being never hunted by the hounds he grows pursy and lazy in the lowlands, but his wiles set the keepers and their traps at defiance. He attains to enormous size and is always in sleek condition. Like Major Dugald Dalgetty, he never misses an opportunity of laying in the provant or replenishing the larder. One instance of his coolness in difficulties we remember. It was a party where the beaters mustered strong, and having lunched freely, in defiance of rule were making a most unholy noise. There was a cry of "Cock!" and a shot, a second cry of "Down!" and a pause, while unsuccessful search was made for the bird. We were uncocking the gun preparatory to leaving our station, when an old fox emerged from the midst of the hullabaloo, with the missing woodcock in his mouth—for he had quietly retrieved it.

It is a sharp descent from the roe to the rabbit, but the rabbit is in every respect a most estimable animal when his ravages are kept within due bounds. He is unwisely neglected by fashionable cooks, for he is excellent when coming from the kitchen in any shape, from the mulligatawny soup to the smothering in onions, with a sauce *à la Soubise*. No animal affords finer shooting practice—the only drawback for novices is that he gets them into the habit of snap-shooting, and he is at his best and brightest among the sandhills rolling down to the beach—with these scattered patches of the prickly gorse the rabbits have been cropping into fantastic forms. The dazed rabbits emerging at the end of a driven covert are mobbed and shot down like sheep. The rabbits bolting across a narrow ride demand as swift calculation of the chances as if you were firing at a streak of lightning. Let skilful shots say what they will, there must still be a large element of luck there. But in the sandhills with their hollows and the patches of whin, with the rank bent grass in which the colonists bask through the day, and which sometimes is thick enough to cover the scuttle to the burrow, both the gun and the quarry have tolerably fair play, though doubtless an expert would lay odds on his shooting. Then there is the exhilaration of the exercise, with its strain on the back sinews: the innocent intoxication of the brine-laden breezes, the wide views out to seaward, with the sails and the trails of steamer smoke, the merry clamour of the seagulls swooping overhead, the gabbling and calling of the waders that are foraging below high-water mark, and on the other side the complaining alarm notes of the lapwings, who, though they have got rid of their cherished nurslings months before, are nevertheless as fussy as ever.

THE COVERTS

We have left the grand battue to the last, because it would tax the ingenuity of a sporting Macaulay to say anything fresh about it. Yet we may cast a passing glance at its picturesque and humorous aspects. There is no more genuinely English sight than the cheery muster before the doors of some great mansion on a day that is expected to make a record bag. There is the host, who, if he understands his duties, is the strategical organiser of it all, and he should be set upon making things pleasant for his guests, and seeing that each man has his fair share of the shooting. He ought to keep the whip hand of the important head keeper, whose looks are anxiously watched by his obsequious satellites in velveteen. Then there is the array of long-gaitered beaters in fustian—an irregular levy, who have been eagerly expecting the great outing in the woods. On the whole they are a well-fed and rosy-faced lot, with sturdy calves and athletic forms. Some of the elders may have warnings of rheumatism in the near distance, and tramp about with a perceptible string-halt ; but they compare favourably with the pallid artisans of the towns, and you can see that their lines have fallen in sanitary places. There are the guns with their carriers and loaders, for the most part as fine specimens of manhood as England can boast, and with eyesight as sharp as their nerves are steady. For at the biggest shoots they are generally picked men, who will make death as pleasant as is possible under any circumstances. Sentimental humanitarians mourn over the butchery of hand-fed pheasants. Why, the hand-fed pheasant is one of the luckiest of living creatures. He is reared from the shell in the lap of luxury, and supplied with all the delicacies of the season, till he chooses to vary his diet by strolling abroad. His retreats are kept undisturbed, and his privacy is never intruded upon, save by the raiding poacher, who must make the venture at his peril. The pheasant must die at last, like all of us, but even at the methodical battue he has a fair chance. And when he falls to the crack shot, it is a case of instantaneous collapse, and he is dead before he rebounds from the grass. Then, if he were grateful for all the care bestowed upon him, he should rejoice to know that he may sell for a mere trifle in warm weather, and furnish the cheapest of dainties for the modest dinner party, as the rabbit is the luxury of artisans in the manufacturing districts. So the pheasant preserver who has reared his birds regardless of expense is a benefactor to his species when he sends them to market.

But to return from the finish to the start. There is the exhilarating walk from the house to the home coverts, through sights that have inspired immortal painters. The skeleton boughs of the lofty trees of the rookery, with the rustle of their few and faded leaves, standing out Corot-like against the sky in the greyness of vanishing mists; the group of gazing cattle standing fetlock-deep in the withered bracken, suggestive of Cooper or Rosa Bonheur; the sheep that have huddled together at the noise of the men and the yelping of the retrievers, with the gleam on the fleecy backs that

Millet has so often given us; or perhaps the herds of half-scared but still trustful fallow-deer reminding us of many a scene by Landseer. The interest changes when the covert is disturbed by beaters, who should make play with their sticks, and be chary of using their voices. We can conceive the consternation in the sanctuary caused by the unwonted inroad. The small birds gathering for their migration are the first to go; there are the indignant protests of jays and magpies; the pigeons take hurried flight for the open; the squirrels scrambling up the trunks, with frequent pauses, finally seek refuge in the tallest trees, whence they peer down at the proceedings. As the line advances, the rabbits and hares hustling together are in startled motion like so many maggots in a mouldy cheese; and the pheasants are running purposelessly to and fro, until one more hysterical than the rest gives the signal for a simultaneous scattering. Then comes the ceaseless crack of the breech-loaders, while breeches are getting warm though the guns are being changed. It is to be hoped that all is going smoothly and pleasantly, but there is always the off-chance of two disagreeables which the most considerate host cannot altogether control. There is the dangerous shot, and there is the jealous shot. The danger comes in chiefly when an excitable man is unfortunately told off to walk with the beaters. In these circumstances he should shoot at nothing except ground game or sky-scrapers, but he is apt to blaze at the birds flying forward breast high, when he may blind a companion or bag a stop.

More common still is the jealous shot, who is a detestable nuisance. By snatching at other men's game, and claiming promiscuously what never belonged to him, he is likely enough to put the coolest of his neighbours off their shooting, and in any case he is pretty sure to ruffle their tempers. Besides, it may be almost taken for granted that he is something of a tailor, and mangles even more birds than he misses. And nothing is more painful to the genuine sportsman than to know that crippled victims are dropping around him beyond sight and search, to suffer and die in lingering torments.

CHAPTER XXII

Curling

FEW people in England are fond of cold. Many of us hold and broach irreproachable theories as to its bracing effect on our frames, but our inward conviction is that it is disagreeable, like many other tonics. We are not all of us skaters, and many of us who are find ourselves condemned in a frost, by our avocations, to the sufferings of Tantalus. We grumble at a mild winter, and submit to it with much philanthropy. It is very different with our relations north of the Tweed —at least, with the dwellers between Tweed and Tay. There there is no sort of hypocrisy in the aspiration of vigorous males after bitter winters. For what is above all others the national game can only be played in national weather. Golf is popular in a sense, and, moreover, it can be played at all seasons, but then it can be only played in certain localities and at a certain cost. But there all the world are curlers: all you ask for the game is water, of which there is no lack; a frost, which used to be no very rare phenomenon, to make the water ice; and a couple of heavy circular stones, polished on both surfaces or on the lower one, and secured to handles. The prime cost is little, something within the means of the humblest peasant, if he is careful in saving, as he is sure to be. A couple of fragments from the neighbouring quarry, a pair of pebbles from the nearest brook, two bits of iron, is all you want—the outlay is a slight expenditure of labour. Of course superior wealth may vindicate itself in a pair of *pierres de luxe*, but the brass and the ornaments go for little, and not unfrequently it is the most slovenly workman who has the most showy tools. When the stones are flawless, roughly as they are used, they bid long defiance to blows and wear and tear. We should say there may be stones in existence now that have lasted, in their degree, like the Sphynx. They may become heirlooms, and be transmitted from generation to generation.

We have no intention of dwelling upon curling in its technical details. Nothing is duller reading than games upon paper, and we should as soon think of illustrating the grace and poetry of the gazelle by exhibiting the skeleton of the animal. It is enough to say each player has a couple of stones; of the two sides each counts there, four, or five players; and the object of each side is to leave one or more of its stones nearest to the mark or "tee," which is forty-two yards distant on the ice. The play is of course directed to "guarding" the good stones of your own party, to removing those of your opponents. But we notice the game as a very characteristic feature in Scottish life. In the first place it diffuses over the breadth of the country a great deal of innocent enjoyment; in the second, it does more to blend classes, to promote kindly feeling between superiors and dependents, than any amount of philanthropic speeches or any number of discourses on charity. Regarded in that view, the curling-pond is the English hunting-field popularised and thrown open to every one, without any of the heartburnings coming of trampled wheat, broken fences, vanished pheasants and fowls, and trapped foxes.

A stranger visiting Scotland with preconceived conceptions of the austerity of the national character would be strangely staggered in them in coming upon a jovial "rink" of curlers. Very justly do its admirers affectionately christen it "the roaring game." In Scotland every sheet of water lies, of course, in hilly ground, and he must hear the players long before he sees them. All lusty men in the prime and vigour of life—for even the old and the ailing are regenerated and rejuvenated for the day—they turn out prepared to be uproarious. With the air so calm and crisp that a child's whisper might be heard a mile away, and while the faintest crack of the ice rings like a pistol-shot, it is *de rigueur* to bellow. The "skip," or captain, who stands by the mark to issue his orders to the men only some forty yards removed from him, bawls as if he were shouting for a life-line from the deck of a vessel in the breakers. Nor is silent obedience the order of the day in the ranks, and the players hail back to him in equally stentorian tones. Every man is equipped with a voluminous broom to sweep the path should the stone show signs of dragging. The stone delivered glides smoothly and more or less swiftly forward with its dull, murmuring sound. On reaching the line where it becomes allowable to apply the brooms, if there seems an absence of powder, its watchful friends are galvanised into supernatural energy, while the unnecessary chorus of "soop her up" wakens the echoes in the adjoining parishes—and parishes are large in Scotland.

The well-pitted sides are bringing the match to a close in the lengthening shadows of the surrounding hills, and excitement has risen to fever height. The dull roar of the curling-stones on the keen ice is accompanied by the frenzied shouts of the partisans as some shot of great moment is being played. Respectable fathers of families, and kirk-elders to boot, are dancing as if they were on hot "girdles" and possessed by demons. The stone delivered, or, rather, barely dropped, from the strong arm of Sandy the smith is gliding forward on its fateful mission. "Soop her up! soop her up!" "Na, na; let abee! let abee!" The brooms are being flourished over the shapely brown boulder from the Burnock Water by fingers that burn to lend it legs and direction. The voice of the skip dominates all: "Leave alane! leave alane, will ye? She's a' there, right eneuch!" And suddenly, as the stone has skirted the very edge of one of the enemy's surest guards, a tremulous movement is to be detected in the handle. The crafty player, with a dexterous turn of the wrist, has communicated the hitherto imperceptible "side." The stone, in a graceful para-

CURLING. *By* LANCELOT SPEED.

CYMBELINE
of

bola, curls gently inwards, takes an "inwick" off the inner edge of another, and circles in to lie "a pot-lid" on the very tee. What yells of applause and triumph rend the air! "Shift that if ye can, my lads!" shouts Bodencleuch in friendly mockery; while Dreepdaily chafes and rages in wild but impotent disgust. That great shot of the smith's has decided the "end" and the game; for in vain does the schoolmaster—with the laird following to neutralise his play—try to break a way to that winning-stone through the advanced-guards of Bodencleuch.

It is interesting to see the stiff-set Scotch features gradually expand, the tight-drawn wrinkles of the mouth relax, the grey eye kindle and beam; illuminated by the joviality within, the very cheeks dimple. Had Sydney Smith ever assisted at a curling-match he must have recanted that heresy of his about Scotchmen being unsusceptible to humour. To be sure, a good deal may pass current in the circumstances that would scarcely bear subsequent criticism, as the manner of Artemus Ward's lecturing eked out its matter. Yet enough would remain, could it only be collected, after a long winter of curling, to give Dean Ramsay materials for another of his volumes. One touch of hard frost in Scotland makes the whole world kin, setting them all by the ears in amicable contest. Each parish and village has its curling club. Challenges fly about thick as snowballs round the doors of the parish school, and the long-standing peaceful feuds are referred to their annual arbitration. The stakes are honour, and generally a subsequent banquet of beef and greens. That is the regular curler's fare, and it has the advantage that it taxes unduly neither the purse of the loser nor the talent of the country Soyer. The cookery is simple, and if it is only careful must be successful. The chef is encouraged by the knowledge that the men he caters for are all connoisseurs in the dishes he provides. He serves strictly *au naturel*, for in the course of the day each guest has found his own sauce on the ice. They intimate approval in practical fashion, and the quantity consumed is stupendous. One sees rare feats of strength and capacity at southern harvest-homes. But appetites seem to wax as you go to the northward, and we should say a Scotch curler in good form occupies the mean between an English labourer at his annual assignation with the roast beef and plum-pudding and an Esquimaux feasting on blubber at his visitor's expense. The drink is strong and simple as the meat is plain. Inebriety is strictly discouraged. Indeed, those seasoned brains strengthened by air, exercise, and a heavy dinner, must drink deep before they reach the limits of temptation. As tumbler after tumbler of strong, sweet toddy goes down, you would say those respectable Calvinists ought to seek their appropriate future in the Northern Valhalla. The best of them would come off not discreditably had they followed Thor in his long pull at the Æsirs' horn. Then they have always—what goes a long way to make a pleasant evening—a common interest and subject. Peer or peasant, every one for the time being is wild over curling ; and although the place of honour in the chair may be yielded to the great man in the parish, yet talent asserts itself, and the most skilful curler is the most respected man. Very possibly he is a labourer, who wears over patched corduroys the high-collared ancient black coat handed down from his grandfather, and with a marked flavour of the chest in which it reposes from Sabbath to Sabbath. Memory is a faculty which might be supposed almost dormant in the most of them from lack of use, yet every man remembers, or swears he remembers, each shot that has been played on that eventful day. Then there are the matches of past years to be referred to, and the weather, for once, furnishes a topic equally natural and engrossing as they meet season after season ; the "lang frosts" marked with white stones, and those melancholy " Green Yules " that stopped the curling and filled the neighbouring kirkyard. After all, if you do somewhat exceed in the boiled beef, the Islay, or the Glenlivet, to-morrow, should the frost but hold, it will give you plenary absolution. But that element of uncertainty which is so apt to mix gall in the cup of the curler—will the weather last ? Matches must be concerted beforehand, and your sport is likewise the sport of the capricious elements. Travellers from Perth to Stirling may have observed among its somewhat sad surroundings a meadow stretching along the line and evidently meant to be flooded on occasion. On those few acres of ground are concentrated annually in Scotland for a season the hopes and fears of half its manhood. That is the battle lake where the annual matches are contested between the players of the North and the players of the South. It is needless to say that Nature, being a woman, loves to throw over those who pin their aspirations to her, and you may generally count on the day fixed for the Royal Caledonian Curling Club match being singularly mild and open. But when she does deign to be propitious, frowning, and chilling, the sight is one to repay the philanthropist or the student of manners for a long journey to the North. Moreover, if he number Scotchmen among his friends, on that day he knows exactly where to look for them, and is sure to have a most cordial welcome from men in the fullest flush of health and spirits.

CHAPTER XXIII

The Attractions of Winter Weather

THERE is a luxury, no doubt, in life in the tropics; and when we are shivering in our English damp and fogs, the islands of the South with their balm-scented breezes will flit before us in visions of the earthly Paradise. We are alive to the charms of cloudless skies; of the checkered shadows under flowery groves in landscapes lit up by floods of sunshine; of myriads of brilliant stars reflected in sleeping seas landlocked within reefs of coral. We can sympathise with the feelings of the tempest-tossed adventurers who, after beating in the teeth of Atlantic gales into the Unknown, exchanged the decks of their straining caravels for a time of blissful repose in the islands of "the Indies"; as we can imagine those seductive memories of the Cytheræan Otaheite that incited the mariners of the Bounty to their memorable deed of violence. But the tropical Edens have their shady sides for men who have been bred in more bracing latitudes. It is all very well for the sensuous aborigines to live in each glowing hour and take little heed of the morrow; to gather their fruits from the boughs within reach of their hands; to dispense with clothing in disregard of decorum; to swing their hammocks of fibre anywhere out of the sun, and dream away the days and the feverish nights. The life must pall sooner or later on men with whom energy is inborn; the heat is enervating, and saps the strength, which is the source of health, good spirits and self-satisfaction; and the lotus-eating immigrants, after a time, might be driven to seek refuge from weariness in suicide.

British folks have a happy knack of adaptability, and can acquit themselves with credit under most conditions. They made the fortune of our fervid West Indian colonies with their own before the abolition of the slave trade and of the sugar duties. They have conquered an empire in Asia and kept it, in spite of the relaxing atmosphere of the plains of Hindostan, where they must swelter through their duties in baking cantonments or stifling courts of justice, and struggle for a troubled sleep under punkahs. They have settled Queenslands, and Georgias, and Guianas, with many a province more or less swampy and sultry; they live, as they make up their minds occasionally to droop and die among mud-banks, mangroves, and malaria, at the mouths of rivers on the Gold and Grain coasts. They take cheerfully by battalions and batteries to scorching rocks, at such stations as Gibraltar, Malta, and Aden, which might be marked on an ascending atmospheric scale as hot, hotter, hottest. Nevertheless, and naturally, they will always show to more advantage in the least genial of latitudes. We have nothing more thrilling in the national annals—though foreigners, by the way, have been running us hard of late years, as the Dutch and the Scandinavians did in former centuries—than our stories of arctic adventure. We see the hardy navigator—an amphibious cross between the bull-dog and the sword-fish, with the tenacity of the one and the dash of the other—standing out into the polar fogs and ice-floes in the bark that was but a cockle-shell in point of tonnage. The timbers might be seasoned oak, and the rude fastenings of well-hammered iron, yet a casual nip of the ice must crack its sides like a walnut-shell. We see the rough skipper and his crew clinging to the tiller and the frozen shrouds, in seas that sweep the deck from stem to stern, and weather that would tear any canvas into ribbons. In the safe little sea-boat, that is slow at the best under sail, they have to bide their time and possess their souls in patience as they lie becalmed under the lee of the ice-cliffs, or dodge the irresistible set of the ice-packs. There was scarcely room to "swing a cat" in the tiny cabin that just served as a refuge. Over-tasked and short-handed as they were, they had often to turn in "all standing," ready to answer the boatswain's call at a moment's notice; and they expected the inevitable arrival of the scurvy on salt junk, weevily ship-biscuit and new rum. Preserved meats and lime-juice were as yet undreamt of; and their medicine and luxury was the quid of tobacco, at once the best of sedatives and stimulants. It is a long stride from those forlorn-hopes of adventure to the well-found and strongly-manned expeditions we have lately been sending out to the Pole. But even with all the appliances that science and experience can suggest or liberality supply, the lives of arctic explorers must be trying at the best; and the soundest constitutions are strained if not shattered. Yet the only difficulty in finding the crews is the picking and choosing in the crush of volunteers; and cheerfulness under perfect discipline does its best to command success, though the sole distractions out of doors through the long dark winter, are constitutionals along the snow-paths kept clear to the "observatory," or sledging-parties carried out with heroic resolution.

For when you change passive endurance into a grapple with difficulties, the spirit will rise irrepressibly to meet them. We have travellers wrapped in the casings of furs and woollens they dare not cast, facing the frozen blasts on the steppes of Tartary, or scrambling up the highest passes in our hemisphere—those gutter-pipes which drain the "Roof of the World."

We can recall a dozen stories of winter-travelling adventures, where we may be sure that the pleasures predominated over the pains, though the adventurers, who were gently born and bred, must have suffered as intensely as they endured doggedly. Such as Lord Milton and Dr. Cheadle hewing their way, with "Mr. and Mrs. Assineboine," through the precipitous forests on the banks of the Fraser River; Major Butler likewise setting his face to the westward across "The Great Lone Land"; Mr. Andrew Wilson carried as an invalid on a litter, along slate-cornices on precipices under the hanging snow-masses in the Himalayan "Abode of Snow"; or Major Burnaby, on his ride to Khiva in the cold that was almost too trying for his Cossack guides. What go far towards nerving the men of the North to the enjoyment of their winters, or of arctic weather, are the pleasures of hope and of contrast. Even the *employés* of the Hudson Bay Company have the prospect of basking through their brief summer day; and the hardiest of us would scarcely care to cast in our lot for life with the Esquimaux. Shaw and Forsyth, and the travellers who have crossed the Hindu Kush, looked forward to a welcome in the Vale of Kashmir, or in the rich vegetation that encircles Kashgar, sacred to the admirers of the Arabian Nights; while Burnaby, when he had left the steppes behind him, drew bridle among the gardens and pomegranate-groves of the Khivan canals. Tourists in Europe have experienced delights of the kind when, after the damp and gloom of a raw Roman winter, they have taken their first spring rides in the Campagna, when it was bursting almost before their eyes into one vivid blush of violets; or when, after a long day and night passed in the old-fashioned *diligence* in the frozen mud on the heights of the Morena, they have rubbed their eyes, with the break of dawn, among the fountains and orange-trees of sunny Cordova. A balmy breath of spring in winter is soothingly refreshing as an oasis in the desert. But comparatively very little heat goes a long way with most Englishmen; and in a really tropical climate they generally feel at their worst. Even an unusually warm summer in England makes the life of too many of our fellow-creatures a melancholy spectacle, till they begin to pick up again with the shortening days.

Very different it is in the beginnings of "our old-fashioned English winter" with men who have wealth, health, and strength in moderation! We believe it is the lightness of feeling, following on the first steady fall of the temperature below the freezing-point, that explains those effusive rhapsodies on "seasonable" jollity which characterise our popular Christmas literature. We are really in excellent spirits, and perhaps the bracing air has gone to our heads. We see everything not precisely in *couleur de rose*, but in the dazzling radiancy of sparkling frost, and are in the humour to listen to absurdities and sentimentalities as sound enough sense to be fitting to the season of the year. But it is the modern school of Christmas writers who are become sickly, stilted, and sentimental; and for that Dickens is chiefly responsible. He began so admirably in a flow of natural humour and pathos, that he was encouraged to parody himself, and so the picturesqueness of "Pickwick" and the city idyl of the "Christmas Carol" came down to the level of the latest of his Christmas annuals. But the early Christmas pictures by masters of genius must touch sympathetic chords in every bosom, and make misery itself often feel sadly mirthful in memory of the frolics of happier times. Without going further back in our literature, take Scott's famous introduction to the sixth canto of " Marmion "—

> "Heap on more wood!—the wind is chill;
> But let it whistle as it will,
> We'll keep our Christmas merry still."

The ring of the metre sounds like the church bells to a devotee, or the dinner-gong to a hungry man. What a striking picture of the kindly joviality that levels ranks and sets a truce to cares! The baron's hall, where the flames from the great log-fire that went roaring and crackling up the vast chimney, flashed their light on merry faces and burnished flagons. The stately baron in the chimney-corner, unbending for once ; the "heir with roses in his shoes," flirting with village maiden with redder roses in her cheeks; the boar's head, bedecked with bays and rosemaries, grinning on the festal board among sirloins and huge bickers of plum-porridge, and wassail-bowls bobbing with the roasted crabs ; the tales of the hunting-field by flood and fell ; the stories of venerable, time-honoured superstitions that made the hearers shudder even in that merry crowd ; the mumming, the singing, the laughing, and the dancing, while the winds that howled and whistled through the trees and the loopholes in the battlements, drove the smoke-wreaths back again down the chimney, and scattered the sparks from the blazing roots. Little recked kinsmen, tenants, and cottagers, of trifling inconveniences like these, in those Christmas gambols that

> " Could cheer
> The poor man's heart through half the year."

Some centuries later, and in " Bracebridge Hall," we see how our old English fashion of keeping Christmas impressed a sympathetic American. The New Englanders, as Mrs. Beecher Stowe shows in her " Poganuc People," have a pretty notion of perpetuating those traditions that were carried over the Atlantic in the *Mayflower*, although the early Pilgrim Fathers were Puritans. But in a new country, with the go-ahead energy that has grubbed the forest and split the trees into shingles ; with its practically-minded men and its hard utilitarianism, its brand-new buildings and its bald-faced meeting-houses, the associations must be lacking that give the season its solemnity. There are no old squires and old Masters Simon ; no old blue-coated serving-men bred under the roof-tree of the hall ; no old polished mahogany dining-tables, or old family portraits whose burnished frames are brightened up for the occasion with mistletoe and holly-berries ; no cellars of rare old wines and ales that flow at the festal Christmas-tide like water ; above all, no quaint old Norman Church, where the pews of oak and the mediæval monuments have been as yet undesecrated by the æsthetic restorer. Then Dickens popularised the Bracebridge Halls—we will not say that he vulgarised them—in his delightful sketches of the Manor Farm.

For though we fancy "the fine old host" dropped his *h's*, though he welcomed that very rough diamond the inimitable Bob Sawyer as a familiar friend, and extended his hospitalities to a seedy strolling actor like Jingle—nevertheless the Manor Farm must live in the memories of Englishmen and their descendants *in sæcula sæculorum*. We cordially echo the hearty sentiment of Mr. Weller: "Your master's a wery pretty notion of keepin' everything up, my dear. I never see such a sensible man as he is, or such a reg'lar gen'l'm'n"; as we assent to the grateful utterance of Mr. Pickwick, when sitting down "by the huge fire of logs, to a substantial supper and a mighty bowl of wassail"—"this is indeed comfort."

But the whole of the winter sketches, of which that supper on Christmas Eve is but one in a series, are as delightful as they are characteristic of manners that are departing. The drive along the frost-bound roads on the outside of the Muggleton mail, after the codfish and the barrels of oysters had been forced into the gaping fore-boot; the change of horses at the inn in the market-town—it was only a slow coach, we must remember—when Mr. Pickwick and Mr. Tupman came so near being left behind, when they had run up the yard to refresh themselves at the tap; the walk along the frozen lanes to the farm; the meeting with the house-party, the reception, the supper, the rubbers, and the hot elder-wine to follow; the wedding next day, and the breakfast that sent the poor relations to bed. Of course there is a dash of Christmas romance in the pretty fancy that elderly gentlemen fresh from town could hold out through the rustic hospitality of the farm, and rise each successive morning all the brisker and the brighter for it. We should surmise that Mr. Pickwick must have been troubled by nightmares after those late and heavy suppers ; while Mr. Tupman was the very subject for flying twinges of the gout. But there can be no question that, for keeping dyspepsia at bay, there is nothing like country life and jovial company at a time when you feel bound to feast and make merry; and there are charmingly natural touches in that scene on the ice which preceded Mr. Pickwick's immersion in the pond. It is a rough English translation of the hearty communion of a Scottish curling-match. Old men become boys again in the biting air, and take to frolicking like carthorses turned out in a meadow. "Ceremony doffs her pride" at the Manor Farm as in the baronial hall; and there are old Wardle and the fat boy, Mr. Pickwick and his faithful Sam, Messrs. Snodgrass, Sawyer, Winkle, &c., all "keepin' the pot a-bilin'," and following each other along the slide as if their very lives depended on it.

Such bright winter pictures have, of course, their sombre side. You tumble out of bed to see the country covered with a dazzling mantle. Every twig and slender spray is enveloped in icy tracery. There are festoons of icicles depending from the window-sashes, and the panes are interlaced with a delicate fretwork that may shame those masterpieces of Moorish art that

ATTRACTIONS OF WINTER WEATHER 301

are still the marvels of the connoisseur. Sparkling in the cold sunshine, it all looks cheerful enough as you contemplate it from a comfortably warmed room, unless, indeed, your soul be set upon hunting, and your horses are fretting in their stalls. But even in the country your pleasures may be dashed by reminders of the existence of suffering. There goes a thinly-clad urchin under the windows, shrugging his shoulders together, and blowing upon his frost-nipped fingers. The birds are gathered into ragged balls on the boughs; the blackbirds and starlings are hopping gingerly about on the lawn, like so many jackdaws of Rheims, blighted under the ban of the church; the very tomtits seem limp and depressed; while the robins, pressed by the cravings of appetite, come almost tapping at the windows as they ask for their crumbs. After all, it may be hoped that the sufferings of those country creatures are nothing worse than may be endured and soon forgotten. These birds will be fed from the breakfast-room windows, and there are still hips and haws in the hedgerows for their fellows. The boy has had a morning meal before turning out of his cottage, and there are worse maladies in the world than chilblains, while exercise will set youthful blood in circulation. But your thoughts travel away to the poor in the great towns, who must rise to fireless hearths and shiver on short commons. After all, such sufferings, like the poor themselves, will be always with us, and in winter time the souls of the well-conditioned must be exceptionally open to melting charity. If you cannot help being bright and cheery yourself, you feel the more bound to consider your less fortunate fellow-mortals. Christopher North put it very neatly and truly in one of the "Noctes" for this month of December. He had been eulogising winter, *more suo*, over a blazing fire before the well-spread board in the blue parlour at Ambrose's; and the Shepherd had been chiming in with the praises of cold and curling—beef and greens. Tickler, sitting in moody reserve, strikes a dissonant note. "This outrageous merriment grates my spirits. 'Twill be a severe winter, and I think of the poor." North answers, "Are not wages good and work plenty, and is not charity a British virtue?" Charity is still a British virtue; while institutions that were then unthought of have been founded, and the organisation of dispassionate relief has been indefinitely extended. We remember, for our comfort too, as a fact incontestably established by statistics, that cold is far less destructive than damp to life and consequently to health; and in the fitful climates of an English winter, we can have but the choice between the one and the other. So let our readers be free-handed with their cheque-books and their purses, and they may give themselves over with easy minds to the joys and the buoyancy inspired by the season.

Even in the metropolis, setting the chances of accidents aside, a hard winter may not be altogether unexciting. There is always something impressive in gatherings in a great city under circumstances that are at once picturesque and unfamiliar. Once we came very near to witnessing a repetition of those grand historical *fêtes* of the Ice-king, when fairs were held on the frozen Thames, and oxen roasted whole were washed down from flowing hogsheads. Had it not been for the works of the Thames Embankment, the brackish tide might have been bound in iron fetters. We missed that stirring spectacle by a hair's-breadth; but before now we have seen skating on the Serpentine by torch-light, when a London feast of lanterns seemed in course of celebration between Albert Gate and Kensington Gardens. The wolves and hyænas were disporting themselves with the lambs—or, in other words, the hordes of roughs from the east were mingling amicably with shop-lads and decent artisans and gay young gentlemen from the clubs of the west. The police mustered strong in case of need, but what were the scattered members of the blue-coated force among so many? There were noise and horse-play, and boisterous merriment; and we do not say that pockets were not lightened here and there, or some differences settled by hitting from the shoulder. But on the whole it was a gay and a good-humoured mob; and even the ladies who ventured out upon the side-walks could admire the humours of the night without much risk of insult. A whole school of Rembrandts and Schalkens would have found endless subjects for their brushes. The bands of skaters skimming along in open order, and the hockey-players, swaying blazing torches overhead, leaving the splashes of flaming resin in waving beauty-lines behind them, till the air and ice seemed to be studded with flights of Brobdingnagian fire-flies; the illuminated circles and the fiery crescents, where a space had been cleared for the graceful evolutions of amateurs surrounded by admiring spectators; the girdling rings of carriage-lamps along the drives; the rows of chairs and tables, with their constellations of candles, where skates were being strapped on or stripped off; the glowing stoves of the hot-chestnut sellers and baked-potato men; the horn lanterns on the roving wheelbarrows, with oranges and apples and lighter refreshments; the cracking of vesuvians and kindling of pipes; the reddening of cigar-tips circulating in their myriads; the reflection of the flickering volumes of light cast faintly and fitfully in the floating fogs—all made up a strange carnival of fire, to the crash of many kinds of Cockney music, from brass bands and barrel-organs to accordions and concertinas.

CHAPTER XXIV

Winter in the North

IT is but a night ticket taken at King's Cross or Euston Square, and we shift the scene to the north of the Border. You roll out of the berth in the "Pullman," or shake yourself clear of your wrappings to contemplate the December morning breaking on the sea or the landward wastes. Sea blends with sky and vapour with dull grey fallow, till you can hardly tell where one begins or the other ends. But there are bright streaks in the reddening horizon to the west, which slowly break into golden bars, and then the disc of the ruddy orb of light rises in all the promise of his frigid glories. It is in the assurance of a life-giving winter day that you hear the hoar-frost crackle under your chilly feet on the railway platform. The double dog-cart is in waiting with the roughed horses : strip their warm clothing, and give them their heads. They spring forward, rattling the pole-chains, breathing smoke if not flame from their nostrils like the swifter coursers of the sun overhead ; and far and near may be heard the echo of their hoofs as they rattle, regardless of their back sinews, along the iron roads. For the black frost has laid a veto on field-labour, and most of mankind who work out of doors must take a holiday perforce. The ploughshare is frozen fast in the crisp furrow; the ditcher might splinter the point of his pickaxe before doing another yard of his drain; the farm pond must be broken to let the animals drink; and as the partridges have gathered to the shelter of the rick-yards, so the snipes and every species of wild-fowl have taken to the shrunken rills of slow trickling water.

It is an involuntary holiday; but is the parish to stand idle on that account, or draw chairs and stools into the ingle-nook to gossip and doze and keep the fireplace warm? Not a bit of it! It is not every day that the canny Scotchman has the chance of giving himself over to enjoyment with a clear conscience. Dreepdaily has challenged Bodencleuch to a curling-match; and already the players, with a long admiring tail, are striding forward over hill and moor, from all the airts, to the trysting-place. The laird, hospitable as he is, somewhat hurries you, nevertheless, over a hearty Scotch breakfast; for he is to act skip or headman himself for his players of Bodencleuch, while the stalwart schoolmaster from over the march discharges a similar office for the men of Dreepdaily. A sharp walk through the policies and past the kirk takes you to the curling-pond. It is a merry scene, set in a frame of silver, that you look down upon from the angle of the path that leads over the brae from the kirk-stile. The pond lies in a hollow, at the foot of a

WINTER IN THE NORTH

broomy knowe, that in the fresh fragrance of the spring is covered with yellow blossoms. Now all nature is as deathlike as well may be. Everything below and around is clothed with a chilly winding-sheet, stretching under the steel-blue glitter of an almost cloudless sky. But long before, you had heard the clamour of voices sounding deep and shrill in the rarified atmosphere, and now you look down on such a gathering of rural worthies as Burns might have sung or Wilkie painted. A burst of welcome greets the laird and his friends, followed by a respectful though a momentary hush. Place for the kirk, and there is the parish minister, and likewise his reverend brother of the Free persuasion; and there is the stout schoolmaster of Dreepdaily, famed as a curler far and near, who dwarfs his "shilpit" but energetic compeer of Bodencleuch. The minister's man, who is likewise precentor, will soon have an opportunity of showing that his sonorous bass is good for other things than pitching psalm-tunes. There are farmers who cultivate and graze their five hundred acres, and crofters who club with a neighbour to hitch up a single "pair of horse." There are keepers from the hill, and woodmen from the plantations; cottagers who get their living among the dikes and the ditches; "mason lads" who have been frozen out of their work; the tailor who has slipped from his board, the shoemaker who has cast his apron behind him, and the smith who has been lured away from his forge, though they might all have been following their indoor avocations. There are poachers and village scant-o'-graces, somewhat shamefaced, and in the meantime on their best behaviour, but feeling that the occasion brings them temporary absolution; and herd-boys and "hafflin' callants," and *id genus omne*. Seldom elsewhere will you see such a gathering of folks of many ages and ranks and creeds and callings, meeting for once on a footing of the most fraternal equality, and indulging in the fullest liberty of joviality, without forgetting good manners and mutual regard.

From curling to cock-shooting, in the alliterative point of view, is a natural transition. While the curling-ponds in the east and south have been bearing for many days, the fresh water in the milder climate of the west coast is still rippling to each gentle breeze. But while the curling sports are still in full swing, a letter reaches you from Argyllshire. The frost has come at last, and in earnest, and the cocks will be following it in flights. Already their harbingers are scattering about in many a hanging copse and many a corrie on the heather braes. And one fine morning a select party of friends, gaitered and shooting-booted, is sitting down to an early repast in a lonely shooting-lodge on the shores of Loch Fyne. A lonely lodge we say; and indeed the sole drawback to the spot is the difficulty of finding beaters in that romantic wilderness. However, the old keeper has done his best, and has mustered, by hook or crook, half a dozen of ill-matched mortals, from a leggy, shock-headed Celt, who has turned out in the scantiest of tattered kilts, to a short-set boy who, in an ordinary way, acts aide-de-camp to any poacher, or shepherd, or gillie. A grander beat than ours, in point of picturesqueness, it would be difficult to find ; and it is as dear to the cocks as to lovers of nature. The ground falls in a succession of long tumbling slopes from the ridge of heather-covered hills to the shores of the loch. From each eminence the eye naturally travels down the estuary as it winds away among the mountains, round promontory, creek, and bay. Most beautiful of all, perhaps, is the immediate foreground. What tempts the woodcock are the multiplicity of springs, and the variety of streams that come down an endless succession of parallel ravines, with rocky banks that are overgrown with wood in many spots. Here the water is leaping down staircases of stone, under mossy cornices fringed with icicles. Elsewhere you can barely hear it murmur as it is lost to sight under the drooping firs and the birchen boughs. And everywhere in those tiny valleys are gushing land-springs, which convert the turf around them into a tiny morass, where the mud will be softened for the "long-bills" in the mid-day sunshine. Between these Scottish nullahs are patches of Highland jungle—the dwarf oak, and the birch, and the spruce and silver-fir, interspersed with old and gnarled hollies, and interwoven with matted brambles ; while the open glades in the heather are dotted over with outstanding trees like the Alpine *wetter tannen*, and with beds of withered bracken, in all the winter hues of their reds and yellows.

Even had our force been drilled and trained to work together, it would be no easy matter to handle it cleverly. The very retrievers at heel sometimes "come a cropper" in scrambling down the sides of ravines; and should a cock be flushed while you are setting your face to the "stey brae," the bird is sure to go away unscathed. Moreover, though there is no snow to speak of, each stone and root is varnished over with its coating of treacherous ice, that gives hold neither to foot nor hand. But there seems to be a providence that saves sportsmen from sprained ankles, and each fall is only a subject for merriment, though the occasional plunge over mid-thigh in a "moss-pit" is a more serious matter. But soon the shooting begins, and the bag mounts; the roe have been bled and hung to trees to be retrieved again; and in spite of immersions, scratches, and falls, beaters and guns are in the highest spirits. Brief space is given for lunch, since days are short and distances are considerable. And we have yet to beat out the famous oak-coppice that hangs upon the side of an almost precipitous valley. How the beaters are to work their way along, where even monkeys with prehensile tails might be puzzled, is for their consideration. They scramble in somehow at the one end in faith, and we trust that they will struggle out at the other. Close beating is a sheer impossibility: but it is hoped that the game, being seldom disturbed, may rise or go forward in place of running back. It is almost worth coming all the way to Loch Fyne to have a single shot at an old blackcock

WINTER IN THE NORTH 311

in these circumstances. Up he rises from among the rocks on powerful wing, his jetty plumage glistening in the sunbeams, skimming the feathering firs with the sweeping pinions that propel him like a rocket shot from a mortar. Clean missed in a flurry by the first gun—cleverly killed by the second; and borne ahead for fifty yards or so by his acquired velocity, you hear him crashing through the branches in the depths, and can mark his course by the showers of ice-dust.

In the dark inclement days of the winter, the moors and forests are left very much to their native denizens. Even the keepers and gillies, when not under surveillance, are inclined to fight shy of the upper hills; and the shepherds, who have to face much fearful weather, strive to keep their flocks in the more sheltered valleys. For there is something appalling in a Highland snow-storm, when the day is darkened with feathering snow-flakes and the air laden with icy drift; when the winds howl down the passes and shriek in the wildest fury as they are caught in the glens and the corries; and when snow-slips and small avalanches are happening everywhere, engulfing each living thing that comes across the path of their descents. Then fox and wild cat take refuge in their earths in the recesses of the cairns, howling and moaning with cold and hunger; and the winged game cower together in the lee of the braes, or scrape for a precarious subsistence on the more exposed banks that have been laid bare by the storm. When the snowfall is suspended and the "lift has cleared," the shepherd must go abroad in fear and trembling. Too many of the fleecy flock so dear to his memory are lost to sight, buried deep under the heaps of gathering snow-wreaths; and in many a quiet nook and corner of the winding stream the backwater will be choked with submerged corpses.

Death is never far from the man who is out in a Highland snowstorm, and it is a risk that the sportsman will not lightly encounter. But *en revanche* there are often, in the dead season of the year, long spells of settled and most exhilarating weather, when the grouse sit wonderfully in the " black frosts," and a vigorous walker may fill a bag satisfactorily. Then, seen in the bright sunlight, the clear summits of the highest hills may exercise an irresistible fascination on him, and he decides for a bold dash at the ptarmigan. If he go by the barometer and sage advice, he may make the expedition tolerably safely. The work will be hard, of course, but scarcely so severe as one might fancy. For by judicious strategy the ascent may be made by the slopes where the snow-sprinkling is comparatively thin, and along ravines whose gravelly and slaty sides offer a comparatively sure footing. And having once surmounted the lower zone of perpetual snow, the sportsman will find himself " travelling," as the Scotch say, on natural causeways that have been swept by the winds, and which are roughly paved with what looks like the *débris* of a stone quarry. Nor should it be so much the sport you look to on those occasions, as the splendour of the sky effects, the grandeur of the scenery, and the romantic

DEAD PTARMIGAN. *By* A. COOPER, R.A.

CATALOGUE OF
MEMOIRS

WINTER IN THE NORTH

excitement of the whole undertaking. Down in the valleys are morning mists and darkness. The bottom of that deep chasm you have left to the right, and where you heard the harsh voice of the raven, is filled with billowy volumes of vapour; but already, though the sun will be invisible to you for half an hour to come, the tops of the " Rocky Mountains " for which you are bound are glowing in all the hues of the rainbow. When the sun does burst into sight, the dazzling radiance of the landscape becomes almost painful, and it is a relief to rest the aching eyes on the shadows thrown here and there by some boldly projecting cliff. There are animated objects enough of interest as you press forward, though there is no time to loiter. The grouse cocks rise wild with their cheery crow. Now and again, as you climb by the banks of the stream, you cross the tracks of the night-hunting otter or the wild cat, or almost surprise those little parties of ducks that have been feeding at their ease in some sequestered pool, where the steepness of the fall has kept the hill burn in motion. As the snow gets thinner, and you leave the region of heather for the stones, the tracks of the mountain-hares are more frequent, and soon they are starting before you each twenty yards, sitting up, kangaroo-like, in their quaint curiosity, and inspecting you with complacent interest over their shoulders. Considering the impossibility of carrying them away, knocking them over would be wanton bloodshed.. You would gladly have bestowed a barrel on that magnificent hill-fox, with the sinewy body and the feathering brush, who, though he supplies his larder as a rule with the hares, must have taken toll many a time from the firstlings of the flock, judging by his size and grand condition. But before you have time to snatch the gun from the gillie who has relieved you of it, he has vanished round the corner of the nearest ridge, to reappear by-and-by on a more distant slope, going pleasantly within himself at a comfortable canter.

The actual ptarmigan-shooting in itself is, it must be confessed, somewhat tame. Although there is little difficulty in finding the birds at first, since they are pretty sure to get up shy and wild, yet they will often return nearly to the spot from whence they were sprung, and wait your second approach comparatively calmly. And as they have a trick of dropping sharply behind the rocks where they rise, you need not scruple to shoot them sitting. But there is something grandly exciting in the sport all the same, as you go scrambling among the rocks and fallen boulders; taking jumps that in cooler blood you would eschew; setting the serious chances of fractured limbs at defiance; and keeping on your legs in shooting attitude as best you can, while swaying your breech-loader in the air by way of a balancing-pole. The sense of taking one's diversion aloft in the blue empyrean, far above the normal regions of a Highland cloudland, is in itself exhilarating enough; and the air you inhale is light as laughing-gas, without being so rarefied as to try the lungs. Then the white ptarmigan, flushed from their perch on the cliffs, go circling beneath your feet round splintered pinnacles and buttresses, eddying over the abyss in the drift of the vapours, like a flight of storm-pigeons. Plunging the eye far down into the profound, there is nothing but those circling specks for it to rest upon, between the slab on which your shooting-boots are slipping and the slopes of heather some couple of thousand feet below. As for the glories of the prospect, you may turn your face as you will. All around stretches a seemingly limitless extent of trackless moor, forest, and sheep-farm, where hill and valley, till they confound themselves in the snowy distance, are veined by the black blotches or silvery lines that mark the lakes or the rivers and burns.

CHAPTER XXV

Winter Ferreting

IT is a natural descent from the clouds, or where the clouds ought to be, to the Lowland coverts. We are in the great preserves, where hares in herds and troops of home-bred pheasants invite the attention of banded poachers, and provoke heartburnings in parishes that ought to be peaceful. Should big *battues* rank among winter pleasures? Hardly, in the sense in which we are writing this article; and poetically as picturesquely, there is a terrible bathos in the droop from days among the ptarmigan in the upper air, to the massacre of pheasants running tame between your boots. Besides, anybody but an enthusiast in slaughter must be *ennuyé* by standing up to the ankles in the half-frozen mud of the rides, or blowing upon numbed fingers at some draughty corner, though he may comfort himself with the assurance that it will soon be a "hot" one. Far more to our mind is the rough-and-ready fun to be found in ferreting in a keen frost. The little party are all on the *qui vive*—from the guns and the keepers with spades and ferret-boxes, to the cock-eared terriers who are admitted to participate

WINTER FERRETING

in the sport, and the more sober-minded retrievers who form the reserve. Hardly a breath of air is stirring : you may almost hear the flutter to the earth of a withered leaf, and so everything is in your favour. And there is something in such commonplace or vulgar amusements as rabbiting and rat-hunting that recommends itself to the vagrant instincts of humanity. For ourselves, we have ferreted in all manner of circumstances, from wheat-stacks and tottering barns upwards. In the mounds under the gnarled boughs of the oaks and thorns in a venerable park, where the rabbits burrowed amicably in the hollow stems among the jackdaws. We have shot on the face of a brae sloping to a precipice dipping sheer into a lake, where each rabbit, as he was rolled over, crumpled into a ball, and pitching over the brink was picked up by a boatman in waiting ; in the dikes dividing fields in the northern Scotch counties, where the piles of loose granite that had been cleared off the land were honeycombed by labyrinths of galleries—where ferrets had to be sent in by the half-dozen to cut the lines of communication, and whence the inmates would scuttle at intervals like the fragments of a bursting shell. And of course we have ferreted in all weathers. But to our fancy, as we said, the pleasantest form of the sport is in the perfect stillness and purity of the clear winter day, in the banks and hedgerows of a richly wooded Lowland country. It is a very fair match, on the whole, between the guns and the rabbits. Scene— for example—under the skeleton canopy of a spreading oak, the leafless twigs forming a lacework against the sky, with a straggling hedge in front and a bramble-grown ditch beyond. The burrow dates from days immemorial; some of the holes have been enlarged by the colony of badgers that take up their quarters there from time to time; and the outlets are so many, and in such unlikely spots, that any attempt at a systematic blockade is impracticable. *Dramatis personæ:* a couple of guns standing back to back under the oak; two others, similarly posted in the field beyond the ditch; three keepers bending in varied attitudes over the burrow, previous to rushing towards the stem of the oak to bestow themselves out of the way; three ferrets who have disappeared in the bowels of the earth; a couple of veteran terriers, their heads twisted on one side, almost to the dislocation of their necks, and each nerve in their bodies quivering with excitement; with as many retrievers that are scarcely less interested, though they do their best to keep up some dignity of deportment. So far as the mere ferreting goes, the terriers, Spice and Ginger, had better have been left at home, since they are more likely to tumble into the way than not. But they are useful in hunting out a ditch or a hedge-bottom; and a miss here and there is of little consequence. *Conticuere omnes; intentique ora tenebant.* The tails of the ferrets have been deliberately dragged out of sight; and all is silence in the meantime.

But as we feel, it is the ominous silence that heralds earthquakes and convulsions of nature. There is a faint

WINTER FERRETING

scraping and a shuffle beneath our feet; the shuffling is succeeded by a rushing to and fro; the scraping grows into a portentous rumbling, as if a working party of gnomes, with picks and wheelbarrows, were mining the foundation of the ancestral oak. The grumbling echoes of that subterraneous chase are now here and now there. If the distracted terriers were to follow their bent, they would be dancing over the surface of the ground like a couple of globules of quicksilver. Even the sportsmen, although they have time to think, or because they have time, are conscious of something of the flutter that thrills on the nerves when a covey of black-game is whirring up all around one. The rabbits have realised there is danger above, and are loth to be forced by any amount of hunting. You can conceive the sudden agitation in those peaceful tenements below, with the stealthy enemies, all teeth, claw, and muscle, following up the remorseless chase with slow, malignant ferocity. Now some stout old buck must be standing fiercely at bay, his bristling back set to the end of a burrow, and his fore-paws hammering viciously at his assailant. You can follow the shifting fortunes of the single combat, for there seems to be but a sod between you and the lists. Next there is a rush of desperation; he has taken a flying leap over the ferret, and is gone by. Then a second fugitive shows his head above ground only to jerk it back again; while a third bounces out of one hole, like a Jack-in-the box, to take a flying leap down another. But at last the general *sauve qui peut* begins. There a rabbit makes a rush for the ditch, and gains the covered-way of matted weeds and thorn, closely followed up by the yelping terriers, to be hustled out again a little lower down ; while a companion dares a straight dash across the open, to be cleverly stopped in due course. The winding-sheet of snow is rent and torn as rabbits tear their way out of hidden issues, to land themselves in the middle of scattering charges ; there is a quick rolling fire, with sharp clicking of the barrel-hinges as the smoking breech-loaders close on the cartridges ; a shower of icy particles from the bushes, falling on the curly coats of the retrievers ; a scattering of floating flick, a cutting of twigs by the driving shot, a crimsoning of the spotless surface. Then the shooting dies away and ceases, as the bolting draws to an end. The terriers are come back from their mad bursts of excitement, with panting tongues and heaving sides : the keepers gather up the slain which the retrievers had already been collecting for them ; and finally, the ferrets reappear one by one, blinking their fiery eyes, and licking their encarmined jowls, to be caught up by the napes of their necks and deposited snugly in the boxes. The exciting melodrama is at an end, so far as that burrow is concerned, when we move on to another, where the scenery has changed with the circumstances. In the hurry and crush of incidents ; in the strained expectation, passing through quick sensations to the sanguinary *dénouement*, keeping all the faculties on the alert, and the blood in swift circulation, there is no time to think of being chilly. And then, when you feel you have had enough of it when the

WINTER FERRETING

lights on the landscape begin to fade as the sun sinks down in the cloud-bank to the westward ; when the ferrets, gorging themselves on the game they have grappled, begin to hang in the holes in spite of powder-flashes, till the keepers have to exercise their shoulders in digging among the stones and roots—you have only to lay down the gun and walk briskly home to the library. If we desire to enjoy luxurious converse with a favourite author, who will bear dozing over, since we half know him by heart, we find nothing more delightful than that time before dinner, when, after some hours of moderate exertion and exposure, we mingle listless reading with languid reverie, and intersperse both with an occasional nap.

CHAPTER XXVI

Winter Fowling

VERY different from the dawdling over rabbiting is wild-fowl shooting. The one may be enjoyed in moderation as a distraction ; as an agreeable digestive after a comfortable breakfast ; as a whet for indolent literary by-play and for dinner, after the fashion of the *avant-table* in Russia or Scandinavia, where spirits and piquant trifles are served up as appetisers. Wild-fowl shooting is a serious business, and we do not know whether, any more than the battue, it ought to be included among winter pleasures. For our own part, we should be inclined to say no ; but it is certain that it becomes a passion with those who devote themselves to it. The successful wild-fowler needs something of the qualities that set up a Hercules going forth upon his labours. In the first place, he must have enthusiasm bordering upon an abiding frenzy. He must have no ordinary endurance, with a constitution of iron ; he must have keen eyes and steady nerves ; he must have coolness and presence of mind to temper his eagerness ; and, before all things of course, he should

WINTER FOWLING

be a deadly shot. In the pursuit of ordinary game the "hit and miss" man may enjoy himself as much as his "crack" companion. But it is heart-breaking in wild-fowling, after having intrigued, manœuvred, and toiled for a single family shot, to see the birds fly away without a feather of their plumage being ruffled. The practical wild-fowler should be as clever with his gun as the juggler who goes through his feats on the slack-rope. Ashore, he must shoot when he has been shivering in spite of his bodily powers; when his feet have been frozen to his stockings, and his stockings congealed in his boots; when he is slipping about in treacherous mud, in a pair of "mud-shoes," or boards that are attached to his boots like sandals; or when he has sunk over the knee in shifting sands, or has been taken aback by a chance while fording a sea-creek. Ten to one, the flight he fires at may come travelling down wind at something from twenty to forty knots an hour. And what a weapon he has to carry! We believe that the most accomplished modern experts declare by preference for a five-bore; and none but those who have been initiated can realise what it is to carry so ponderous a piece of metal through a long day's heavy walking in the face of blustering weather. Even the most accustomed shoulder may ache, and the bare recoil must often be serious. And if the fowler has to contend with such difficulties ashore, what must it be afloat? In loch-shooting, of course, if you can, you will choose a calm day, and so your difficulties are lightened in place of being aggravated. But off the coast, though scarcely a zephyr may be stirring, there may, nevertheless, be a heavy ground-swell. And then you must take aim from a dancing platform, and make your flying practice by knack or instinct. Imagine a man shooting grouse on a drive as he balanced himself on the oscillations of a see-saw, and you have a moderate notion of the chances of sea-fowling under circumstances that are fairly favourable.

Then for the requisites in point of constitutional hardihood. Mild weather saddens the fowler's heart, and his spirits go up with the fall of the thermometer. It is indispensable that he should dress himself warmly, yet, for his own sake, he must not make his wrappings too cumbersome. He will have to crawl or worm himself along when making his stalk, and yet he may have to lie *perdu* for minutes or half-hours, more or less, without moving a muscle. Even in a boat he must not so over-hamper himself with top gear as to prevent the heavy gun coming easily to his shoulder; and yet a bitter wind blowing off the sea or the salt marshes may be searching his marrow through pea-jacket and jersey. Keeping the feet dry is out of the question; and his only certainty about the best pair of waterproof wading-boots is, that they will infallibly doom the wearer to partial immersion. Gloves, as everybody knows, are sadly in the way when it comes to fingering a lightly-set pair of triggers; and half-frozen feet and half-frost-nipped fingers must trouble the calm pleasures of expectancy.

The successful wild-fowl shooter must necessarily

be an enthusiast ; but we believe that most gentlemen who take to the sport, follow it more or less in *dillettante* fashion. That is the experience of Mr. Colquhoun, the veteran author of " The Moor and the Loch," who observes that the rustic who has only the single barrel of an old-fashioned weapon to depend upon, grudges no expenditure of patience in the attainment of his ends. He has familiarised himself with the haunts and habits of the wild-fowl, and lays himself out deliberately to circumvent the birds. He watches for a pot-shot, dwells deliberately on his aim, and, for the most part, does damage proportionate to the pains he takes. While the gentleman, somewhat impatient of delays and inconveniences, and trusting to the killing powers of his tool, with the reserve of a second barrel, often scares the birds in his rash approaches, or fires too precipitately at an excessive range. Mr. Colquhoun's advice for wild-fowl shooting on inland lakes, is as simple as it will be found to be satisfactory. After expatiating on the birds' quickness of hearing, &c., recording his observations as to their keenness of scent, and counselling the sportsman as to his equipments, he tells him how the stalk may be most surely accomplished. When you have detected the birds you propose to try for, take their bearings exactly by marks upon the shore in relation to another placed further inland. Then make a *détour* to come unperceived behind the inner mark. From that of course the final approaches have to be made, with an astuteness even greater, if possible, than that which is indispensable in deer-stalking. Should there be divers, you take advantage of their temporary disappearances to run forward between times to a succession of ambushes like the "stations" of some pilgrimage to a Catholic shrine.

Often, no doubt, there is excitement enough in that sort of sport; but to us, considering the suffering that may be involved, too much is staked on result. As in deer-stalking, through no fault of your own, you may be balked even of a miss at the last moment. We like better another form of the sport when questing for ducks. You follow the springy drains, keeping fifteen yards from them, and about forty in advance of an attendant who walks close to the trench. It is deadly work covering the plump, full-fed mallards and their mates as they first rise in their heavy flight; and there is intense satisfaction in surprising a wild goose. When gathered into flocks, as you see them generally, the geese are among the most suspicious of created things; and the man who has stalked a flock with its vedettes and sentinels set, may plume himself on no ordinary achievement, unless some lucky accident has befriended him. While a wild duck, fired at from an ambush in the gloaming, as he wings his strong flight overhead to his favourite feeding-grounds, is as hard to hit as he is hard to kill. Even heavy pellets, striking at certain angles, have an extraordinary knack of rolling themselves up harmlessly in the down.

We scarcely care to diverge to long-shore shooting, which, though by no means an uninteresting subject in itself, is a sport left for the most part to professionals. It may be followed, by the way, with great success in the Dutch polders and marshes ; in the sand-dunes of the Flemish seaboard, and in some of the north-western departments of France. On the mud-flats and sands in our own eastern counties, and on the sand-banks and bars at the mouths of the brackish estuaries, among the floating sea-weed, in sharp frosts at the commencement of the winter, the bag may be filled with a wonderful variety. Stalking along under cover of the sand-hills and sea-walls ; stealthily turning along the bends of the creeks, where the waters are sinking with the reflux of the tide ; crouching in bloodthirsty expectancy as you see a flight skimming towards you along the beach—you may kill herons, curlews, ducks, and plovers, with many a species of diver and wader, of which some may be as rare as the most of them are common. Nor shall we embark on board one of the handy little yachting craft, of which the crew is but a man, with possibly a boy, but which, nevertheless, have most elastic accommodation below, while there is actually room on deck for the dingy, which is often towing astern. The cabins of these are snug places enough, as they are assuredly compact ; but the owners, amateurs and town-bred though they may be, always strike us as being among the most venturesome of British mariners. We take it for granted that the skipper is proof to sea-sickness, and it may be assumed that he is equally confident that he was never born to be drowned. For to say nothing of the notion of being capsized in a squall, which he would scout as an outrageous impeachment on his seamanship, there are the probabilities of his grounding upon a bank in one of the fogs, which are accompaniments of the weather most favourable for sea-fowling. He pursues his sport on the borders of the crowded waterways, where fleets of coasting craft are continually plying ; and may be awakened out of the sleep he has dropped into on his watch, to find his boat cut down to the water-line, while he is being submerged by a strange cutwater. Moreover, he may have to run in a sudden gale for moorings in some river mouth or harbour of refuge, by no means always easy of attainment. As a set-off against these probable or problematical dangers, is the " pleasure " of alternately sitting up in the biting air on the deck, glass in hand, behind a swivel-gun or a battery of heavy breech-loaders ; and diving down into the tiny cabin to be toasted before facing a fresh spell of the cold.

CHAPTER XXVII

Winter in the Shires

WE have been writing of winter sports and pleasures to be followed for choice among the frost and snow; but, oddly enough, the winter sport *par excellence* of the English gentleman comes to a stand-still in our genuine winter weather. A frost is not unwelcome to the fox-hunter in the spring and after an open season, when he has well-nigh ridden his horses to a standstill, and half his stud is gone on the sick-list. But frost in November or December, when the winter is young and hopes are fresh! It is certainly not quite so trying as it used to be in the days of the mail-coaches and post-chaises, when the hunting man in the Midlands was practically storm-bound in the streets of a dull provincial town; when the sole resources were over-eating and hard drinking, the billiards by day, the rubber by night, and smoking countless cigars in the stables in dismal contemplation of the hocks of the steeds. Now a man takes his ticket to town by express train, and while he finds a sympathetic chorus of growlers in his club in St.

James's, is always within reach of a telegram. But even comparatively fortunate as he is, that season of suspense is a sore trial to him. His sweet temper is fretted with hope deferred. He goes to bed restless, after anxious looks at the skies, and sees his horses casting themselves in their stalls in his perturbed nightmares; or wakens in disappointment from Tantalus-like dreams, where he has been following the hounds to the music of the horn. To make matters worse, notwithstanding these worries of his, in place of losing flesh he has been laying it on. When men of frugal minds have been calculating weights somewhat too closely in making their purchases, half a stone more is a serious annoyance. But such time of probation must come to an end, and at last the weather has shown unmistakable signs of relenting. A tremor of expectancy has run through the hunting counties, and the first meet after the yielding frost has been advertised to come off at the kennels.

And we do not know that the successors of the immortal Leech could find more inspiriting subjects for their pencils than in the humours of the grand gathering after the involuntary rest. It has become apparent that the weather has fairly broken, and there is even some prospect of scent on the grass and the fallows. There is a general coming up from all parts of the country; for though squires and farmers have had their graver avocations to distract them, yet they too have been vexing their souls over missed chances of sport. Each man is on the alert, and the horses are decidedly more so than is agreeable. Even the cover-hacks seem to have quicksilver in their heels, which is all very well; and the horses in the vehicles of many fashions which are pressing forward to the muster, are tossing the foam about their chests and rattling their frothing curb-chains. Sober old hunters, warranted steady when sold, and carrying certificates of irreproachable character in their faces and ordinary demeanour, are indulging in gay and unaccustomed gambols; while the giddier youngsters, although they may "be free from vice," are showing themselves playful as kittens, and as full of tricks as so many monkeys. We think it is Mr. Benjamin Buckram, who remarks in "Mr. Sponge's Tour," in discussing the character of the redoubted Hercules, that if a gentleman gets spilt, it does not much "argufy" whether it is done from play or vice. And not a few gentlemen now seem to be much of that way of thinking, as their mounts, catching the contagion of excitement in the crowd, disport themselves like fresh-caught mustangs from the Texan prairies. Here is a silken-coated young one on his muscular hind-legs, gracefully improving on the antics of a dancing-bear, and threatening to topple back upon a rider who has scarcely nerve to bring him back to his bearings. Another, arching his crest and tucking in his haunches, shows an English edition of the Australian buck-jumping trick; while most of them are lightly laying back their ears, or shooting flashes out of the corners of their eyes, and not a few are unpleasantly ready with their heels. But if it is all in good temper on the part of the steeds, the same can hardly be said of the riders. The jostling, and the chance of a humiliating accident, throw some gentlemen off their mental balance, who are already uneasy as to the "safety of their seats"; and it would appear that some lowering clouds are flitting across the general hilarity. But the hospitality of the worthy master brings incipient unkindness to a check. The meet at the kennels means a meeting on the lawn, where the disappearance of the frost is demonstrated conclusively by the cutting up of the turf and furrowing of the gravel. The long tables are spread in the old oak hall, among family portraits, under polished rafters and scutcheoned panels. The genial host goes about among his scarlet-coated guests, hail-fellow-well-met with everybody; and the ladies of the household, as they do the honours of the tea and coffee, light up the sombre old banqueting-hall with their smiles. There is a pretty lively clatter of knives and forks, intermingled with the clash of cups and glasses. Those who do not sit down to the more substantial fare, gather round the decanters on buffets and sideboards; while the liveried serving-men are busy out of doors handing brimming tankards to yeomen and outsiders. If the horses are full of fire and oats, their exuberant spirits will soon be counterbalanced by the circulation of jumping powder among the gentlemen of the hunt; and if sharp retorts were bandied a few minutes before, there is a general drowning of all unpleasantness. Only, should there be a find, and should the numerous field get fairly away with their fox, a wise man will do well to take a line of his own, though at the chance of having to face some extra fencing. A crush in a lane or a cannon in a gap, may possibly entail awkward consequences.

One of the show meets of the season is a characteristically English spectacle, which must impress the intelligent foreigner who desires to study our manners or to pass our choicer horse-flesh in review. In a good country, whether in the shires or the provinces, he will see as high-bred hunters as money can procure; while some of the hacks and the pairs in phaetons and double dog-carts, are models of symmetry and style after their kinds. He will be struck by clean-built thoroughbreds that look smaller than they are till he comes to see them extending themselves over formidable fences, and laying the wide-stretching enclosures behind them in their stride. He will admire the serviceable animals that carry those substantial farmers, who manage to see a sufficiency of the sport though they stick for the most part to gates and lanes; and transfusing their intelligence into the instinct of the fox, ride knowingly to points rather than on the sterns of the pack. And he will understand the universal enthusiasm for the sport when he marks how the rag-tag and bobtail turn out for the fun from the market-towns, the villages, and the solitary hamlets, mounted upon anything, down to broken-kneed ponies and ragged-coated donkeys fed on furze. But our article lies rather in the snow and on the ice than in sloppy pastures and holding fallows. So we shall not follow the hounds as they draw from cover to cover ; and as for the tale of the run, has it not been often written by men who were themselves unapproachably in the foremost flight, but who are gone beneath the turf they used to gallop over ? The shades of the departed warn us to be silent, from Nimrod of the *Quarterly*, mighty among literary hunters, to the lamented Colonel Whyte-Melville, lost to us by an accident in the hunting-field. The hunting-field in the south, as the curling-pond in the north, brings many classes together in a kindly communion of tastes and sympathies ; and long may it continue to do so. The greater and the more unreserved the kindly intercourse of the sort, the less is it likely that revolutionary legislation will sow dissensions among those who were born to be friends—will banish all but utilitarians from rural England, and subvert the time-honoured landmarks that our fathers religiously preserved.

www.ingramcontent.com/pod-product-compliance
Lightning Source LLC
Chambersburg PA
CBHW032043220426
43664CB00008B/835